D1035376

From Streetcar to Superhighway

Technology and Urban Growth

A series edited by
Blaine A. Brownell, Mark S. Foster, Zane L. Miller, Mark Rose, and
Howard J. Sumka

Mark S. Foster

From Streetcar to Superhighway:
American City Planners and Urban Transportation, 1900–1940

Temple University Press

Philadelphia

Temple University Press
© 1981 by Temple University. All rights reserved
Published 1981
Printed in the United States of America

Library of Congress Cataloging in Publication Data

Foster, Mark S
   From streetcar to superhighway.

   (Technology and urban growth)
   Bibliography: p.
   Includes index.
   1.   Urban transportation policy—United States—
History. 2.   City planning—United States—History.
I. Title. II. Series.
HE308.F65   711′.7′0973   80-27202
ISBN 0-87722-210-X

HE
308
F65

DEC 15 '86

For my mother and the memory of my father

178976

WITHDRAWN
EMORY & HENRY LIBRARY

Contents

Series Preface

The automobile is one of the most frequently cited examples of a specific technological innovation that has, in the space of only a few generations, changed the shape and character of American cities (and many urban areas elsewhere in the world) and altered patterns of living and perceived dimensions of space and time. Sprawling suburbs and congested downtown streets seem vivid testimony to the motor vehicle's power. We are now in the habit of regarding this dramatic change as proceeding inevitably from the imperatives of the innovation itself. In reality, this considerable impact is more complex and less direct.

Many decisions that shaped the impact of the automobile on American cities were made by businessmen, elected officials, and ordinary citizens—who bought cars, voted for highway construction and improvements, and criticized transit companies. But city planners were called upon to deal more specifically and explicitly with the new innovation than any other group, and it is important to know what they thought of the motor vehicle and how they envisioned its role in American life.

In this book, Mark S. Foster develops several of these themes, focusing in particular on city planners, automobiles, and public transportation during the four decades between 1900 and 1940. City planners, seeking to direct urban growth along more desirable lines, brought a general American sense of optimism and environmentalism to the consideration of key issues such as declining property values, poverty, and rapid decentralization. As the trolley and then the automobile had facilitated the development of urban ecology and social structure, it appeared to city planners that automobiles might also play a role in shaping a new city, or at least a prosperous one. Technological optimism—in this case the conviction that engineered refinements of the automobile and the street would eliminate the problems of traffic jams and pollution—contributed to the popularity of the automobile in planning circles. Once automobile and trolley operators cooperated in shaping the fast-growing urban fringe, the new city would begin to emerge. Physical control of the urban fringe, or so ran the reasoning, would inevitably lead to desirable lines of development for the social and economic city, presumably the object of so many plans and hopes and so much old-fashioned political maneuvering.

The program of city planning between 1900 and 1940 never achieved these goals, and only rarely did city planners as individuals influence the course of urban development. Part of the failure rested with the planners themselves and with those who employed them. Planners operated as consultants and as employees in understaffed and poorly financed city offices. Inevitably, they served those who hired them, producing small plans for limited improvements and entertaining petitions for zoning variances. Competition for funds and influence overwhelmed city planners, who often lacked both a professional identity and an entrenched position in urban bureaucracies and political circles.

Nor is it certain that planners could have reshaped cities or rescued mass transit from decline, even had the appropriate resources of influence, patronage, and expertise come quickly to hand. By the late 1920s, trolley lines were largely in-place and trolley operators continued to suffer from their reputations as bandits of the public. As trolley ridership declined, operators enjoyed neither a reputation for good service nor more general symbols of legitimacy susceptible to manipulation in the political arena. The working of the urban political economy, with its emphasis upon individual choices, also conspired against city planners, who might have sought to rescue the trolley as part of a city redevelopment package. City planners and their plans were no match for the ambitions and schemes of real estate operators, utility company officials, street builders, and indeed the trolley operators themselves, who were eager and anxious to serve urbanites who in large numbers were selecting home and business sites at the edge of the city. By 1940, relates Foster, "cities seemed farther from viable solutions to urban transportation needs than ever before."

The impact of technologies such as the automobile and the trolley upon society and upon cities is thus both strikingly obvious and tremendously complex. As either broad phenomena or as specific innovations, these technologies were a response to and reflection of urban society and culture at a particular time, and also agents for social and cultural change. More generally, so dramatic was this capacity for inducing change that specific technological innovations did not long remain precisely the same in terms of how they were applied or perceived. On the other hand, the application—and to a large degree, the generation—of new technologies occurred within an existing societal and cultural framework, which placed greater value on mobility than on stability and on expansion rather than on controlled growth.

The Technology and Urban Growth Series attempts to focus on the critical role of technology in the city-building and urbanization processes and to explore the complex interrelationships between technology, society, and ways of living and thinking in the urban setting. This series is inaugurated with this volume.

The Editors, Technology and Urban Growth Series

Acknowledgments

As every author quickly learns, preparation of a book is truly a shared experience. To those who have given their time, insights, resources, hospitality, and encouragement, I express profound gratitude.

I owe my deepest debt to two inspirational teachers who guided my first efforts to become an historian. Lyle W. Dorsett believed in my potential and provided years of encouragement during my quest to become a productive scholar. In addition to lifting my spirits when I was discouraged, Franklin D. Mitchell taught me many of the rudiments of scholarship. Both men provided splendid examples of perseverance and hard work.

Several professional colleagues and friends played important roles in preparation of this book. Mark H. Rose read three versions of the manuscript and provided countless valuable suggestions for improvement. Fellow automobile historian Blaine A. Brownell generously shared many of his original ideas and critiqued an early version of the manuscript. John Hancock similarly labored over two of my early efforts and provided many valuable suggestions. Other scholars who survived exposure to various forms of the manuscript include Zane L. Miller, Tom Noel, Lyle Dorsett, Rickey H. Whitelaw, and William H. Wilson.

During several extended research trips, I exhausted the patience of countless archivists and their staffs. Among the dozens of helpful people I met were Joe Oldenberg of the Burton Historical Collection at the Detroit Public Library; Gould Colman, Jane Gustafson, and Kathleen Jacklin of the Cornell University Archives; Ray Geselbracht of the Roosevelt Library in Hyde Park; Archie Motley of the Chicago Historical Society; and William Lind and the entire staff at the National Archives in Washington. Joe Boskin and Sam Warner, Jr., of Boston University permitted me to test emerging ideas in a stimulating seminar and provided warm hospitality while I was in Boston. I made many new friends during the course of my travels. Fellow scholars who critiqued my ideas include Paul Barrett, Warren Belasco, John Clark, Donald Davis, Diane Ghirardo, Patricia Haines, and John Ryan. Several research assistants helped me effectively use limited time in various cities. Robert Jooharigian of Detroit and Clarisse Poirier of Boston were particularly helpful.

In an era of rampant inflation, few scholars can effectively pursue their studies without ample financial and institutional support. The Ford Motor Company Fund awarded a substantial grant and made no effort to influence my judgments. Among the officers at Ford, Leo J. Brennan, Jr., of the fund and Vice President Richard Shackson were particularly encouraging and enthusiastic. A University of Colorado Faculty Fellowship provided a year's paid leave. The Eleanor Roosevelt Institute awarded me a grant-in-aid that allowed me to make a critical follow-up research trip. My colleagues at the University of Colorado at Denver have uncomplainingly endured my absence from meetings and reluctance to assume committee responsibilities during the past two years. Leona Rozinski and Joan Smith, two indefatigable members of our office staff, typed portions of various versions of the book and saved me from some of my most egregious errors.

Finally, I have had the singular good fortune to work with Kenneth Arnold, editor-in-chief at Temple. He patiently examined several "final" drafts of this book and made valuable suggestions for improvement. At times, I have stubbornly resisted changes, and I accept full responsibility for the book's shortcomings. To those who have generously helped me, and to others I have not named, I owe my heartfelt thanks.

M. S. F.   Denver, Colorado
                                                    August 1980

From Streetcar to Superhighway

Introduction

Many observers of the contemporary urban scene believe that America's response to the challenge of the city has failed.[1] Escalating crime and unemployment rates, steadily worsening physical blight, and ever-increasing demands for social services are among the serious issues faced by harassed city officials. In the past two decades, newspaper headlines have documented major urban crises in all parts of the country, from the bankruptcy of New York City to major race riots in Los Angeles.

Although less overtly dramatic than some other urban issues, intracity transportation is one of the most important problems facing local officials. The general public has been acutely aware of the friction between advocates of public and private transportation only since the Arab oil embargo of 1973. Yet for the past eighty years, public officials have debated over whether to promote mass transit, the automobile, or a combination of the two.

Despite its persistent popular appeal and support from politicians, the automobile has been the subject of harsh words from social critics for more than twenty years. In 1958 John Keats noted the pervasive influence of the automobile in post-war America with his oft-quoted remark that it had become "demonstrably more important to us than our human wives, children, jobs, and even our food."[2] Lewis Mumford portrayed its impact upon the cityscape in dismal terms in 1961. That the automobile had polluted the air and wreaked visual havoc on the urban environment for years was bad enough. Far worse, feckless public officials who should have known better had tolerated and even abetted this automobile "invasion." Mumford scorned the highway engineers and city planners who, by "allowing mass transportation to deteriorate" and by building superhighways and massive parking garages, had "helped destroy the living tissue of the city." According to Mumford, the auto industry and oil companies formed a powerful cabal whose artful propaganda hypnotized responsible city officials and induced them to "dismantle all the varied forms of transportation necessary to a good system." He perceived the planners' compliance as almost a conspiracy.[3]

Other critics suggested that opponents of the automobile comprised only a tiny liberal clique, whose views were directly countered by the preferences of the overwhelming majority of Americans. What the anti-automobile crusade amounted to, according to B. Bruce-Briggs, was an undemocratic effort by "elites" to "drive the other guy off the road, particularly when he was not as sensitive, educated or prosperous as [they] were." Bruce-Briggs believed that affluent suburbanites objected to the "lower-class slob who jammed highways in his old Chevy with his wife in curlers and his squalling brats beating on the rear window."[4] These self-appointed elites devised elaborate rationalizations to try to force the "lower-class" element into mass transportation. Their most common arguments were that cars were polluting, unsafe, and destructive of urban landscapes. However bombastic this rhetoric, pro-mass-transit public officials driving to work alone in air-conditioned automobiles might squirm at the element of truth it contained.

The clashing perspectives of public transit enthusiasts and defenders of the automobile inspired this study. If the two sides have anything in common, it is that they emphasize recent developments and generally lack historical insight. Proponents of each view implicitly assume that urban transportation policy in the United States evolved largely by accident, and that no logical principles guided those responsible for it. Most popular writers who have analyzed the role of the automobile in the urbanization process emphasize its encouragement of suburban sprawl after World War II. Historians have taken a longer view, and several perceptive studies have explored the response of the American public to the motor vehicle before 1940.[5] But no work has fully examined the changing perspectives and reactions of city planners to the rapid evolution of urban transportation technology in the prewar period. I hoped to discover whether planners were more prescient than the public at large about the probable impact of the automobile upon the urban environment, and whether their views made much impact upon public policy in the urban transportation field.

The majority of American planners emphasized the automobile's potentially beneficial impact on the urban environment from the beginning of the twentieth century. Advocates of mass transit occasionally clashed with proponents of the automobile, but most planners believed, at least through the Depression, that both forms of transportation could thrive. If there was a crisis in urban transportation before World War II, it was seldom reflected by any sense of urgency in planners' public policy recommendations. Essentially, planners' responses to urban transportation problems assumed a piecemeal, uncoordinated character, which contributed to the rise of the automobile as the primary mover of urban residents.

For a variety of reasons, many of them beyond their direct control, planners exerted only a limited impact in shaping the twentieth-century city. The automobile was but the latest of a series of technological advances that significantly affected urban evolution. Steam railways, trolleys, structural steel, elevators, and the telephone permitted significant expansion of usable urban space. While structural steel and the elevator allowed rapid vertical growth, a variety of railway improvements enhanced horizontal growth. Many steam railroad systems were established during the nineteenth century, and street railroads advanced from the relatively slow horse-drawn lines of mid-century to the more efficient cable and electric systems of the 1880s and 1890s. By the time automobiles appeared in significant numbers in the early twentieth century, much of the technological infrastructure of the industrial city was already firmly in place.

But if the physical framework was largely established, important fixtures still needed to be attached. Early in the twentieth century, urban decisionmakers devoted much of their attention to providing new services that significantly enhanced city life. The first decades of the new century marked large-scale expansion of electric, gas, sewer, and telephone lines, particularly in newer areas.[5] Even in the older sections of American cities, engineers and planners faced complex problems of coordinating the underground access routes of old and new services. Thus, transportation was but one of many crucial urban issues then challenging planners.

A number of factors limited planners' potential impact. Politics frequently prevented active intervention in urban transportation. The planning profession grew rapidly between 1900 and 1940, but individual planners and professional organizations experienced constant, energy-draining struggles for formal recognition and for adequate funding and authority to effect their programs.[7] In the maelstrom of both local and national political settings, planners were invariably pitted against seasoned politicians and more established bureaucracies. Those interests were generally slow to recognize a need for comprehensive planning. Planners were usually under intense pressure to develop prompt solutions for immediate urban problems.

Many present-day urban critics are at a loss to explain why earlier urban decisionmakers allowed many fine mass transit systems to deteriorate or disappear altogether. Even assuming that early-twentieth-century planners could have prevented their decline, this argument ignores much. By 1910, mass transit companies often had enormous economic power and unsavory public images; by championing their cause, planners might have jeopardized what little influence they possessed. In addition, mass transit spokesmen did not promote their industry effectively. As street railway patronage and financial strength waned in the 1920s and 1930s, trolley officials adopted a seemingly inconsis-

tent strategy of simultaneously proclaiming the industry's good
health and lobbying for public assistance. The latter pleas usually
fell on deaf ears. Although precedents for assistance to large
utilities existed, public officials saw that accommodating the
automobile was more in keeping with the American ideal of
private responsibility, since individuals would be providing their
own means of transit. As automobile historian James J. Flink
noted, "the general adoption of the automobile was the most important reform of the pre–World-War-I era, an especially attractive reform to Americans because it did not involve collective
political action."[8] Politicians also possessed an incentive for consciously promoting the automobile: they could widen streets and
build highways during current terms in office, rather than initiate
construction of far more expensive mass transit systems that
might not be functioning until years after they lost reelection
bids.

Present-day urban critics fault the automobile for contributing
to inner-city decay by encouraging both homeowners and
businessmen to abandon central locations in favor of the suburbs.
This observation reflects the cheap wisdom of perfect historical
hindsight. Many turn-of-the-century observers viewed the inner
city very differently, as a social menace from which the masses
should make every effort to escape. If mass transit and other
technological advances helped initiate decentralization, so, they
believed, could the automobile more rapidly promote that end.

While the automobile was an expensive toy for the rich in
1900, quickly dropping prices and mass production placed it
within reach of most American families by the 1920s.[9] Parkway
construction, which may have appeared elitist to some social
critics in 1900, seemed by the 1930s to be a democratic response
to urban transportation needs comparable, perhaps, to providing
subways in 1900. Unable to solve the problems of inner-city
congestion, planners eventually shifted their attention to outlying

areas of the cities. Urban decisionmakers initiated major street and freeway programs in the 1920s and 1930s under the assumption that by building roads in advance of housing development they could control the impact of the automobile as an urban transportation tool and also direct the pace and pattern of the outward migration process.

Today there are 120 million automobiles on American streets and roads, and it is easy to perceive certain fallacies in planners' original assumptions. In 1940, the so-called "automobile problem" was not nearly so apparent, since there were but 27.5 million cars on the road. Given that urban decisionmakers had wrestled with the far more urgent problem of surviving the Depression and would soon face the severe headaches of World War II adjustments, perhaps we should not be too critical of their general failure to anticipate the flood of automobiles that in the postwar period jammed new automobile facilities. Passage of the Interstate Highway Act in 1956, which financed massive freeway systems through the hearts of our cities, sealed America's commitment to the automobile as the primary mode of urban transportation.[10] For better or worse, planners ultimately accepted the sprawling form of the mid-twentieth-century city. To better understand the evolution of their thinking over the past eighty years, we should begin with an examination of the turn-of-the-century urban milieu that they hoped to reform. Urban decisionmakers of varying persuasions generally agreed that they faced a brutal urban environment. If they could not significantly change it, they at least hoped to escape it.

1 The Turn-of-the-Century City

Life in the turn-of-the-century American city was not as idyllic as popular imagination would have it. For most urbanites, it was downright perilous. The tens of thousands living in the slums of New York's Lower East Side and Chicago's Maxwell Street District vastly outnumbered the fortunate few who resided in Victorian mansions on Fifth Avenue in New York and Michigan Avenue in Chicago. To many residents, the cities were "frightening and unnatural phenomena. Their unprecedented size and vast, uprooted populations seemed to suggest the uncontrolled forces unleashed by the Industrial Revolution, and the chaos that occupied the center of modern life."[1] Such conditions were by no means the discovery of contemporary scholars. When naturalist writers uncovered urban poverty, some genteel Americans recoiled with shock and horror. Few passages in American literature capture the squalor and crowding of the slum more vividly than Stephen Crane's famous description of a tenement in *Maggie: A Girl of the Streets*:

> Eventually they entered a dark region where, from a careening building, a dozen gruesome doorways gave up loads of babies to the street and gutter. A wind of early autumn raised yellow dust from cobbles and swirled it against a hundred windows. Long streamers of garments fluttered from fire escapes. In all unhandy places there were buckets, brooms, rags, and bottles. In the street infants played or fought with other infants or sat stupidly in the way of vehicles. Formidable women, with uncombed hair and disordered dress, gossiped while leaning on railings, or screamed in frantic quarrels. Withered persons, in curious postures of submission to something, sat smoking pipes in obscure corners. A thousand odours of cooking food came forth to the street. The building quivered and creaked from the weight of humanity stamping about in its bowels.[2]

Working conditions and temptations of the city received equally penetrating treatment from other urban naturalists. Upton Sinclair's *The Jungle* (1905) pungently describes the losing struggle for survival in Chicago's stockyards by the proud, strong, hard-working Jurgis Rudkus, a recent immigrant from Lithuania. James T. Farrell's *Studs Lonigan* (1932) features the dreary life of a lower-middle-class Irish youth growing up in the same city.

Undoubtedly, one of the most frustrating facts of urban life at the turn of the century was lack of personal privacy. Crowding was a fact of life for almost everybody, but the poor suffered most. Frequently a dozen or more people shared two or three tiny, unventilated rooms in miserable tenements. While some former residents of European cities were used to such conditions, count-less immigrants and native migrants from small towns and rural backgrounds were undoubtedly horrified. According to housing reformer Jacob Riis, New York's Lower East Side, which con-tained 290,000 persons per square mile, was the world's most densely settled living area. In 1910, citywide density in New York was 23,179 persons per square mile; Boston contained 17,795, and Chicago held 16,723 persons per square mile.[3]

Social, economic, and political factors explain much of the distress experienced by the "masses," and the sheer ugliness of the urban environment accented their plight. Slums were conspic-uous in all but the newest cities, and industrial plants polluted the streams with their offal and the air with their smoke. In pre-zoning days, residential buildings stood next to blacksmith and butcher shops, and many urbanites lived adjacent to garbage dumps.[4] Streets and boulevards reflected the chaos of urban affairs. Iron-rimmed wheels and horseshoes shrieked against cob-blestone streets day and night, contributing to the babel of noise. Horses, which were still vital for transportation and hauling freight, burdened sanitation and health departments. In New York City, they dumped 2.5 million pounds of manure and 60,000 gallons of urine onto city streets each day, and 15,000 dead horses had to be removed at public expense each year.[5]

However forbidding the aesthetic environment of the typical industrial city of 1900, that was where most of the new jobs were, and millions of newcomers streamed into urban America annually. A variety of technological advances profoundly affected the physical growth of cities and promised increased comfort for residents. Innovations such as structural steel and the mechanical elevator had already permitted construction of sky-scrapers much taller than the six- to eight-story downtown build-ings of the mid-nineteenth century, and post-1900 construction escalated vertical growth. While gas and arc lighting for streets and buildings had been popular for some years, the availability of cheaper electricity encouraged white-collar employers to push back the night even farther. In the home, indoor plumbing and steam heat made urban living more tolerable, at least for those who could pay.

But probably no technological advance exerted as profound an impact upon the daily routines, outlooks, and opportunities of urbanites as did changes in urban transportation. Prior to the introduction of the horse-drawn streetcar in about 1840, most urban dwellers traveled by foot. Omnibuses and hansom cabs were available, but because one-way fares were usually at least ten cents and most urban workers earned little more than a dollar a day, these modes of travel were limited to the affluent. Horse-drawn streetcars speeded up travel somewhat, but fares usually remained beyond the means of working-class urbanites. The late nineteenth century marked advances in street railway technology that enormously enhanced its impact. The first significant step in mechanizing street railways was the introduction of the cable car in the 1870s. The cars were pulled by underground steel cables that operated on a conveyor belt principle. Cable cars were an improvement over horse-drawn streetcars and were well suited to cities with steep grades and mild climates, like San Francisco.

1. Late-nineteenth-century urban planners hoped to alleviate conditions such as these in New York. Long before the post–World-War-II suburban boom, planners envisioned opening up large areas of the urban landscape for single-family homes, hence bringing sunlight and fresh air to working-class families. Photograph by Jacob A. Riis, Jacob A. Riis Collection, Museum of the City of New York.

13

2. Another view of the squalor that early-twentieth-century urban planners hoped to overcome by promoting decentralization. Photograph by Jacob A. Riis, Jacob A. Riis Collection, Museum of the City of New York.

3. A street scene from New York's Lower East Side from around 1890.

Early in the twentieth century, American planners assumed that rapid decentralization, abetted by either the trolley or the automobile, would enable them to eliminate much of the crowding endemic to eastern cities. Photograph by Jacob A. Riis, Jacob A. Riis Collection, Museum of the City of New York.

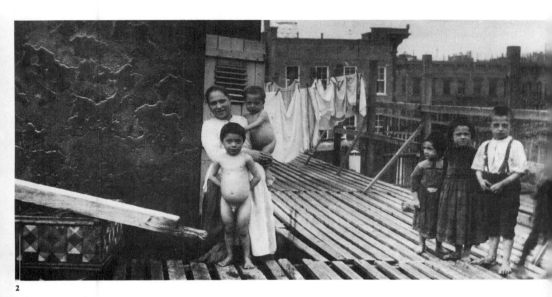

2

3

Unfortunately, they were not particularly reliable mechanically, and inclement weather hampered their performance. The successful harnessing of electricity to the streetcar, beginning in Richmond, Virginia, in 1884, was the key advance that assured the trolley's indispensability. By 1900 urban leaders regularly boasted about their street railways and nearly every American city of 25,000 or more had at least one trolley line. Rising wages, and the fact that in most cities one-way trolley fares were a nickle or even less, finally made the trolley accessible to large numbers of workers.[6]

The period between the 1880s and World War I was the golden age of America's electric railways. Between 1890 and 1920 trolley patronage in America leaped from 2 billion to 15.5 billion passengers annually.[7] Total trolley ridership grew almost 700 percent during a period in which the nation's urban population increased roughly 150 percent.[8] Riding "habit," or the frequency with which the average urbanite actually used the trolley, also increased dramatically. By 1920, residents of several of the nation's most densely settled cities rode the trolley an average of nearly once each day.[9] The streetcar became the chief mode of transit for nearly all classes and ages: businessmen commuting to their offices; industrial workers going to factory jobs; housewives on family errands; and children traveling to and from school. Entire families frequently boarded trolleys for weekend trips to the countryside at special excursion rates.

Luckily for the electric street railway, it emerged during one of America's most dynamic periods of urban growth. The rate of growth between 1900 and 1920 was less than that between 1870 and 1900, but the 1920 census revealed that, for the first time in history, a majority of citizens resided in urban areas.[10] Though cities such as New York and Chicago had long been immense, the first two decades of the century marked the emergence of new urban giants. In that brief span, Detroit grew from less than 300,000 to nearly a million residents. Los Angeles, an overgrown village containing slightly more than 100,000 people in 1900, emerged as the Pacific Coast's largest city by 1920, with just under 600,000 residents.[11]

Far more significant than mere increases in size was the new direction of growth. By the 1920s, observers reported that the fringe areas of American cities were growing faster than the central cities.[12] Between 1910 and 1920, population growth within the 29 largest central cities averaged 25.1 percent, while the average rate at the fringes was 32.7 percent. In some cities the differentials were startling. While Chicago grew by 23.7 percent in that decade, the surrounding area's population increased by 76.3 percent; similarly, Detroit more than doubled its central area population with an increase of 113.3 percent, but its fringe area grew by 254 percent.[13]

Observers of American urbanization generally agree that advances in transportation technology keyed horizontal expansion.[14] Until the 1840s, the outer limits of the built-up areas of even the largest cities were seldom more than two miles from their centers. As increasing numbers of immigrants poured into the eastern cities during the 1830s and 1840s, more people competed for fixed amounts of space. Thus residents of eastern cities welcomed the almost simultaneous introduction in the 1840s of horse-drawn trolleys and steam railroads, not only for the speed and comfort they added to commuting, but because they encouraged the beginning of residential decentralization on a very modest scale.[15]

Introduction of the electric trolley on a massive scale unquestionably speeded up the process of decentralization between 1880 and World War I. The city dweller of 1880 may have dreamed vaguely of a small frame house in the suburbs with a garden and white picket fence, but day-to-day reality was his struggle for survival in the inner city.[16] For the working-class urbanite, physical mobility meant escaping from poverty and perhaps from other ethnic groups; his horizon often stretched only as far as new neighborhoods a few blocks away.[17] Electric street railways permitted the gradual migration of middle- and working-class Bostonians into suburbs such as Roxbury and Dorchester in the late nineteenth century.[18] Conservative piecemeal extensions of transit service meant that, in Boston at least, local patrons seldom had to walk more than a quarter of a mile to reach transit facilities.

Late-nineteenth-century urbanites perceived the fledgling suburban movement as mainly accommodating the needs of the well-to-do; but it was also a phenomenon of growing importance to less prosperous city residents.[19] Between the late 1880s and World War I a number of industrial suburbs appeared on the urban landscape. In the Chicago area, Pullman and Gary were founded by manufacturing concerns.[20] In addition, the rise of electric interurban railways in the same period fostered the creation of many brand new suburbs, often miles from the central cities.

Social critics who lament the ultimate decline of the street railway often forget that early trolley promoters, seeking profits first and foremost, were often far more interested in selling land than in providing unified transit systems. Interurban railway boosters and land developers made natural partners. Trolley promoters frequently kept future routes a closely guarded secret while buying huge tracts of land along projected rights of way. With the fanfare of announcing the new proposed routes, values of adjacent property often multiplied quickly. In some cities, many individual trolley promoters built lines connecting residential neighborhoods with central districts. In Chicago, for example, fifteen separate companies provided street railway service as late as 1897.[21] While some made handsome profits, the overall result was a lack of coordination and chaotic conditions on downtown streets, created in part by the presence of the streetcar tracks of several competing companies.

Significantly, mass transit promoters often made handsome profits from land sales even when they lost money in providing actual service. In theory at least, the sale of lots for residential development provided the street railways sufficient patronage to assure attractive returns on their investment. In the late nineteenth century, real estate interests and trolley promoters combined to develop huge areas of Brooklyn, Boston, Chicago, and many other large cities.[22] This method of development continued in the early twentieth century. In the Los Angeles area, a syndicate formed by Henry E. Huntington purchased 50,000 acres of land in the San Fernando Valley alone, and he developed thirteen brand new towns in the metropolitan region between 1902 and 1917. Largely as a result of such real estate promotions, by World War I Huntington's Pacific Electric Railway Company was the most extensive interurban system in the world.[23] Between 1918 and 1922, Oris and Mantis Van Sweringen parlayed possession of a 1,400-acre tract east of Cleveland and an ability to persuade a local street railway to extend its lines to their property into the famous community of Shaker Heights. That some automobile suburb planners have imitated the community's imaginatively conceived winding streets for sixty years does not obscure the fact that Shaker Heights was originally a "trolley suburb."[24]

With the advent of the electric railway, urban leaders did everything in their power to stimulate investment in local street railways. By arranging low-interest loans, offering cash subsidies and parcels of city-owned property, and agreeing to long-term franchises at fares that seemed to promise handsome profits, civic leaders believed they were assisting economic growth through real estate development and were providing their cities with the most up-to-date transportation services for the foreseeable future.

In the early years, politicians who arranged franchises and helped bring the first electric trolleys to cities were heroes. Grand openings of new streetcar routes occasioned gala civic ceremonies. Most patrons enjoyed the relatively smooth, comfortable ride, and the clanging bells reassured proud civic leaders that everything was indeed up to date in their cities.[25]

Electric railways appeared at first to promise only improvements to life in urban America. In 1897 the Massachusetts Street Railroad Association proudly reported that "there is no known method of conveyance by which large numbers of persons can be transported through the street with so much expedition, and safety to themselves and other travelers, with so little noise, confusion, and dirt, and with so little obstruction and wear and tear of the street, as by the electric railway."[26] Trolleys offered yet other competitive advantages over their horse-drawn predecessors. They were cleaner, and they did not suffer heat prostration in the summer months. After all but the most severe winter blizzards they could plow paths through city streets. While mischievous youths occasionally halted cars by tampering with overhead connections or greasing rails on uphill slopes, motormen were able to remedy such vandalism in minutes.

Unfortunately, predictions that electric trolleys would ease street traffic problems soon proved incorrect. A 1901 editorial on Boston's congestion optimistically suggested that "undoubtedly the new [street] railway is a material relief to the traffic of the city at large."[27] But it also noted that in laying their lines the street railways often inconvenienced local traffic for weeks, or even months, and that poorly-laid tracks frequently constituted hazards for pedestrians and other vehicles. Most important, within a few years after new lines were laid, so many trolleys entered central districts that more people and competing vehicles jammed the same narrow streets.

Criticism of the trolley industry took many forms, but its tone shifted markedly around 1900. In the 1880s and 1890s there were occasional complaints from newspaper editors about drunk or discourteous motormen, drafty or stuffy cars, and frequent accidents. Although these charges did not disappear after 1900, the emergence of the progressive movement signaled a new and more fundamental challenge to street railways and other large public utilities. Leaders of the movement challenged the right of large corporations to pursue profits at utter disregard for the public welfare.[28] Street railways provided a particularly inviting target for the wrath of reformers. By the turn of the century many street railways had been transformed from shakily financed operations competing against several other local companies into huge profitable monopolies with absolute control over public transportation on city streets.[29] As patronage and profits increased rapidly, critics launched efforts to tame the growing "monsters." Politicians who a few years earlier had eagerly offered street railways longterm franchises on nickel fares now viewed that fare as yielding unconscionable profits and initiated campaigns for lower fares and public ownership. They observed that the nickel fare still prevented many laborers, who were potential supporters, from using the trolleys. In the late nineteenth century, Detroit's Hazen S. Pingree, one of America's most colorful "reform" mayors, tried to force the local street railway lines to lower their base fare to three cents.[30] While the working classes and certain newspapers gave Pingree overwhelming support, the city's "influentials" and largest newspapers opposed him. In a scathing attack typical of turn-of-the-century muckraking prose, Pingree vilified the trolley interests and their friends: "The snake editor of the *Free Press* will slip and slide around on the sidewalk in the slime of the reptiles and vipers which he will discover this morning trailing themselves over the sidewalks of Detroit and in and out of the Council Chamber."[31]

Large corporations absorbed abuse from many quarters in this

period, and street railways received a generous share. Frederick
C. Howe lambasted the so-called "public service" corporations:
"The private monopolies which supply light, heat, transportation,
and power are another cause of poverty. They collect such tribute
as a corrupt alliance with the city sanctions."[32] Even prominent
fiction writers attacked street railways. Theodore Dreiser presented a very unflattering picture of the machinations of an un-
scrupulous trolley magnate in *The Financier* (1912) and *The
Titan* (1914). Yet some thoughtful observers believed that criticisms of large utilities went too far, and that overreaction by
politicians worked to the long-term disadvantage of the public.
Nelson P. Lewis, a civil engineer and planner from New York,
worried that street railways, which had basked in the glow of
public favor and lucrative franchises in the 1880s and 1890s,
risked the wrath of intransigent city councils and public utility
boards in the early twentieth century. Lewis feared that "the
pendulum [of public opinion] would swing too far in the other
direction," and that city officials would reject even reasonable
franchise and rate requests from the trolley companies.[33] Lewis's
fears proved prescient. Indeed, while a majority of city residents
continued to depend upon the trolley for most of their urban
transportation until the 1930s, investors found firms in other,
unregulated, industries more profitable and inviting even before
World War I. By that time, public discontent with the street
railways was evident at many levels.

Given the crowded conditions and depressing physical environments in many cities, it is not surprising that Americans
welcomed any technological advances that promised to spread
out population and convert more adjacent land to urban uses.[34]
Thus civic leaders and public officials welcomed the automobile
revolution in the twentieth century, just as they had heralded

advances in street railway technology in the nineteenth. The Duryea brothers introduced the first operating automobiles to the United States in 1895.[35] Until at least 1900, when there were 8,000 registered cars in the country, most Americans considered them little more than toys for the rich.[36] Driving anywhere was an adventure in the early days, perhaps even more so in rural than in urban areas. Turn-of-the-century roads were designed for horses and buggies; automobiles found virtually impassable the deeply rutted country lanes, which were bumpy and dusty in the summer and became quagmires in the rainy season. Farmers, whose horses were easily startled by the clatter of gasoline engines, were often unfriendly, if not downright hostile.[37] Even on city streets, the gasoline-powered carriages suffered frequent breakdowns and appeared unfit as a functional mode of mass transportation.

Nevertheless, the automobile attracted ardent supporters from the very start, and a number of enthusiasts envisioned its enormous potential for changing patterns of urban transportation years, even decades, before the fact. Influential writer and magazine editor Ray Stannard Baker stated flatly in 1899 that "the experimental plaything has become a practical necessity." Baker compared the cost of owning and operating an automobile to that of buying and maintaining a horse and carriage; over five years, the automobile cost 20 percent less. Baker enthusiastically noted that the electric automobile was "practically noiseless and odorless and nearly free from vibrations."[38] In 1900 playwright Cleveland Moffett predicted not only the greatness of the automobile, but also its future negative impact upon street railways: "Trolley lines are wondering if automobile buses and coaches are destined to war against them, as they have warred against the railroad."[39]

To fight the automobile's image of exclusiveness, enthusiasts stressed its utility. One industry spokesman pointed out in 1900 that as the automobile increased in popularity, public demand for good roads would evolve. Construction of streets and roads passable in all weather benefited everybody, whether they lived in country or city, and whether or not they owned an automobile.[40] Although he stressed the automobile's function as a "vacation agent" and the joys of automobile touring, William F. Dix also pointed out its potential for facilitating intracity movement of people. Because the automobile was not confined to trolley tracks, it could occupy any unused portion in the street. This allowed the automobilist to use any street in the city; hence, if traffic on one street was jammed, he could find another, less crowded one. In effect, the automobile would supplement the city's rail and trolley facilities. Dix suggested that automobiles were cleaner, quieter, and more flexible than streetcars. In certain situations they could replace the "cumbersome, gigantic [street] railway [cars] departing at infrequent intervals."[41] Automobiles and trucks would similarly provide greater speed and flexibility in the movement and delivery of commercial freight.

An extremely important outgrowth of the automobile revolution was that the motor vehicle opened up formerly inaccessible areas for urban use. Full appreciation of the automobile's potential for encouraging suburban development would not be evident until the 1920s, but some perceived this connection two decades earlier. Winthrop E. Scarritt, president of the American Automobile Association, suggested in 1903 that the key to opening up the city rested with lowering the price of the automobile. "With the coming of the low-priced automobile you will find [suburbs] building up with homes, each on its ample plot of ground and inhabited by a family for whom the cost of living will be reduced to a minimum, and the pleasure of existence enhanced immeasurably."[42] By opening up suburban land, wrote James J. Flink, "the automobile seemed, to proponents of the innovation, to afford a simple solution to some of the more formidable social problems of American life associated with the emergence of an urban-industrial society."[43]

The belief that a middle-class family could save money by abandoning the city for the suburbs also convinced a few people to move. One former city dweller told of selling his Chicago home for $25,000 in 1909 and buying one of comparable quality in suburban La Grange for $7,000. His new home was some distance from trolley or steam railroad lines, so he purchased an automobile to commute to work. He professed delight with his financial windfall.[44] His decision clearly presaged one important future role of the automobile in urban development.

The automobile multiplied the amount of land accessible for commercial and residential uses several fold. Interurban railways had allowed development of land located miles from downtown areas, but such development was generally limited to space located within a few blocks of the lines, which were often miles apart: the automobile permitted development of the large areas in between.[45] Thoughtful observers such as Chicago architect and planner Daniel H. Burnham praised the potential of the automobile for opening up the cities very early in the new century.[46]

Late-nineteenth- and early-twentieth-century developments in technology promised exciting alternative living environments to urban Americans, and changes in transportation led the way. Even as new opportunities within industrial America drew increasing numbers of people to metropolitan areas, the electric trolley and the automobile made physical escape from the crowded inner city a possibility for some urbanites. The steam railroad and electric street railways first allowed city builders to look beyond the physical limits of the walking city. The automobile revolution commenced with a bang and a sputter, but its influence on the urban environment was gradual in the first two decades of the twentieth century. Prescient observers perceived that it could be the key to turning vague dreams of spacious suburban homes into reality for countless urbanites. "Automobility" not only excited many urbanites, it gained an important place in the minds of civic leaders and city planners as well.

2 The Planning Movement's Early Years

Planning occupied a curious position in turn-of-the-century American culture. On the one hand, the country possessed even in 1900 a more significant planning tradition than many realize today. City planning was philosophically consistent with the chief impulses of the progressive movement, one of which was to bring a sense of order to the urbanization process.[1] On the other hand, the dynamics of individual decisionmaking within the nation's modified laissez-faire economic system contravened large-scale planning.[2] A major factor behind planners' lack of impact was that they took their first hesitant steps during a period in which cities were already experiencing enormous social, political, economic, and physical changes. Hence, planning commissions endured limited or nonexistent budgets and possessed small staffs, and urban politicians frequently derided or ignored their recommendations.[3]

Perhaps the most important reason planners exerted little influence on urban affairs in the early years was that the emerging profession was wracked by disagreements and simultaneously pulled in many directions.[4] City Beautiful planners promoted civic centers and lovely boulevards, while others, labeling themselves more "practical," advocated short-range programs to benefit the disadvantaged. In addition, a variety of urban needs, including water, sewers, and basic health services, preempted scarce resources; transportation was but one of many issues they faced.[5] Disagreements within the profession clearly spilled over into the arena of urban transportation, particularly the issue of whether or not to promote innovations in rapid transit. Some believed subways and elevateds created more problems than they solved. It would be inaccurate to argue that planners preferred the automobile before 1920, but a few perceived the motor vehicle as a means of mass transit well before the "Jazz Age.'

Planning's impact on the urban landscape appeared very limited in the early twentieth century, but America possessed a tradition of planning that reached back for many years. A number of colonial and frontier towns were officially platted with areas set aside for public uses. Among the important American cities manifesting varying degrees of planning from their founding were Philadelphia, Savannah, Salt Lake City, and Washington. By far the most grandiose, and in many respects the most enduring, city plan was French designer Pierre L'Enfant's layout of the capital, presented to Congress in 1798.[6] Unfortunately, the demands of commercial and industrial enterprises for convenient space often overwhelmed the good intentions of founders in Washington, as in many other cities.[7]

In contrast to those who planned their cities from the beginning, a number of nineteenth-century civic boosters and civil engineers made heroic efforts to replan the physical evolution of cities whose development was well underway. As early as 1818 Detroit civic leader Augustus B. Woodward designed a plan of wide radial streets leading out from what is now Cadillac Square several miles into the surrounding wilderness. Many farmers resented his plan as uninvited interference. In their view, wide boulevards, which often bisected irregularly platted farms, were visionary.[8] In 1844, when Boston had a population of roughly 100,000, local engineer Robert F. Gourlay predicted a city five times as populous in fifty years. Even more important, he realized that with irregular topography, limited space, and narrow streets, downtown traffic congestion would be a nightmare. Gourlay imagined a subway under the downtown area, either pulled by steam engines or pushed by compressed air.[9] Though few paid attention to Gourlay's futuristic proposals at the time, turn-of-the-century Bostonians probably wished otherwise. By the time they shared Gourlay's vision of a subway through heavily built-up areas, land acquisition and construction created enormous financial burdens and difficult engineering problems.

Nineteenth-century city planning was generally modest in

scope and had little effect on transportation. Many proposals now considered forerunners of the twentieth-century planning movement envisioned little more than amelioration of the worst conditions created by excessive crowding in slums. The park plans of Andrew Jackson Downing and Frederick Law Olmsted inspired visions of "breathing space" and a taste of country life for thousands of unfortunate slum dwellers, but they did not attack basic problems. Turn-of-the-century housing reformer Lawrence Veiller held few illusions that tenement housing codes would bring instant utopia to the destitute of New York. At best, if adequately enforced, they would help provide at least a minimally civilized living environment.[10] As historians Stanley K. Schultz, Clay McShane, and Jon A. Peterson have demonstrated, civil engineers took huge strides in providing sanitation and the most basic public health services before 1900.[11] But important as these advances were, they exerted little direct effect upon the appearance of cities.

Americans owed much to European planning thought. Some historians have argued that the origins of city planning can be traced from the dawn of civilization.[12] Greek, Roman, and medieval town builders demonstrated ingenuity in the use of urban space. As noted earlier, Americans owed thanks to a Frenchman for designing the national capital. Daniel H. Burnham's famous twentieth-century design for Chicago drew heavily from Haussman's nineteenth-century plan for Paris. Englishman Ebenezer Howard's concepts about the detached "garden city," presented at the close of the nineteenth century, wielded enormous influence upon twentieth-century American planning thought. Howard envisioned self-contained, independent suburban towns of 30,000 to 50,000 residents. The towns would be separated from major cities and from other suburbs by wide "greenbelts" containing parks and farmland. A crucial element in Howard's theoretical exposition was his insistence that the towns contain their own small industries, which would permit residents to live close to their jobs.[13] While Howard's American disciples copied many of his ideas and borrowed his terminology, too often the so-called "garden cities" became mere appendages to large cities, whose residents were forced to make time-consuming daily journeys to their jobs in central districts.[14] Nevertheless, early-twentieth-century Americans found much support in European planning theory for their commitment to the suburban movement.

In 1900, American planners possessed little group awareness and no formal organizational structure. After the first official city planning commission appeared in Hartford in 1907, the profession emerged very slowly.[15] Like so many of the progressive reform groups evolving at about the same time, city planning organizations attracted large numbers of amateurs. Engineers, landscape architects, housing reformers, lawyers, and public service commissioners dominated the ranks of those who attended the first national conference on planning, held in Washington, D.C., in 1909.[16] Those who wrestled with transportation problems in metropolitan areas invariably pursued separate careers and viewed their planning efforts as a sideline. John Nolen was a landscape architect and park designer with a private consulting practice in Cambridge, Massachusetts. Although Nolen was interested in planning large cities, most of his commissions involved replanning small and medium-sized towns and presenting New Town proposals.[17] Charles Dyer Norton, an early supporter of the Burnham Plan in Chicago and an inspiration behind the New York Regional Plan of the 1920s, was secretary to President William Howard Taft, a businessman, and a banker. Alfred Bettman, influential chairman of the Cincinnati Planning Commission, was a prominent attorney and an expert on zoning and public utility franchise law.[18]

Like the founders of other nascent movements, pioneering

planners had little or no formal training.[19] Harvard University offered a single course in city planning in 1909, but four years later the *Journal of the American Institute of Architects* lauded that institution for providing "the first full and complete recognition" to the new profession. Even so, the journal called for expanded educational efforts, geared toward bringing at least the most basic concerns of city planners to the attention of the general public.[20] There were more concerted moves toward professional organization after the first national conference on city planning.[21] John Nolen saw the day of the "generalist," or amateur in city planning, coming to an end. In 1911 he predicted an increased trend toward specialization that would bring a new sense of professionalism to the movement.[22]

To many planners, it seemed that professional recognition and a sense of achievement were painfully slow in arriving. Before World War I, a number of planning commissions emerged; while they produced large numbers of plans, their achievements were far more impressive on paper than in practice.[23] In 1916, Chicago planner Walter D. Moody lamented that "city planning, as such, is not now recognized as an established profession. . . . The element of scientific promotion is comprehended by few and hence given no place by the many."[24]

Planners exerted little physical effect upon American cities, in part because they confronted myriad problems and controlled little money. In the early twentieth century few cities had planning staffs, and those that did seldom provided anything approaching adequate funding. Boston officially organized a city planning commission in 1915, but in 1920 its annual appropriation was a mere $4,676.[25] Although Los Angeles became a leader in regional planning in the 1920s and 1930s, a city planning commission was not chartered until 1920. In the early years, more than 150 volunteers staffed the Los Angeles commission, but their attendance at meetings was spotty and their participation was often desultory.[26] The Los Angeles body did not become an effective organization until it was significantly streamlined by the new city charter of 1924. In Chicago, the Burnham Plan of 1909 had stimulated initial enthusiasm for a planning commission. Yet in 1920, businessman Charles Wacker observed that the city council had provided only $100,000 for planning during the previous ten years, and that if local business groups had not donated twice that amount, little progress would have occurred.[27] Problems of uncertain funding plagued planning staffs in even the largest cities for many years.

The conflicting pressures of great expectations and limited resources forced planners to make difficult choices. Historian Mel Scott argued that "perhaps no other profession had to contend with so many rapid technological advances, so many startling changes in urban areas, and so many unfamiliar technical and legal problems as the city planning profession encountered just after its founding."[28] Planners realized that they needed to develop both a comprehensive philosophical framework and a set of concrete, practical objectives, but they soon learned the difficulty of achieving either. Some dreamed up bold futuristic schemes for urban utopias, but political and financial realities suggested cautious, limited proposals for minor adjustments. The conservative approach might do little to change the city in the short run, proponents argued, but it would give fledgling planning commissions time to establish themselves.

In the early part of the twentieth century, some thinkers assumed planners could effect little change unless they possessed broad powers. Burnham's 1909 plan for Chicago was particularly far-reaching in scope, and no single statement had a greater impact upon planners' consciousness than his famous dictum, "Make no little plans; they have no magic to stir man's blood."[29] Others called for the power to implement such visions. John

Nolen urged creation of permanent planning commissions, with guaranteed appropriations and authority to reserve land, borrow money, and hire specialized consultants when needed.[30] Professional architects such as Burnham and Nolen could well afford to take such an expansive view of the parameters of planning, since they could fall back on lucrative private practices should their public recommendations be rejected by uncooperative city councils.

However, most planners thought in less grandiose terms than Burnham and Nolen. Students of the movement have noted that early planners feared alienating local business leaders, whose support was often crucial. Mel Scott suggested that planners were wary of being labeled "visionaries" by businessmen, politicians, and other civic leaders; therefore, they generally eschewed the luxury of "adventuresomeness" of thought.[31] In a similar vein, historian John Hancock concluded that planners had little choice but to work within the "commercial-expansionist" mentality of the times.[32] Furthermore, planners had to work very carefully within municipal bureaucracies. Official and quasi-official planning staffs existed only at the whim of unpredictable city councils. For this reason, some thoughtful planners doubted that planning commissions should possess binding authority. These strategists feared that more firmly entrenched city departments would sabotage nascent planning organizations that they perceived as poaching in their territory. Reflecting this view of political reality, the Massachusetts Metropolitan Plan Commission suggested in 1912 that its powers should be limited to examining plans of other governmental agencies and expressing approval or disapproval. The commission specifically disavowed any intention of wielding final authority, seeking only ". . . to effect coordination of the plans of two or more agencies whenever this is desirable."[33]

In the years before World War II, the "conservatives" appeared to carry the day. Historian David R. Goldfield argued that, "despite the Progressives' deep commitment to social and political reform, their methods were conservative in that they sought to modify the grave injustices of urban society without altering that society."[34] Certainly, few planners challenged existing political structures, and they quickly learned that final authority rested with mayors and city councils. Even the most established and renowned planners often avoided risking their precarious positions of influence by pushing their ideas too forcefully. John Nolen, who argued for legal authority for planning boards, wrote to a younger member of his consulting firm that he "always refused to agitate for adoption" of plans in cities in which he had worked.[35] Most likely Nolen perceived that local enthusiasts could more effectively promote planning ideas than could professional outsiders.

Nolen's detachment, whether feigned or real, reflected the fact that, in other respects, planners negotiated from positions of weakness rather than of strength. The nature of their "product" precluded effective bargaining. Once they presented their plans, they had little but the pressure of public opinion with which to negotiate for adoption of their proposals. The disposition of Virgil Bogue's 1911 plan for the development of Seattle exemplified this problem. Opponents of the plan charged that formal approval would be a mistake, because it would coerce the city into constructing specifically designed civic improvements for many years to come. In effect, they called it rigid and inflexible.[36] Subjected to a civic referendum, the Bogue Plan lost by nearly two to one. One student of the plan's history suggested that the real reason for its defeat was that voters realized they could take its attractive suggestions and ignore the rest, without committing themselves to the whole package. Even though defeated at the polls, the plan may have triumphed in the long run, as much of

Seattle's subsequent development closely followed its most basic recommendations.[37]

On occasion, planners themselves spoke candidly about their weaknesses and disadvantages. George Kessler, one of America's most famous landscape architects, admitted that the chief impetus for planning was negative: "City planning, at least in its element of park and parkway development, is a matter of rebuilding or reconstruction, pulling down the efforts, the mistaken efforts mostly, of earlier times."[38] An even more critical obstacle was the negativism with which the general public viewed any costly plan that possessed intangible or remote benefits. When Edward H. Bennett prepared an elaborate city plan for Detroit in 1913, the *Detroit Times* predicted failure because civic leaders regarded it as "visionary and prohibitive." The paper correctly anticipated that "the plan when paid for will probably be tucked away some place."[39] The Detroit Plan Commission itself admitted the barren results of its early planning efforts. An annual report pointed out that five different city plans were prepared between 1900 and 1918; while "interesting from a historical standpoint," they were otherwise worthless, and they now "occupied valuable storage space in the city garage."[40] Although the cost in dollars for preparing plans was usually negligible, failure to produce practical results for money spent hurt planning in the long run in Detroit and other cities.

Of even more concern to some planners than financial problems limited authority, or even specific projects, was the philosophical issue of what the guiding principles of city planning should be. Even before 1910, profound disagreement emerged between proponents of the City Beautiful idea and those who urged planners to pursue more pragmatic, immediate goals.[41] Those favoring beautification held the upper hand during the first decade of the twentieth century. Planners were inspired by visits to the Columbian Exposition in Chicago in 1893 and the World's Fair in St. Louis in 1904, where they studied the prominent displays of dazzling public monuments, illuminated by the latest advances in street lighting.[42] Between 1900 and 1910, such famous landscape designers as Frederick Law Olmsted, Jr., Charles M. Robinson, and George Kessler presented plans for extensive renovations of central business districts in a score or more of large and medium-sized American cities.

City Beautiful advocates generally believed that large-scale redevelopment of the core city was the key to improving the urban environment. That the root of urban problems in America lay in the social, economic, and political disintegration of urban centers seemed self-evident.[43] Their plans projected multi-million-dollar civic centers, miles of elaborate radial parkways, and hundreds of acres of park space.[44] Advocates of the City Beautiful believed that their programs would achieve two distinct ends. Construction of stunning civic centers, monuments, and parks would galvanize residents to higher levels of achievement, and even the very poor would eventually join the economic mainstream. On an even higher level, beautification of downtown areas would inspire succeeding generations to overcome parochial squabbles and unite to develop cities worthy of the new and vibrant American civilization.[45]

Others within the emerging community of planners were less optimistic. A revolt against emphasizing civic centers and public monuments appeared as early as the first national planning conference in 1909. By 1912 the forces of the "city practical" counterrevolution were dominant. New York planner George B. Ford articulated their views when he questioned whether planners could permit cities to spend money on "frills and furbelows, when only a step away the hideous slum, reeking with filth and disease, rotten with crime, is sapping the very life-blood of the

4. A downtown Chicago street scene from around 1910. Chaotic, crowded streets existed before the mass popularization of the automobile. Courtesy of the Chicago Historical Society.

5. The lakefront rehabiliation of former railroad yards next to Chicago's Loop symbolized the finest tradition of city beautification. This is Grant Park around 1910. Courtesy of the Library of Congress, Washington, D.C.

city." Ford labeled city beautifiers' plans for "extravagant public monuments" a "perverted use" of the poor man's taxes. He insisted that the money would be far better spent providing needed social services for the poor.[46] Fellow New Yorker Arnold Brunner, a member of the American Association of Architects, joined Ford's challenge to the beautifiers at the 1912 conference. Brunner charged that "the City Beautiful movement failed—failed because it started at the wrong end. . . . Since utility and beauty go hand in hand, let us insist on utility."[47]

Regardless of their philosophical orientations, many planners cited inadequate transportation as the single greatest obstacle to creating a humane urban environment. Frederick L. Olmsted, Jr., complained in 1910 that planners were entirely preoccupied with developing adequate city streets, but John Nolen argued that such an emphasis was entirely warranted. "No other feature is so permanent, no other so difficult to change. Streets also have the most direct and intimate influence upon the economic, sanitary, and esthetic development of city life."[48] Most early-twentieth-century planners realized that street layout created the framework for the future spatial evolution of their cities. Badly planned streets and inadequate thoroughfares could prevent orderly development of outlying areas and seriously inconvenience future generations.

Given the lack of unity among planners regarding even the most basic issues, it is not surprising that they arrived at no consensus in urban transportation. By the end of the nineteenth century, however, they were at least developing some notions of what would not work. Specifically, they realized that, even aside from political considerations, the electric trolley was no magic cure for urban congestion. If anything, the streetcar intensified crowding of downtown streets, at least in large cities, because it permitted more people to concentrate quickly at a given point. In large cities like New York and Chicago, downtown streets were jammed by horses, carts, and milling pedestrians. Trolleys on narrow streets simply added to the chaos.

Even before the introduction of the trolley, some nineteenth-century municipal engineers believed they could solve congestion problems by providing additional levels for traffic. Engineers experimented briefly with steam locomotives on elevated tracks in New York after the Civil War. This effort failed partly for environmental reasons, as sparks and soot from locomotives showered pedestrians.[49] However, electricity promised a cleaner form of transport and created fewer fire hazards. As a result, some turn-of-the-century planners believed electrically powered elevated cars or subways might solve congestion problems. The first subway in America opened in Boston in 1897; initial layouts for systems in New York and Philadelphia soon followed.

A few planners urged subway construction in almost all of America's large cities. Alfred Bettman, influential Cincinnati planner and lawyer, believed that modern rapid transit facilities, either above or below street level, were crucial for large, rapidly growing cities. While admitting that both subways and elevated lines were extremely expensive, and that few cities could afford complete systems in the beginning, Bettman urged city governments at least to start their systems immediately, since rapid transit would be more expensive later. As Bettman put it, "a wise city will not wait until the evil effects of inadequate transportation facilities are upon it."[50] In 1902, nationally renowned transportation consultant Bion J. Arnold advised Chicago to build a modern rapid transit system, estimating a cost of between $85.5 and $90 million.[51] Twelve years later, little had been done, and Arnold projected the total cost of the same system at $130 million. Realizing the difficulty or impossibility of building a complete system in 1914, he urged the city to raise between $30 and $50 million and begin immediate construction of a system's core. Arnold's "incremental" strategy was to build the core, then add to it piecemeal as finances and political realities permitted.[52]

Apart from urging construction of elevateds and subways for what they perceived as sound business reasons, some transit planners recommended them as a means to decentralize cities. New York transportation engineer George B. Ford believed that city dwellers should be distributed over a much wider area, and that rapid transit was the critical element permitting them to move quickly, comfortably, and inexpensively about the city.[53] Although he later perceived superhighways as the best means to decentralize cities, New York planner Edward M. Bassett wholeheartedly supported Ford's praise for subways in 1913, declaring that "rapid transit is the only thing that will bring low rent and sunny homes to working people in great cities."[54] In the early twentieth century, planners generally believed that decentralization was an unmixed blessing.

Most who endorsed construction of rapid transit facilities mistakenly assumed that new facilities could be self-supporting. A handful of planners anticipated public transit companies' future financial difficulties, and urged public subsidies even for existing mass transit lines. However, a larger number believed that transit companies were in good financial health and could attract capital for rapid transit construction without help. Transportation consultants in some cities argued that large increases in trolley patronage made subway construction both feasible and imperative. The New York planning firm of Barclay, Parsons, and Klapp noted that ridership on Detroit's lines tripled between 1904 and 1913, and argued that revenues from increased patronage could finance upgrading of existing facilities and building of subways.[55] While such an argument appeared valid in 1915, severe wartime inflation and fixed fares soon rendered it obsolete.[56] But old ideas die hard. Despite increasing evidence of its invalidity, the "self-help" argument for providing rapid transit lingered into the 1920s, and it even surfaced occasionally in the 1930s.[57]

Today it seems evident that subways only made sense in a handful of large, highly centralized cities, but some transportation consultants of the past assumed that construction of rapid transit was inevitable in most cities. Supporters of this view pushed Bettman's and Arnold's recommendation that construction of subways could hardly begin too soon. Harland Bartholomew, a young planner from St. Louis, insisted in 1917 that as cities approached the million mark in population, construction of rapid transit, either above or below the street, was imperative.[58] The Los Angeles Department of Public Utilities rejected rapid transit in 1913, but shifted its stance the very next year. Utilities experts urged that the city begin construction when its population reached one million; building preferably would commence when the population was only 750,000.[59] Even in the smaller cities, local planners often assumed the inevitability of eventual construction of rapid transit lines. In 1911, when Seattle's population was but a quarter of a million, Virgil Bogue concluded that streetcar lines, "wherever found, would generally be rebuilt as either subway or elevated in the course of time."[60]

Despite urgings that comprehensive rapid transit was crucial to the formation of humane urban environments, a number of planners resisted subways and elevateds even early in the century, sometimes for political reasons. Planners shared both much of the optimism of reformers and many of their suspicions, particularly concerning large public utilities. As Stanley K. Schultz and Clay McShane show, many early planners had long years of experience as professional city engineers; as engineers, some planners possessed intimate knowledge of the machinations of both politicians and public utility officials.[61] Street railway interests were frequently involved in deep, secret, and occasionally corrupt franchise negotiations with public officials, and it was inevitable that some planners distrusted both groups. More significantly, planners who were inherently suspicious of street railways were naturally wary of supporting proposals for any new rapid transit facilities that would be controlled by presumably corrupt monopolies.

Even in the early twentieth century, there were thoughtful critics who opposed subways and elevateds for substantive reasons. The deeper they probed the issue of rapid transit, the more complex it appeared. Simply superimposing new subway lines over existing, but frequently outmoded rights of way would invite disaster. They noted that, more often than not, nineteenth-century street railway systems were jerry-built collections of tracks built by several competing companies. John Nolen commented in 1919 that "the first discovery in almost every city where systematic studies have been made for the improvement of transportation has been that the street railway system is poorly planned, and will not permit of such a routing of the railway lines as is necessary for thoroughly good service. These conditions are found in their most aggravated form in the central areas toward which the lines converge."[62] In most cities, therefore, almost all trolley lines led directly downtown and forced nearly every streetcar to pass through the center of the city whether or not logic necessitated its presence there. With hundreds of streetcars crowding central districts, elevateds or subways might at first appear to be the natural solution. Simply get the rumbling monsters off the street, and downtown traffic could become "normal." Sober-minded realists feared that any rapid transit system that followed the comparatively inexpensive rights of way of older streetcar lines would quickly become obsolete.

Others charged that any type of central-district-oriented rapid transit system would court obsolescence by exacerbating downtown congestion. Unless new routes permitted crosstown patrons to avoid downtown areas, subway and elevated lines would simply multiply the number of persons crowding into the central districts. Chicago architect and planner Alfred J. Roewade opposed Bion J. Arnold's 1902 plan for a subway system largely on these grounds. Roewade argued that the subway plan would not improve conditions for pedestrians and teamsters in the central district, and he urged using the money to increase traffic capacity by widening narrow downtown streets.[63] Reviewing his city's experience with subways, New York planner Ernest B. Goodrich noted in 1915 that "it has been pretty well demonstrated that rapid transit has increased congestion. We normally have designed rapid transit systems to decrease congestion, but the desire always seems to be to get to the central point. We go there because we have greater opportunity to get what we want. More people come to the center when we get rapid transit than they [sic] did before."[64] John Nolen supported Goodrich in a nearly identical statement three years later.[65]

Some transportation experts even doubted that rapid transit lines would help to decentralize the city. Both foreign and American planners adopted this view. To be sure, building high-speed lines far out into the countryside might permit the sale of small lots and bungalow homes to thousands. But British town planner Raymond Unwin noted that improved rapid transit facilities also attracted more people from the country into the city.[66] Unwin, like his predecessor Ebenezer Howard, and their American friend John Nolen, believed that beneficial decentralization would occur only when job locations as well as residential areas were spread out. Rapid transit lines that simply lengthened the distance of one's journey to work solved no problems and threatened to create new ones. Historian Joel A. Tarr observed that it was evident even at the turn of the century that construction of rapid transit facilities did little to help the poor escape the central city.[67] Hence, long before the automobile became commonplace, many influential planners and transportation consultants articulated strong reservations against ambitious rapid transit systems.

Even very early in the century, some planners perceived the automobile's potential for moving masses of people. With the numbers of motor vehicles growing geometrically between 1900 and 1920, some of the most respected planners in America placed a good deal of faith in autos' ability to contribute to the healthy spreading out of the nation's metropolitan regions. They believed that "automobility" would lead to decentralization of housing and the amelioration of social disorders; meanwhile, trucks and motor buses would help revive decaying central cities.

One of the most ambitious early regional plans in America was Burnham's plan for Chicago. The Burnham proposal clearly emphasized the central role of the automobile in future regional transportation. His prophetic vision of the future projected not only a complete system of wide radial thoroughfares leading from outlying areas into the central core, but a series of circumferential highways, the most distant being fifty miles from the downtown area. Although Burnham failed to anticipate problems that the automobile would create, he was at least a decade ahead of his peers in anticipating the needs of both through traffic and intra-city movement.[68] And Burnham was even farther ahead of his contemporaries in attempting to direct land use rather than simply serving existing needs.

Less ambitious in regional terms was Virgil Bogue's 1911 design for Seattle, which evidently assumed a key role for the automobile. Wide boulevards were a tradition in urban development long before the advent of motor vehicles, and their purposes transcended the mere movement of traffic. In keeping with existing traditions, Bogue projected a waterfront boulevard 300 to 500 feet in width, with other city boulevards a minimum of 160 feet wide. While Bogue hoped they would possess the greatest possible aesthetic appeal, he made it plain that their primary purpose was the functional movement of vehicles. Trees and shrubs might be planted in portions of boulevard rights of way not immediately paved, but "in such locations only as will enable the future development of roadways to be made with the greatest freedom when traffic demands."[69] Clearly, future needs of motorists were to supersede any aesthetic considerations.

No American planner supported the automobile more forcefully than Nelson P. Lewis, chief engineer of the New York Board of Estimate. According to Lewis, the automobile had a beneficial impact upon the cityscape for several reasons. By discouraging further centralization, it helped diffuse land values and "stabilize" real estate. Lewis argued before the national planning conference of 1915 that intelligent policing of traffic flow and regulation of vehicle size would "permit a much greater volume of traffic to be accommodated with safety on the same street." In addition, more extensive use of the private car would "result in a better knowledge on the part of the citizen of his city and its environment."[70] Rather than exacerbate congestion, the automobile would, in Lewis's view, reduce it. By World War I, in response to increasing numbers of automobiles and pressure from automobile enthusiasts, city governments had vastly improved local streets.[71] Lewis perceived a direct relationship between streets and automobiles; spreading automobile traffic onto more city streets would encourage urban governments to improve the streets and beautify them by planting more trees and shrubbery.[72]

An important factor behind the planners' approval of the automobile was their assumption that they could always guide its evolution as the servant of mankind. At the 1915 planning conference, C. M. Talbert of St. Louis argued that because numbers of automobiles were increasing "gradually, if rapidly . . . a great many of the problems will solve themselves."[73] A year later Lewis once again emphasized that "the development of the motor vehicle appears on the whole to present no problems to highway officials, especially problems relating to street congestion."[74]

Such euphoric predictions of the future impact of the automobile did not stand unchallenged. Planner Ernest B. Goodrich directly contradicted Lewis by arguing that the automobile would increase rather than relieve future traffic congestion. Dr. Werner Hegemann, a Berlin planner visiting the 1915 conference, made a telling point in charging that the automobile divided American city dwellers into two classes, the "barons," riding not horses, but automobiles, and the "common people," who depended upon public transportation. He feared that once the wealthier, more influential classes adopted the automobile, they had little incentive to fight for improved public transportation. Hegemann believed that promoting the automobile would hurt mass transit, and that living space for the masses would be restricted to areas close to central districts, which could be served profitably by streetcars.[75]

More significant than the arguments of planners for or against the automobile was that the majority of planners did not perceive that the motor vehicle, like other great technological breakthroughs, permitted both concentration and the outward movement of households and business firms. In the early years of the planning movement, few doubted that decentralization was anything but a blessing, and they welcomed any technological advances that assisted such a pattern of growth. Clearly the planners' perception of the impact of the automobile upon public transportation was not measurably more prescient than that of the general public. Of more immediate significance to the evolution of urban transportation was that while most planners acknowledged the key role of the trolley in moving large numbers of urbanites, a substantial number opposed providing private companies the incentives to improve services sufficiently to keep

pace with modern needs and demands. This may have been largely a matter of planners following the line of least resistance, as
some present-day critics have charged.[76] But the evidence suggests that this criticism of the planning profession is simplistic.
Numerous and urgent challenges kept planners from concentrating full attention upon what was happening in urban transportation. Even more to the point, many planners consciously rejected
rapid transit for carefully articulated reasons. At the time, at
least, their arguments appeared tough-minded and soundly
reasoned.

3 Transportation and the Changing City

By the 1920s the suburban trend was evident to nearly everybody. This powerful movement had profound effects on urban transportation, many of which were barely noticeable even to experts. In retrospect, it is obvious that significantly lower population densities, combined with greatly expanded service areas, sounded the death knell for many street railways. But transportation officials and city planners largely overlooked this reality. Street railway officials emphasized the superiority of the trolley in transporting large numbers of riders in congested districts, and virtually ignored the fact that automobiles were establishing new patterns of traffic movement in outlying areas.[1] Similarly, mass use of the automobile, at least as a tool for urban commuting, caught too many experts by surprise. For these and other reasons, neither street railway managers nor public officials took effective action to bolster mass transit systems during the 1920s.

By 1920 the modern industrial city had emerged and had already incorporated many of the technological systems fundamentally affecting its physical growth.

Except for the emergence of the over-fifty-story skyscraper, the downtown area had achieved much of the appearance it possesses today. Even so, American cities experienced important changes during the decade. Most were growing, although at very uneven rates, and growth in some older cities slowed significantly during the 1920s. Between 1920 and 1930 Boston's population increased by only 33,000, from 748,000 to 781,060. Seattle had been a boom town in the three decades between 1890 and 1920, enjoying a seven-fold increase, but during the 1920s its population grew by less than 20 percent. Other cities, including Washington, D.C., and Denver, experienced similarly declining growth. However, the 1920s brought spectacular population gains in other cities. Between 1920 and 1930, Detroit's population jumped from under 1,000,000 to 1,568,662, thanks largely to the rapid growth of the automobile industry.[2] During the same period Los Angeles's population more than doubled. Southern California's boom, more broadly based economically than Detroit's, rested upon a combination of petroleum discoveries, tourism, health care, real estate speculation, motion pictures, agriculture, and light industry.[3]

Of far greater significance than overall area growth rates was where the growth took place. Virtually every important American city's fringe areas experienced more rapid expansion than core cities after 1920. Local booster publications bragged about central-area growth during the 1920s: ever-taller skyscrapers, increased parking space, thousands of additional square feet of office and storage space, and so forth. But new and exciting types of growth also occurred on the fringes. The same publications proudly listed the numbers of new housing starts, miles of new streets, electrical conduits, and gas and sewer lines on the cities' outskirts.[4]

Historians, urban geographers, and other social scientists have heatedly debated the question of when American cities began to decentralize. Two reliable studies suggest that the origins of decentralization can be found in the nineteenth century, or even the eighteenth.[5] Kenneth T. Jackson observed that nineteenth-century cities exhibited a systematic pattern of population movement toward the periphery.[6] Nevertheless, while demographers cannot pinpoint the years when more Americans actually left than entered the inner city, they are virtually unanimous in the view that the process intensified in the 1920s.[7] Up until 1920, while cities were growing more rapidly than rural areas, population growth was greater in the central cities than on the fringes. During the next decade, a significant change occurred. While core-city areas grew at a rate of 24.2 percent, the surrounding ring areas grew by 33.2 percent.[8]

Fringe areas expanded more rapidly than core areas in virtually every major city during the 1920s; yet demographers have uncovered some interesting variations. Leo Schnore revealed that whereas before the First World War many new residents moved directly to the urban core, in later years they bypassed the center of the city to settle directly on its fringes.[9] There were many reasons for this. First, as already noted, transportation improvements made the inner city more accessible from the fringe areas. In addition to providing an alternative means of commuting along traditional suburb-to-downtown corridors, the automobile allowed quick, convenient access between home and job locations in outlying areas. Social factors also contributed to this new pattern of urban growth. One of the most obvious was rising racial and ethnic tensions. During the prewar years successive waves of immigrants settled in core cities; World War I and its aftermath brought the decline of immigration and an increase in the number of black migrants to the inner city.[10] One result was that during the 1920s many native whites moving to metropolitan areas from the country bypassed the traditional pattern of residential succession. Instead of starting at the core and moving slowly outward as their economic and social status improved, they created new, mostly white, suburbs.[11]

Fringe-area growth was impressive in all cities, but active real estate promotion and the automobile combined to create a spectacular degree of horizontal growth in Los Angeles.[12] The remoteness of local subdivisions astonished some observers. During the height of the real estate boom of the 1920s, incoming motorists often encountered staked-out subdivisions more than thirty miles from the heart of the city. According to a local wag, some tracts were "so far out that not even Hollywood's pistol shots reverberated through the pastoral solitude."[13] The city's population more than doubled during the 1920s; among its better-known suburbs, Beverly Hills grew 2,485 percent, Inglewood grew 493 percent,

Huntington Park grew 445 percent, and Glendale grew 364 percent.[14]

As noted earlier, the impressive suburban development that preceded World War I was due largely to the efforts of real estate, utility, and street railway promoters. Although real estate and utility promoters continued to play prominent roles in the suburban boom of the 1920s, the automobile became developers' chief ally. Hindsight makes clear that the explosion of auto-mobile suburbs signaled the demise of the electric railway. In the 1920s, however, the overall growth of urban areas, and the fact that the majority of urban residents still depended on trolleys, obscured this reality. During the 1920s more people used the streetcars than ever before or since. Between 1920 and 1923 ridership of electric railways inched upward from 15.5 billion patrons to a peak of 15.7 billion. Thereafter, patronage declined, although very slowly; in 1930 ridership still amounted to 13.1 billion passengers for the year.[15]

A tapering off of street railway patronage concurrent with rapid urban growth signaled the beginning of the industry's decline; however, the robust health of the motor bus, a new means of public transportation, shrouded the impending demise. The census did not list the motor bus as a carrier of revenue passengers until 1922, when buses transported 404 million; by 1930 they carried 2.5 billion passengers. Thus combined patronage on electric railway and bus lines reached a peak of 17.2 billion riders in 1926 and declined to 15.6 billion riders by 1930. In effect, then, the bus took up much slack in street railway patronage.[16] One may speculate that, had the bus not appeared when it did, public officials might have realized the weakness of the mass transit industry and provided financial support at a critical moment. But given the social, economic, and political conditions of the 1920s, such intervention would have been highly unlikely.

In the early years of the evolution of the gasoline-powered motor bus—roughly between World War I and the mid-1920s—trolley operators usually viewed the new invention as an intruder rather than an ally. During World War I, jitney buses appeared on city streets in large numbers. These large automobiles, carrying up to a dozen passengers, often operated along heavily traveled streetcar routes. Trolley companies legitimately argued that the unlicensed private citizens driving these vehicles robbed them of vitally needed patronage. Jitney operators retorted that they were simply practicing free enterprise. As a result of trolley company pressure, and because hundreds of jitneys operating without schedules jammed city streets, many city councils subsequently outlawed them as a public nuisance.[17]

By the early 1920s, however, some street railway officials believed that the motor bus was not necessarily a competitor, but might instead be an ally in their effort to retain control of urban transportation. The bus provided mass transit officials a flexibility they had not possessed earlier. It permitted street railway managers to provide temporary service in rapidly developing but lightly settled areas, while they decided whether or not to expand trolley lines. Officials could experiment with a variety of crosstown routes, and eliminate unpopular or lightly traveled routes with little delay or inconvenience to patrons.[18] In addition, buses were more maneuverable than trolleys in congested areas, and their greater maneuverability made possible faster and more frequent service.[19]

Many mass transit companies experimented with buses during and after the 1920s, and those that did not often suffered. Trolley executives in Atlanta generally ignored the bus and chose to pour most of their resources into upgrading streetcar service. Although the Georgia Power Company won the American Electric Railway Association prize for the "most outstanding contribution to increasing the advantages of electric transportation in an American

city" in 1927, mass transit patronage in Atlanta declined precipi-
tously during the "Jazz Age."[20] Nevertheless, mass transit
spokesmen in many American cities realized that greater speed
was a crucial attraction in their effort to maintain mass transit. As
one of them observed in 1927, "There is no use trying to satisfy
car riders with what satisfies us. We must deliver the kind of
product that satisfies them."[21] In many respects, the motor bus fit
their requirements. In retrospect, the bus may have hurt the mass
transit industry, in that it lulled industry officials into believing
they were making innovations adequate to compete with the
automobile.

Given perfect hindsight, it seems startling that many, perhaps a
majority, of trolley company executives touted the industry's
good health and bright future during the 1920s. Their optimism
was reinforced by studies that employed statistics in imaginative
ways. Influential transportation consultant John Beeler published
a study in 1925 revealing that per capita use of trolleys increased
as population in metropolitan areas grew.[22] Beeler argued that
since American cities were growing rapidly, all would be well in
the transit industry. A 1930 study compared ridership figures in a
carefully selected group of ten large cities in 1920 and 1929. The
report observed that while aggregate population in these cities
had increased by 16 percent, total public transportation patronage
had grown 33 percent.[23] The latter study ignored several unpleasant realities. First, it measured population figures only in
central cities, ignoring the fact that much of the gain in ridership
came from patrons in outlying areas. In addition, the report
glossed over the fact that its 1929 figures included bus riders,
while its 1920 figures did not. Finally, it ignored the fact that
by 1929 overall figures for public transit usage were clearly on
a downward trend.

Present-day critics might find it tempting to contend that during the 1920s spokesmen for the trolley industry deliberately

misled their workers and patrons, and that in the process they fooled themselves. Unquestionably, for purposes of satisfying investors, attracting capital for upgrading equipment, and maintaining employee morale, corporate officials chose to emphasize the bright side of their situation. Industry publications unquestionably pandered to their readers' hopes, yet their tone conveyed strong conviction. A 1927 *Electric Railway Journal* editorial was typical:

> Only a few years ago the electric railway industry was laboriously struggling up the road to recovery, carrying a staggering load of public burdens cumulatively imposed. . . . Today those who are in a position to view in perspective the ground gained are united in the conviction that the turning point has not only been reached but has been definitely passed.[24]

Such expressions of optimism came not only from industry representatives, but also from transportation consultants as well. In 1928 Robert F. Kelker of Chicago, who prepared transportation plans for many American cities during the twenties, expressed a similar view. While admitting that the automobile had caused patronage losses on trolley lines in many cities, he insisted that by upgrading facilities, increasing speed, and employing aggressive marketing tactics, the industry could win back many of its former patrons.[25]

A central assumption of transit industry representatives was that the "masses" would always require public transportation. As one observer in Chicago put it, "Chicago for one hundred years to come will need all the surface and elevated lines, all the subways and buses that we will be able to supply to take care of its teeming millions."[26] Sidney D. Waldon, a former automobile company executive and chairman of Detroit's Rapid Transit Commission, agreed. He argued in 1928 that the trolley would have to be the backbone of urban transportation systems until replaced by subways.[27]

Despite such broad currents of optimism within the street railway industry, other observers were deeply pessimistic about the trolley's future. A number of influential and sober-minded realists concluded that the trolley was in serious jeopardy. Profits, which had seemingly rolled in effortlessly between the 1890s and World War I, were increasingly difficult to achieve, especially when the riding public demanded better service at the same low fares. Trolley company officials found it increasingly difficult to attract capital investment to upgrade their facilities and match their chief competitor, the automobile. As Lucius Storrs, managing director of the American Electric Railway Association, noted, fixed fares on long-term franchises had returned to haunt the industry. The inflation of World War I forced trolley companies to pay far higher prices for capital equipment and labor, but they had to make do with the same gross revenues.[28] At federal hearings on the state of the industry in the summer of 1919, noted investment broker Roger W. Babson testified that nobody but "anonymous losers" like "your Uncle Dudley" and municipalities were investing in the trolley industry.[29] The "smart" money was invested in newer, less regulated industries. Street railways were indeed caught in a double bind. If trolley companies desired to attract capital for reinvestment, they had to emphasize profits; but that strategy would backfire if the public used such publicity as a lever to demand lower fares.[30] To pessimists, it appeared that their industry could not win.

Other industry spokesmen argued that the street railways suffered from unfair property taxation and unrealistic street improvement clauses in their franchise agreements. Stone and Webster Public Relations Manager L. R. Nash noted that street railways paid "special burdens," not assumed by other industries, amounting to an average of more than 5 percent of their operating revenues. Although imposts on street railways varied markedly in each city, they included franchise fees, taxes on net or gross receipts, license fees for cars, track, poles, and wires, and annual maintenance charges for street lighting, paving, cleaning, drainage, sprinkling, snow removal, bridge repair, and traffic regulation. In addition, mass transit companies usually provided free transportation for a variety of municipal, state, and federal workers.[31] Many of these obligations were imposed upon street railways at the turn of the century, when they held a virtual monopoly over street traffic. When many companies were making healthy profits and street maintenance costs were low, company officials accepted such imposts as minor irritants of little consequence—a small price to pay for advantageous long-term franchises. But with the coming of heavier motor vehicles and paved streets, these maintenance costs became substantial. Trolley company officials believed they were also discriminatory. As C. D. Emmons, president of Baltimore's United Railways and Electric Company, viewed it, "The motor vehicle that is competing with [us], in many communities, has free use of the paving for which the electric railway pays."[32]

Some urban observers who worried about the future of the street railway believed that changing social customs worked to the industry's disadvantage. While optimists pointed to increased riding "habits" in certain cities, pessimists observed that by the late 1920s widespread ownership of radios often kept entire families in their living rooms or front porches during leisure hours. In former years, families had taken trolley rides to country parks for picnics and swimming. By the 1920s, they were likely to make the same trips by automobile. The rise of neighborhood theaters and commercial strips along outlying highways also kept people off trolley lines serving downtown areas, where the primary entertainment and retail facilities had been located in earlier years.[33]

Other well-wishers feared the mass transit industry was finally paying for the negative public image it had developed during earlier years of prosperity, and that the public would vent its frustration against the industry when it was most vulnerable. Owen D. Young, chairman of the board of General Electric, a major supplier of trolley equipment, observed in 1928 that "it is indeed a rather dull morning when the public, in one form or another, does not threaten to lick the industry before the day is done."[34] Popular writer Raymond Thompkins, reflecting on the woes of the street railway industry the same year, believed that the trolley was already revealing signs of rigor mortis. "Millions of able-bodied men living today remember when rapid transit first arrived with a whoop, sputter, and clang, chasing horse-cars and horses off to the scrapheap and the glue factory. It is not yet fifty years old in this country. But already its movements grow slow and jerky, it complains of pains in the head, and in many cities men snicker when they speak of it as rapid."[35] If industry loyalists were not yet ready to write its obituary, knowledgeable observers had deep misgivings over its future by the end of the 1920s.

Street railway defenders were keenly aware of the auto-mobile's influence upon physical growth and other facets of urban life; but while some of them admitted its negative impact upon mass transit, most stridently rejected the notion that it could lead to the trolley's downfall. Industry publications insisted throughout the 1920s that the automobile alone could never provide sufficient transportation for all family members in a modern city. While Dad might drive the family car to work, Mom had to run errands and shop, and the kids had to get to and from school. Hence, as the editor of the Pacific Electric Railway's magazine viewed it, most urban trips would continue to involve mass transit.[36] Schenectady Railway President Edwin M. Walker was even more optimistic. He argued that once automobile buyers fully realized the enormous expense of owning and maintaining their new devices, they would realize the folly of their ways and return to the more dependable, inexpensive streetcar![37]

Before World War I, trolley officials had generally assumed a casual, patronizing attitude toward the automobile; by the 1920s their views reflected ambivalence, along with respect for a major new competitor. A few officials tried to downplay the negative impact of the automobile upon street railways, but others acknowledged the benefits it brought to the lives of urbanites by opening up the surrounding countryside for recreation and other purposes. Although its chief purpose was to tout the trolley, a 1925 editorial in *Electric Traction* conveyed the mixed feelings of industry officials. While insisting that high maintenance costs, congestion, and inadequate downtown parking would induce many urban automobilists to return to the trolley, the editorial admitted that those factors had not slowed ever-increasing automobile sales: "We must have our automobile, too, for there is no disputing the fact that a good car is a very enjoyable and healthy luxury."[38] And a 1930 American Electric Railway Association study forthrightly praised the automobile for so increasing the efficiency of farm labor that millions were able to migrate to the city. Whether on the farm or in the city, the report concluded, "the individual has been given a flexible mobility which had never before been imagined."[39]

Street railway officials sensed that a fundamental reason for the automobile's popularity was the aggressive public relations and sales techniques employed by the new industry, and they consciously imitated their chief competitors. Many trolley companies actively courted the patrons they had taken for granted a decade earlier. They expanded public relations staffs, improved courtesy courses for car operators, built safety islands in streets for waiting patrons, upgraded equipment, and adjusted their routes. Street railway managers took these changes seriously and introduced each innovative program with flair. James A. Gregg, sales manager for the Toledo Community Traction Company, described the changing role of the modern trolley executive in 1926: "Ten years ago he was in the engineering business. Today he is in the merchandising business."[40] Cynics urged trolley officials to spend their money refurbishing decrepit older cars rather than the industry's tarnished public image.[41] Although unfriendly critics still viewed the industry's overtures toward the public through jaundiced eyes, by the end of the 1920s mass transit officials had largely abandoned their earlier arrogance.

A few street railway spokesmen so advocated positive thinking that they were determined to perceive threats to the industry, even that of the automobile, as advantages. Britton I. Budd, president of several Chicago-area lines, argued that although the automobile was a serious competitor, it made people far more mobile; in addition to using the automobile, urbanites would also take more trolley rides.[42] After World War I, downtown traffic became increasingly congested, and some mass transit spokesmen argued that the automobile was losing its advantages over the trolley in speed, convenience, and comfort. As a result, many railway representatives maintained that automobile ownership was nearing its saturation point. A 1926 editorial in *Electric Traction* claimed that the anticipated leveling off of automobile ownership would have a positive effect on the trolley industry: "The trend in the larger cities is now clearly shown in an increase in streetcar riding, and even the interurban operating out of cities is profiting by growing congestion on the highways."[43]

However much they may have desired to support these views, pessimists within the trolley industry were deeply worried about the effect of the automobile upon street railway patronage. Lucius Storrs noted in 1920 that rapidly declining costs of ownership and operation had put the automobile within reach of millions who would not have considered such a purchase a few years earlier.[44] Some mass transit industry spokesmen also realized that, in light of the general prosperity of the 1920s, the expense of getting from one place to another was a factor of decreasing importance for many urbanites. A 1925 *Bus Transportation* editorial pointed out that even blue-collar workers were buying automobiles, and expectations of luring them back to the bus or streetcar with low fares were increasingly unrealistic.[45]

Other mass transit officials sensed that their service was increasingly unattractive to patrons because trolleys and buses seemed very slow compared to the automobile. Before World War I and automobile mass marketing, public transit riders tolerated average speeds of eight or ten miles per hour with only occasional grumbles. By the 1920s, with suburban areas sometimes located ten or more miles from central districts, these speeds became increasingly unacceptable.[46] And street railways were even slower in the central districts. An independent transportation consulting firm disclosed in 1925 that for journeys of less than two miles in Washington, D.C., the trolley's average speed was only 4.1 miles per hour. The average pedestrian could travel the same distance at a speed of 3.7 miles per hour.[47] The fact that downtown traffic congestion also inconvenienced and frustrated automobile owners provided small comfort to realists within the transit industry.

While mass transit struggled, the automobile flourished. During the 1920s the number of registered automobiles in the United States almost tripled, increasing from 8.1 million in 1920 to 23.1 million nine years later.[48] In 1920 there was one automobile for every thirteen Americans; by 1929 there was one for every five. A primary reason for the democratization of automobile ownership was the sharp drop in initial purchase price. Between 1913 and 1923, a period in which the overall price index doubled, automobile prices fell sharply. By 1923 the price of the Model-T Ford, which sold for $600 in 1913, had declined to $393. Even more startling were price decreases by Ford's competitors. Chevrolet lowered its sticker price from $1,200 to $495; Overland Motors reduced its base price from $1,495 to $515![49]

Although American farmers had briefly resisted the automobile at the turn of the century by the 1920s they adopted it with enthusiasm. In fact, per capita automobile ownership was higher in the country than in the city. Without an automobile, a rural family was nearly as isolated in the 1920s as it had been in the 1890s. Depending upon the availability of mass transit, the urban family could still move about in some comfort. The nearly 600,000 registered automobiles in New York City in 1930 represented only one for every twelve residents; Boston and Chicago boasted one for every eight persons. Nevertheless, ratios in other cities actually surpassed the national per capita ownership figure. In Detroit and Seattle there was one automobile for every four residents; in Los Angeles, one for every three.[50]

The automobile received accolades from the vast majority of urban observers during the 1920s. Landscape architects often favored it because it made sylvan parks more accessible and increased public demand for these facilities; and such yearnings unquestionably increased their contracts and commissions.[51] Chambers of commerce touted the automobile for boosting tourism and urged state legislators to accomodate the flivver by constructing adequate highways to their cities and throughout their regions. Automobile caravans organized by local businessmen crossed difficult terrain with a view toward extending commercial contacts in nearby cities and publicizing the need for good roads. A 1920 California study estimated that automobile tourism accounted for $74 million in new business for the Golden State.[52] And friends of the automobile industry were well prepared to meet head-on what small opposition it encountered during the

1920s. Confronted by charges that the automobile caused the slaughter of tens of thousands of people annually, defenders pointed out in 1929 that the number of automobiles had multiplied a hundredfold in the past twenty-five years, yet traffic fatalities had increased but tenfold.[53] While deploring needless deaths, defenders insisted that the automobile was safer than ever before and deftly turned fatality statistics into justification for much higher expenditures for safer, more modern highways.

By the mid-1920s the automobile was assuming a role as a mass carrier of urban dwellers. This may have surprised advocates who had long emphasized the automobile's utility on the farm. The public was familiar, for example, with advertising photographs of automobiles being used to power stationary farm machinery. While the automobile industry consciously and aggressively created urban markets, it made no particular effort, at least during the 1920s, to promote the car as a commuting tool for urban workers. Although former Packard Motor executive Sidney D. Walden labeled the automobile "the magic carpet of transportation for all mankind," he suggested very strongly that it was not well suited to urban mass transit. As Waldon noted in 1924, "We have seen its great efficiency for individual rapid transit defeated by the very number of persons trying to take advantage of this new medium of transportation."[54] Few, if any, automobile executives promoted the motor vehicle as a direct competitor of the street railway. In fact, before World War II, automobile spokesmen and motor club representatives frequently cooperated with street railway officials, traffic engineers, and planners who were trying to promote more efficient, speedier public transportation. They participated in meetings dealing with rerouting and schedule changes for mass transit vehicles, implementation of more efficient systems of traffic signals, and policing of traffic flow. On at least one occasion they even supported a publicly financed subway system in Detroit, the auto capital of the world.[55]

Overt expressions of delight over penetration of the mass transit market came from outside of the automobile industry. Some of those who cheered the rise of the automobile obviously had a stake in its fate. Predictably, highway engineers promoted its acceptance and increased use, in the city as well as in the country.[56] Because it opened up the urban landscape on an unprecedented scale, realtors also perceived the automobile as creating more investment and sales opportunities. Only occasionally did praise of the automobile assume overtones of hostility toward the mass transit industry. Stanley McMichael, an aggressive Southern California real estate subdivider, gloated in 1928, "The world—in America at least—is on wheels. Street car strikes no longer frighten us, for there are enough motor cars to carry the entire population to work every day, if the occasion requires."[57] McMichael may have stretched his point, but a national survey taken in 1923 revealed that 52 percent of persons owning automobiles used them for commuting to and from work.[58]

Clearly the automobile became an important means of mass transportation during the 1920s, yet a variety of urban observers argued that its most important beneficial effect was in shaping the cityscape. It is hardly surprising that motor club officials and superhighway designers eulogized the automobile. They pointed out the obvious: that it permitted settling of huge areas of land between mass transit lines, and that it greatly enlarged the "radius of action" of its owners. In other words, with the flexibility of the automobile, the owner could work, shop, and enjoy recreation almost anywhere he chose, and at any time.[59] Even Lewis Mumford, later one of its severest critics, praised the automobile in 1925: "The tendency of the automobile is within limits to disperse population rather than concentrate it; and any projects which may be put forward for concentrating people in greater city areas blindly run against the opportunities the automobile opens out."[60]

What these observers failed to note were some of the intangible, yet vital appeals of the automobile. During the 1920s, the American fascination with the motor vehicle both as technology and as a status symbol deepened. As historian Blaine Brownell observed, "the motor vehicle was a more impressive piece of machinery than a radio, more personal in its impact than a skyscraper or a dynamo, and certainly more tangible than electricity."[61] Automobile historian James Flink criticized manufacturers for overemphasizing credit purchase of cars. A 1926 survey revealed that Americans spent 18 percent of take-home pay on car payments.[62] While advertisers oversold credit buying, they ignored yet another appeal of the automobile to urban commuters: by choosing whom, if anyone, they rode with, drivers enjoyed a degree of privacy previously unknown.[63] Perhaps even more important in the eyes of many buyers, they could avoid close contact with people from other racial and ethnic groups, at least while in transit.

With all these advantages, there was growing realization in some quarters during the 1920s that the automobile could create, as well as solve, urban problems. Few criticized the impact of the automobile upon rural areas. After all, the countryside was large enough to hold the automobile, and the citizens' greater mobility hurt only a few small-town merchants.[64] But its impact upon the city was more immediate and obvious. The automobile jammed narrow streets designed for nineteenth- or even eighteenth-century types and volumes of traffic. Robert Whitten, a nationally recognized housing and traffic expert from Cleveland, observed in 1920 that automobiles occupied up to twenty times as much street space per passenger carried as did the streetcar.[65] Charles R. Harte, a civil engineer, scored the inefficiency of the automobile in congested areas with an interesting analogy: "It is a good deal as if our ladies and our men, also, wore a hooped skirt arrangement ten or twelve feet in diameter and went through the sidewalks. If that were done we should have a riot immediately."[66] Even motor club officials admitted that automobiles had exacerbated congestion problems in downtown areas. A Pennsylvania Motor Federation executive, R. C. Haldeman, observed in a 1927 speech to street railway representatives that downtown on-street parking was both selfish and time-wasting.[67]

An occasional urban observer found fault with the automobile's aesthetic impact on the city. Criticisms were intriguingly varied. The Public School Principals' Association of Newark, New Jersey, complained that the constant noise of vehicles operating on rough pavement interfered with classroom activities in many schools.[68] While critical of "superfluous noise" in a 1926 speech, Chicago businessman Charles H. Wacker also believed that it was absurd to talk of beauty in the modern city when there was so much smoke in the air. He blamed motor vehicles for part of the problem, noting that "we should not overlook the ever-growing menace to health from the fumes emitted by . . . thousands upon thousands of automobiles."[69] A few urban critics cited undesirable land uses that accompanied the automobile's increasing popularity. At the 1928 gathering of the American Society of Civil Engineers, several prominent members noted that, prior to widespread use of the automobile, major streets leading into and through cities contained fine residences and were a delight to travel. Now heavily traveled, they were almost in-variably zoned for business use. In addition to adding to the cities' severe land-use problems caused by excess business zoning, such development usually created ugliness where beauty once prevailed.[70] According to another critic, overzoning for business, ugly strip development, and an excess number of auto-

mobiles robbed motoring of much of its appeal: "The long, slowly moving line of automobiles leaving or entering a large city on a
hot summer day makes motoring anything but a pleasure."[71] But
until the 1960s, few paid serious attention to such critical views.

In certain respects the fate of mass transit mirrored other economic trends of the 1920s: beneath a facade of prosperity lay the
seeds of decay. A variety of circumstances camouflaged the decline of the street railway. Rapid population growth in urban
areas helped hide the fact that smaller proportions of urbanites
relied on the trolley for their important journeys. New patterns of
urban growth, unprecedented at least in magnitude, made effective responses by mass transit companies nearly impossible. It
was not simply for lack of attention that mass transit systems
declined in the American city during the 1920s. Ironically, a
number of planners, transportation engineers, and even transit
officials seriously considered modern rapid transit systems as a
solution to the ills of urban mass transit. The fact that they consciously rejected subways and elevated lines underscores the
complexity of the problems they confronted.

4 The Planners and Transit

The overwhelming majority of urban planners gave up visions of reconstructing urban cores in the 1920s, opting instead to exercise their creativity by shaping suburban environments. This was to some extent a response to political, economic, and social realities: many planners realized that, with limited resources and authority, they could exert the greatest impact in areas where they did not have to correct past mistakes.[1] Most planners, however, genuinely welcomed the opportunity to try to shape the new suburban landscape from the very beginning.

The planners' absorption with suburban development significantly affected their perceptions of urban transportation. In any event, there was little traffic engineers and planners could have done for transit during the 1920s. Private investors showed little interest in either traditional mass transit or modern rapid transit, which included subways and elevated lines.[2] In addition, there was little public money available for upgrading urban transportation systems. During the 1920s, urban traffic congestion intensified so rapidly that planners and traffic engineers worked in a crisis atmosphere. The public demanded solutions to immediate problems, and the seemingly minor adjustments required to ease automobile flow appeared irresistible, especially in contrast to the long-range, expensive alternative of modern fixed-rail rapid transit.

Finally, it is unlikely that planners and traffic engineers would have backed rapid transit proposals even under more favorable circumstances. A handful supported downtown-oriented rapid transit plans during the 1920s; however, most consciously rejected even the concept as an enormously expensive symbol of an outdated form of transportation technology. Subway and elevated systems are extremely inflexible once constructed. Thus, planners believed, while they made sense in a handful of densely settled cities with slowly growing populations and static growth patterns, they were out of place in the dynamic, rapidly changing urban environment of the 1920s.

The early 1920s was a period of rapid growth of organized planning, as a 1924 survey revealed. Of some 233 cities examined, 110 boasted planning commissions. More important, of those cities with planning commissions, 75 possessed official city plans, and all but 21 of the plans had been developed between 1920 and 1924.[3] The decade also brought rapid growth of established planning commissions in large cities. The Chicago Plan Commission's budget multiplied fourfold between 1920 and 1930. The Boston City Planning Board's annual appropriation grew from under $5,000 in 1920 to over $33,000 a decade later. In Los Angeles, the Regional Planning Commission, which was founded on a meager budget of $7,000 in 1924, boasted a budget nearly ten times as large just five years later.[4]

Yet planning organizations experienced increasing difficulty in effectively confronting urban problems. A primary reason was that planners took account of increasing numbers of complex and often unresolvable issues; the planning process thus required time and resources not available to them. Most planning commissions were organized shortly after World War I, just at the time when urban problems were becoming regional in character. City councils, which frequently financed planning commissions, expected results that directly benefited the cities. In a word, councilmen too often took a narrow view of urban problems. British town planner Thomas Adams pointed to just such a difficulty when he urged Boston planners to realize that unless they considered suburban needs they could not realistically hope for lasting solutions to inner-city problems.[5] The Detroit Bureau of Government Research concluded in 1924 that no significant strides could be made in solving issues facing the metropolitan area until planning functions were organized under some type of unified regional authority.[6]

Even in cities where local decisionmakers realized the need for regional planning, the responses were often years behind the need for coordinated and massive efforts. Although Los Angeles founded the nation's first regional planning commission in 1922, its president lamented two years later that the local real estate boom created enormous numbers of new subdivisions, "coming like a sea wave over us." About all regional planners had time or energy to do, he suggested, was to gain rights of way out in the country for adequate streets and highways before profit-crazed realtors choked off any such advance planning by laying out thoughtlessly conceived subdivisions.[7] Even after the real estate boom collapsed in the mid-1920s, other problems sapped Los Angeles planners' strength. By 1930, a local planner complained that 90 percent of their time was consumed by zoning variance cases and minor street changes; he stated that local planners did some replanning, but little original planning.[8]

The refractory problems facing planners in Los Angeles were typical of the energy-draining challenges to planners throughout the country. Drawing up zoning ordinances and examining proposed variances consumed most of their time. A dozen other important issues competed for their attention and limited resources. Among the most important were housing, public health, parks and recreation, acquisition of water resources, and assuring adequate railroad and shipping terminal facilities. In addition, local planning commissions were often founded for the primary purpose of developing master plans. Hence, planners were challenged to produce comprehensive answers to complex problems over very short periods of time. Even though urban transportation was invariably a central component of any master plan, they were able to devote but a fraction of their time to it.

A few energetic planners were stimulated by their boundless, open-ended visions, but many were oppressed by their pedestrian, time-consuming tasks and the capriciousness of the political process. Planners often spent months educating city councilmen about the urgency of their projects, only to have elections occur at the moment planners' efforts were on the brink of success. Hard-won allies would lose their seats, and planners would have to commence the education process all over again with newly elected councilmen.[9] As he temporarily left office in 1926, Boston Mayor James M. Curley, a steadfast friend of the city planning board, observed that it had been treated badly. The city council had frequently derided its recommendations and denied its requests for appropriations.[10]

Historians of the planning movement have frequently observed that planning commissions were so preoccupied with survival and with developing enabling legislation that they tended to work within the context of existing institutions. Mel Scott concluded that planners were "less adventuresome in thought" than present-day critics might wish, because "the materialism of the times was inimical to philosophic probing."[11] Blaine Brownell concurred with this view, arguing that urban planners had no choice but to work within the conservative guidelines set down by "commercial/civic elites."[12]

The fact that planning commissions possessed insufficient legal authority to implement plans undoubtedly encouraged conservative thinking, but some observers believed that their lack of clout induced an ennui that destroyed any creativity. In a complaint reminiscent of earlier years, a Chicago planner noted in 1926 that lack of political muscle prevented his commission from gaining funds needed to effect one plan after another.[13] Other observers, however, suggested that planners themselves merited criticism. An occasional critic charged that lack of official responsibility induced planning bodies to handle their advisory duties carelessly. Cincinnati City Manager C. O. Sherrill had little good to say about his experience with an advisory traffic planning body in 1928. He charged that planners and citizens without specific tasks in urban government kept the public "in an uproar" due to publicity given hastily devised and irresponsible recommendations.[14] Sherrill's complaint undoubtedly reflected frustration over the fact that the planning advisory group itself constituted yet another level of bureaucracy and may well have added red tape to the increasingly complex task of governing a city.

As in earlier years, some planning advocates still argued that the very fact that commissions had little authority was what allowed them to survive at all. In their view, commissions armed with potent legal authority could not escape even greater hostility from more firmly established municipal departments.[15] Businessman Charles H. Wacker, chairman of Chicago's commission, urged his colleagues to avoid lobbying city councils for funds to effect specific recommendations. As Wacker saw it, that task was the responsibility of the politicians.[16] Although they often represented business associations or commercial groups with their own effective lobbying activities, private planners apparently sensed the dangers of direct involvement in pushing for legal authorization. Some consciously took an elitist stance, refusing to push their plans aggressively on the grounds that such activities compromised their professional dignity. Thus British planner Thomas Adams piously noted in 1920, "There is no comparison between the salesman and the professional man. The former is out to sell his *own* products and the latter is merely advocating that a plan should be prepared by *someone*. Engineers and architects who amount to anything do not go about the country seeking jobs like salesmen seek orders. . . . If cities want to negotiate for your services let them come to you."[17] Yet this detachment had drawbacks. A critic suggested that planners possessed few of the skills needed to enlist public enthusiasm. As H. A. Overstreet observed in 1928, planners lacked the art of dramatic literary presentation: "The report of a city plan ought to read like a novel; too often it reads like a half-resuscitated law book."[18]

The distractions of internal differences and external constraints led some planners to become discouraged over their profession's past performance and future prospects. In a 1924 letter to John Nolen, planner Russell V. Black complained of "a certain ineffectuality of much that is being done. . . . So much planning now seems like attempting to stem a flooding river with shovelsful of mud."[19] However, they occasionally managed to focus some attention upon broader issues, including the key challenge of how to respond to increasingly rapid decentralization in metropolitan regions. By the end of the 1920s, the great majority of American planners endorsed decentralization as a positive social objective, although some arrived at this view through a circuitous route. Core-city problems were becoming increasingly time-consuming and complex, and solutions seemed beyond grasp. Rebuilding central districts, the glittering vision of turn-of-the-century city beautifiers, seemed a romantic dream to many planners by the 1920s. Some grew frustrated over trying to solve core-city problems because of cost. Even minor alterations of physical settings in downtown areas often required tens of millions of dollars.[20] Such planners of earlier years as Daniel H. Burnham and Virgil C. Bogue had devoted some attention to suburban development; now many planners were tempted to devote almost all of their attention to outlying areas. As Robert H. Whitten argued in 1924, "We have been considering too exclusively the replanning and regulation of our badly built towns."[21] A handful of planners actually urged abandonment of central districts as a conscious social goal. Speaking in this vein, John A. Beeler, a highly influential transportation consultant, argued in 1925 that central districts were "losing their desirability due to modern developments, and business was showing a tendency to migrate to more accessible quarters. This tendency should be encouraged."[22]

In contrast to their discouragement over the future of the older inner cities, many planners eagerly tackled the challenges in outlying areas. Even big-city planners sensed and shared the mounting enthusiasm. Pittsburgh Chief Engineer Morris Knowles acknowledged that planners would exert their primary influence in small towns and outlying areas near big cities, where they would not have to devote most of their energy to correcting the mistakes of the past.[23] Many of America's renowned planners, such as John Nolen and Harland Bartholomew, who owned and managed private consulting firms, devoted most of their professional attention in the 1920s to plans for smaller towns and regional suburbs. Even those who would later become severe critics of decentralization touted its possibilities. Lewis Mumford argued in 1925 that "instead of setting our minds and hands to make the big city more titanic than ever, we should attempt rather to stimulate and direct the forces that make toward a wider diffusion of population and well-being."[24]

Planners in some of the newer, rapidly developing cities believed that they had a special opportunity to open new trails in planning thought. At the height of the local real estate boom in 1924, Los Angeles planner Gordon Whitnall, an arch proponent of decentralization, informed the national conference of city planners that western planners had learned from the mistakes made in older eastern cities and would guide their eastern colleagues in planning the horizontal city of the future.[25] Six years later, Denver planner Walden E. Sweet echoed Whitnall's regional chauvinism in observing that "to avoid the evils of congestion and overcrowding attendant upon excessive use of land, Denver has aspired to spread widely rather than reach high."[26]

A few planners actually argued that decentralization would not hurt downtown areas; rather, it would help by permitting more "efficient" use of land, creating greater physical mobility, and eliminating unnecessary traffic in densely settled areas. Instead of fighting horizontal growth, downtown interests should recognize its overall effect of enhancing regional prosperity. Resentment against suburbanites who worked in and derived their income from the city, yet contributed no tax dollars to the maintenance of crucial municipal services, was short-sighted, or so went the argument. As New York's Nelson P. Lewis argued in 1923, "This feeling is due to lack of appreciation of the extent to which every town and hamlet outside an important urban district stimulates its growth and ministers to its prosperity."[27] Yet he cited no specific evidence of how suburbs nourished the central city.

Other planners suggested that there were negative effects from overly rapid, haphazard decentralization. In 1922, S. Herbert Hare, a Kansas City landscape architect working closely with prominent land developer Jesse C. Nichols, was helping to create one of the most beautiful suburban developments in the nation. Yet even with his primary attention focused on the suburbs, Hare admitted that cities could not simply continue expanding, "leaving unsolved problems in the blighted districts near the center."[28] Pittsburgh traffic planner Louis W. McIntyre shared Hare's concern, pointing out in 1928 that excessive decentralization left a wake of small, scattered business units and economic losses due to excessive overhead costs and wasteful competition.[29]

A few planners voiced outrage over the fact that some of their colleagues appeared to be almost joyfully abandoning central cities for the suburbs. Robert H. Whitten accused some traffic consultants of simply acquiescing to the deterioration of central districts by permitting both public transportation facilities and streets accommodating automobiles to become so jammed and inefficient that people and businesses would be forced out of the central districts. He charged that a policy of "handicapping the centers in every possible way" was a short-sighted means of effecting decentralization. What minimal traffic relief it created would be only temporary. While admitting that some horizontal growth was desirable, he voiced the hope that it could be done "without strangling the patient."[30] Even Miller McClintock, one of the foremost enthusiasts of accommodating the automobile, chided his planning colleagues for frequently accepting arguments for decentralization rather than engaging in "bold planning suited to the necessity."[31]

As the automobile and automobile planning prospered, advocates of subways and elevated lines became a distinct minority; yet they articulated a wide range of arguments in support of rapid transit. Since promoting decentralization was clearly a popular objective, some proponents of rapid transit systems continued to argue that subways would encourage that pattern of growth. John P. Fox, a Boston transportation consultant, suggested that "real rapid transit should be used to spread out congestion and extend cities in the right direction along carefully determined lines. And this spreading out cannot be undertaken too soon. . . . All over the world the larger cities are in need of the powerful influence of rapid transit lines to decentralize business and direct future growth."[32] Fox was not alone in his assessment of the potential impact of rapid transit. The Seattle City Planning Commission argued in 1928 that modern methods of mass transportation had so profoundly altered former concepts of time and space that virtually all territory within metropolitan regions could be opened up for urban land use. There was neither necessity nor excuse for crowding.[33] The Seattle report, whether purposely or not, was vague about just what types of "mass transit" would effect decentralization, but it appeared to include subways, elevateds, trolleys, buses, *and* automobiles.

Another justification for rapid transit lines heard occasionally was that they made economic sense. William Trimble, a local transit engineer, urged Seattle to build a new system in 1926. One of Trimble's chief arguments was that the surface lines had been losing patronage for several years and that an adequate system of subways and elevateds would cause an immediate 10-

percent jump in patronage.[34] Close study of his report reveals fuzzy thinking. Trimble stated that a four-mile subway could be built for between $3.62 and $4 million—at a time when most transit studies projected costs of between $3 and $7 million per mile.[35] He also failed to provide any clear statement of how the required funds would be raised. Sidney D. Waldon, chairman of Detroit's Rapid Transit Commission appealed directly to the financial self-interest of local manufacturers in his attempt to enlist support for rapid transit. He pointed out in 1927 that as Detroit spread out, the average worker traveled five to ten times farther between home and work than thirty years earlier. Long, tiring daily commutations adversely affected worker productivity. Waldon urged manufacturers to spend less money and energy trying to motivate tired workers and to pay more attention to proposals for building fast, comfortable transit facilities that would deliver workers to their gates refreshed and ready for a solid day's work.[36]

A handful of planners simply assumed that, because central business district congestion was growing visibly worse almost daily, cities had little choice but to provide modernized rapid transit. Waldon articulated this position forcefully in 1926: "History has proven over and over again that we pay for adequate facilities whether we have them or not. We pay through delays and reduced efficiency. We pay through nervous wear and tear, through loss of property in blighted areas, and lessened values. And as a last resort we pay enormously for a few defensive measures that too often fail because [they are] inadequate."[37] Edward Dana, general manager of the Boston Elevated Railway Company, shared Waldon's view. He categorically predicted in 1930 that the backbone of the transportation system in very large cities had to be rapid transit.[38] And traction magnate Henry I. Harriman, a fellow Bostonian, echoed Dana's view in suggesting that effective rapid transit systems could only be provided by underground facilities.[39]

Ironically, advocates of rapid transit systems probably damaged their chances for success by their conscientiousness and their insistence on thorough, long-range planning. Waldon pointed out in 1923 that the greatest mistake of past transit planning was that earlier systems had been constructed on a piecemeal basis, one or two lines at a time.[40] Not only did most pro-transit planners voice this sentiment, but they persuaded city councils to incorporate specific provisions in city charters preventing *any* rapid transit construction until such plans were both completed and officially adopted.[41] This seemingly logical position, sound from the standpoint of professional ethics, proved disastrous in the rough-and-tumble of urban politics of the 1920s. Advocates apparently anticipated little or no serious opposition to the principle of improved rapid transit for the masses. They soon discovered that voters who were quick to approve the principle of rapid transit were loath to back up these straw votes with bonds necessary to finance new facilities. Planners also learned the hard political lesson that opponents of rapid transit could stall official adoption indefinitely by attacking any published plan at a single weak point.

In time, pro-rapid transit planners learned to compromise, but by then it was usually too late. By the end of the 1920s opinion, even within the planning profession, was turning increasingly against core-city oriented, comprehensive new systems. By the onset of the Depression, a majority of planners opposed "old-fashioned" elevateds and subways for many reasons; the most important was their belief that rapid transit would ultimately exacerbate rather than cure congestion in central districts. In effect, they believed it would accelerate the centralization that many hoped to avoid; rapid transit construction and congestion fed upon one another. Central district congestion created demands for subways; once built, the subways enhanced downtown property values, which in turn encouraged construction of new skyscrapers. These attracted still more people, creating congestion once again, and a demand for additional subway lines. New York transportation consultant Daniel L. Turner observed that construction of the East and West Side subway lines in New York in the early twentieth century had created precisely that effect. Rather than considering increased patronage of rapid transit a benefit, Turner emphasized the new headaches it caused. The new subways had not relieved congestion; rather, they accelerated increases in traffic and in a short time "created a worse congestion than before."[42]

While some planners criticized only carelessly designed proposals, others disapproved of rapid transit in principle. Housing reformer Clarence Stein argued that as long as central districts continued to grow and attract more business and workers, there was no way to avoid continuous breakdowns of transit facilities in large cities. Stein perceived rapid transit as both a waste of money and an unfortunate distraction from creative thinking about future city building. In 1925, he strongly criticized multi-million-dollar transit designs, arguing that the money should be used on education, culture, art, and recreation, rather than on proposed alterations that "do no more than make the physical side of congestion barely tolerable."[43]

Other planners and traffic experts criticized subways as symbolizing both outmoded technology and past mistakes in judgment. At their best, subways provided temporary palliatives for intolerable traffic congestion in urban cores. In 1927 John Ihlder scored the subway as "like the outside fire escape, now happily tending to disappear, a confession of failure to build properly."[44] Although Waldon soon thereafter changed his mind and became a passionate advocate of subways, even he criticized them in 1924. He observed that traffic consultants in older, larger cities, with no guiding precedents, had been forced to adopt subways in desperate efforts to remedy congestion.[45] In Seattle, prominent city engineer Reginald H. Thomson was determined not to let his city fall into any such error. In 1925 Thomson acknowledged that proponents of Seattle's rapid transit plan had pressured him to support subways; they had argued that the publicity received by the city for undertaking such an ambitious project would amply compensate for any losses due to unsuccessful operation. Thomson replied that, in light of Seattle's unfortunate experience with municipal ownership of street railways, any such "advertisements" should be avoided.[46]

Other critics contended that subways and elevateds served only the interests of downtown merchants and employers. Detroit City Plan Commission President Judson Bradway warned against building subways in 1923, at least until the city effected adequate zoning regulations to control building of skyscrapers downtown.[47] In Chicago, George C. Sykes, representing west side businessmen who would not be served by any proposed subway lines, charged that the local transportation companies were still dominated by landowners and business interests in the Loop District who "dictated transportation policies . . . to the injury of other areas."[48]

Outlying area and suburban commercial interests could be just as self-centered as downtown businessmen. In Los Angeles, the San Fernando Valley Improvement Association supported regional rapid transit plans—but only if those plans included direct lines between its district and the downtown area.[49] In one city after another during the 1920s, specific rapid transit proposals often received enthusiastic business support only from those firms directly served. In contrast, although proponents of urban road building did not emphasize this point, automobiles could provide direct access at much less public expense to far larger numbers of commercial enterprises in metropolitan areas than could fixed-rail rapid transit. This unquestionably stimulated business support for major street and superhighway programs in the 1920s and after.

Surprisingly, there was significant opposition to rapid transit construction even from the proposed beneficiary, the street railway industry. Much of this opposition revolved around cost. A 1924 article in *Electric Railway Journal* pointed out that elevated lines were ten times as expensive as conventional streetcar lines, while subways were fifty times as expensive.[50] The Detroit street railway consistently opposed plans for comprehensive rapid transit for several reasons. First, they feared that a proposed $280 million comprehensive regional plan was so expensive that it would necessitate a fifteen-cent subway fare. William B. Mayo, general manager of the local trolley lines, believed that the majority of mass transit riders would prefer riding the surface cars, as long as they maintained their cheaper fare.[51] Second, street railway officials were unimpressed by projections of speeds possible with subways; they were quite sure they could match proposed subway performances with minor improvements in the street railway system—at a fraction of the cost. Finally, they feared that subway construction would cause extended disruption of all public transit service through torn-up streets. By the time subways could be in operation, many former trolley patrons might well have been converted to the automobile, never to be won back, however efficient the newer subway service might be.[52]

All in all, the 1920s marked a giant step backward in the prospects of fixed-rail rapid transit in most American cities. Transportation planners and the general public considered speci-

6. Chicago's Loop elevated line in 1924. Rapid transit "solutions" to urban congestion did not automatically enhance the urban environment. Courtesy of the Chicago Historical Society.
7. Construction of a subway extension in New York around 1927. The cost and inconvenience of building rapid transit systems in congested American cities during the twentieth century were enormous. New York Regional Plan Association Records, Department of Manuscripts and University Archives, Olin Library, Cornell University.

fic proposals for rapid transit lines and found them lacking.[53] The reasons varied with place and time, but a brief analysis of the responses in two cities reveals why rapid transit plans failed.

Detroit provides a clear example of the failure of subway proponents to sell their panacea. During the mid-1920s, planners and traffic experts in that city presented some of the most advanced concepts in rapid transit design. Their ideas were examined closely—and in many cases copied—by traffic experts all over the country. But by 1929, local rapid transit boosters had so alienated the public that even a modest proposal for conventional subways was decisively rejected by voters.[54] Detroit area planners started off with inordinately high hopes and grandiose, expensive transit schemes. By the time they presented reasonably inexpensive transit proposals, any initial public enthusiasm had long since vanished.

Detroit's long, colorful history of controversy over street railway operations appeared to be ended when the city took over the local lines in 1922. One of the chief reasons voters approved municipal control was that the privately owned company had failed to provide service extensions to rapidly growing areas of the city. As Detroit continued its boom growth in the early 1920s, city officials realized that they would somehow have to meet these demands or face the voters' wrath. Consequently, Acting Mayor John C. Lodge created the Rapid Transit Commission in December of 1922. He charged that body with the task of examining transportation needs in the entire region and designing a "master plan."[55] The newly formed commission was a seemingly incongruous coalition of automobile company executives, transit industry spokesmen, architects, lawyers, and businessmen.

Sidney D. Waldon, a retired automobile company executive, chaired the commission; no mere figurehead, he tirelessly promoted its objectives on nearly a full-time basis. In mid-1923 the commission revealed its recommendations to the general public.[56]

Its comprehensive transit plan was startling in scope. The core of the proposal was a system of subway lines beneath the central district. In addition, the plan established 65 miles of surface rapid transit lines, which would be carefully integrated with some 563 miles of trolley lines by 1950.[57] Without question, the most exciting, innovative feature of the proposal was the manner in which it dovetailed surface rail rapid transit with facilities for the movement of automobiles. Rights of way 205 feet wide were to be acquired in a radial pattern extending fifteen miles from downtown. A median strip 84 feet wide accommodated high-speed rail rapid transit cars. The remaining 120 feet contained generous widths for limited access highways along both sides. All crossings at grade were eliminated; cross traffic passed either above or below the right of way by means of viaducts. Enthusiasts believed the design provided the safest, fastest rapid transit system in the world. In theory at least, both public transit and automobiles were permitted to travel for several miles in a rapid, uninterrupted flow.[58]

In the first months following publication of the plan, enthusiasm ran very high. The proposal also attracted significant attention from traffic planners in other cities. In October 1925, Waldon reported that planners from other cities were visiting Detroit to study the proposal at a rate of almost one a week. Transportation experts from Chicago, New York, Denver, and Seattle all made pilgrimages to the motor city that year.[59] Waldon received invitations to address such prestigious organizations as the National Municipal League, the American Road Builders Association, and the American Electric Railway Association. Yet it was clear even then that most of the enthusiasm centered on the superhighway rather than on the fixed-rail elements of the design. Waldon himself suggested as early as 1923 that rail lines would play a secondary role: "Adequate highway capacity for the movement of motor vehicles may stave off the requirement of mass transportation on rails for many years, but if the right-of-way is sufficient, and the capacity of the road surface again becomes inadequate, part of the right-of-way *can* be given over to rail transportation of rapid transit trains that will relieve the pressure upon the highway paralleling its line."[60] Waldon may have emphasized the more immediate possibilities of implementing the highway phase of the plan because of pressure from his former colleagues in the automobile industry. Although it hardly needed to be told, Waldon reminded the city council early in 1924 that the economic future of Detroit depended upon the usefulness of the automobile.[61]

It is highly likely that Waldon initially emphasized the automotive side of the transit plan through sincere belief; it is just as probable that he did so in order to ingratiate the Rapid Transit Commission with the city's most potent business moguls. Waldon quickly realized that implementation of the plan depended at least in part upon the commission's continued existence and credibility. Initially scheduled for extinction upon presentation of the transit plan, the commission had carved a slender niche for itself in local government; Waldon had no desire to jeopardize that position of influence by antagonizing his former associates. Thus, the push for actual construction of rail lines could be put off for some time. At the same time, the commission had to demonstrate its effectiveness in order to augment its potential influence, so Waldon adopted the strategy of making the biggest possible splash while spending a small amount of public funds. In April 1924, he recommended a tactic of acquiring rights of way for future construction, rather than risk the commission's precarious position of influence.[62] Actual construction could wait until the political climate was propitious. In annual reports to the city council throughout the decade, the commission presented constant reminders of how much money it "saved" the city through right of way acquisition.[63]

8. Subway proponents frequently encountered arguments against the cost and delay involved in implementing subway plans. This 1928 *Detroit Times* cartoon supports the views of those who advocated the less expensive, more "prompt" Miller-Schorn "rapid transit" proposal. Courtesy of Detroit Public Library.

8

Inevitably, the commission had to face the thorny issue of selling the rail portion of the transit plan. In August 1926, the commission proposed a scaled-down version of the original plan, with 46.6 miles of rapid transit lines; the projected cost was $280 million, including equipment.[64] Both the mayor and city council balked at the enormous sum and refused to place the issue on the November 1926 ballot.[65]

Local politicians sought cheaper, more immediate solutions. Late in 1925 two transportation engineers had presented what appeared to be the politician's dream: an inexpensive solution that could be installed during their terms in office. Henry Miller and Nicholas Schorn proposed a cut-rate express system for surface cars, which they claimed could double their speed. Streetcars would stop only once each half-mile, and they would pick up and deposit passengers at specially designed safety isles in the center of the street, which could be reached only via pedestrian subways. At an estimated cost of but $250,000 to $300,000 per mile, the system was clearly intended as a substitute for the subway. Miller and Schorn argued that "only time could tell" whether Detroit would *ever* need comprehensive rapid transit. They believed future innovations in transportation technology might make the large-scale proposal of the commission "obsolete and economically a blunder."[66] In the meantime, their system promised immediate relief of traffic.

The Miller-Schorn proposal was for years the Rapid Transit Commission's *bête noire*. Waldon and his close colleague, John P. Hallihan, opposed it from the very beginning, suggesting it would produce only temporary relief in traffic movement and would prevent Detroit from effecting a long-range cure.[67] Yet other interests enthusiastically endorsed the Miller-Schorn plan. Del Smith, manager of Detroit Surface Lines, favored trying the system on an experimental basis.[68] John Lovett of the Michigan Manufacturers Association stated that his associates favored it "almost unanimously because it offers rapid transit quickly and economically without imposing additional tax burdens."[69]

Late in 1927 the system was installed on a limited trial basis on Jefferson Avenue. After several months, results were mixed; the Rapid Transit Commission labeled it a flat failure, while Miller-Schorn proponents lauded its time savings and insisted it would prove even more beneficial if installed citywide.[70]

However conscientious the Rapid Transit Commission's reasoning, opposition to the Miller-Schorn plan gained it nothing but enemies. Edgar M. Robinson of the Jefferson Avenue Improvement Association observed that the commission had been promoting rapid transit in theory for years, but when a practical system was actually installed, it provided only criticism.[71] Members of the city council became so angered at the commission that they seriously considered eliminating it altogether.[72] The *Detroit Times* joined the attack, charging that commission members thought only in terms of traffic problems fifty or seventy years in the future and ignored immediate needs.[73]

As the 1920s drew to a close, rapid transit attracted less and less support in Detroit. To its chagrin, the Rapid Transit Commission discovered that subways drew opposition even from those who supposedly benefited the most: owners of property near the proposed lines. When voters rejected a proposed $54 million bond issue for subways in 1929, a good part of the overwhelmingly negative vote came from property owners along the proposed routes, who feared much higher taxes.[74] One owner of an apartment building apparently spoke for many of her neighbors when she stated: "They say there will be an increase in valuation on property near the subway. Try and get it. That is all bosh. They also say there will be an increase in rent. Try and get that too. Why, how can a workingman pay it on $30 to $35 per week? . . . It will be the people who own the half-paid-for property that will suffer to see it all go for taxes." Another Detroit resident argued that those who stood to gain the most, namely downtown merchants and fringe-area manufacturers who would be directly served by the proposed lines, should become philanthropists and present their city with a "model unit" of a rapid transit system.[75]

These seemingly endless, fruitless struggles portended the fate of rapid transit in Detroit. After the city council refused to place the $280 million plan on the ballot in 1926, rapid transit promoters suffered an uninterrupted string of defeats. Perhaps anticipating these difficulties, proponents of rapid transit began abandoning their insistence upon complete and comprehensive layouts in the mid-1920s. Long before Detroit's first major referendum defeat for rapid transit bonds, Willard Pope, vice president of the Rapid Transit Commission, expressed willingness to compromise. In 1925 he argued for building at least the nucleus of the larger system that would be needed in the future.[76] Sidney Waldon, by then one of the firmest supporters of comprehensive transit in America, endorsed Pope's perception of political reality in 1927: "Apparently . . . it would be safer to start [Detroit's] rapid transit system by the construction of but a single line."[77] By the late 1920s, however, proponents had lost whatever slim chance they once had of effecting rapid transit in Detroit. In the late 1930s, the Rapid Transit Commissin proposed a series of increasingly modest subway plans, only to be rebuffed at every turn.[78]

Although the particulars varied, the outcomes of contests over rapid transit in other American cities during the 1920s were much the same. In Los Angeles, public transportation moguls faced two difficult problems: providing adequate service over one of the largest metropolitan regions in the world, and coordinating the flow of intra- and interurban trolleys through Los Angeles's extremely narrow downtown streets. Although they never realistically confronted the first issue they struggled mightily, if unsuccessfully, with the second.[79] Prior to 1920, street railway executives and public officials generally agreed that the city's relatively small population and low population density did not warrant the enormous cost of an elevated and subway system.[80] Nevertheless, some experts assumed that it was merely a matter of time until such facilities would be needed.

A combination of factors precipitated serious discussion of subway plans for Los Angeles in the early 1920s. As the number of automobiles jamming narrow downtown streets multiplied rapidly, downtown merchants and street railway officials begged for relief. In addition, an aborted effort in 1923 to construct a stub-end terminal beneath Pershing Square for the Pacific Electric's interurban line to Hollywood ended in confusion and failure.[81] As a consequence, a 1924 city ordinance forbade any rapid transit construction until a comprehensive plan was officially adopted by the city.[82] The city council appropriated $40,000 for a complete study of local transit needs, and the contract was awarded to the Chicago firm of Kelker, de Leuw, and Company.

Early in 1925 the firm presented its recommendations, calling for construction of 26.1 miles of subway and 85.3 miles of elevated lines within ten years. Fixed-rail facilities were to be supplemented by feeder bus lines; the complete transit system would cost $133,385,000.[83] To its credit, the firm did not try to persuade its clients that rapid transit could be self-supporting. It forthrightly admitted that the region's relatively small population and low population density precluded that possibility. Rather, the firm argued that the principle of public subsidies for local transit had been established in other cities even before downtown street traffic problems became acute.[84]

A handful of advisory bodies, civic groups, and prominent citizens supported the proposal. The president of the Los Angeles Traffic Commission observed that several large eastern cities had started their subway systems when their populations approached one million; if Los Angeles was to follow their example, it should begin construction promptly.[85] Other proponents of rapid transit appealed essentially to civic pride. One member of the Municipal League argued that if New York could build a subway system under rivers and through solid rock, Los Angeles, which faced far less formidable physical barriers, should be able to create a comparable network.[86]

However, the transit proposal's critics were more numerous, influential, and articulate than were its friends. A subcommittee of the prestigious City Club rejected even the principle of rapid transit. After raising the query, "What is rapid transit for?" the majority report stated that if it was for the purpose of relieving congestion, it would fail. Pointing to increased congestion in eastern cities following subway construction, the report expressed the hope that Los Angeles would lead the way in developing a community of "local centers and garden cities, where the need for daily long distance travel would be minimal."[87] Gordon Whitnall, a nationally renowned local planner, concurred. Though Whitnall had supported the principle of rapid transit as recently as 1925, he totally reversed his position a short time later.[88] In particular, he criticized the inflexibility of rapid transit. While a fixed-rail system might make sense in a region where residential patterns and work locations were identifiable and relatively stable, and where population growth had leveled off somewhat, none of these characteristics marked Los Angeles's urban development by the late 1920s. According to Whitnall, there was a great risk that even the most comprehensive, well-planned rapid transit system would be obsolete soon after completion.[89]

By the late 1920s, proponents' hopes for rapid transit in Los Angeles faded. The 1925 transit plan quickly became obsolete as the city grew and changed with startling rapidity. Other concerns competed for the planners' time: a major street plan, designs for a new Union Station, and creation of viable city and county zoning codes. In 1930 advocates of rapid transit called a conference for the purpose of promoting comprehensive transit in the region.[90] Yet their energy seemed exhausted. They passed brave resolutions favoring fixed-rail lines, gave press conferences to newspapermen, and disappeared quietly. Perhaps Donald M. Baker, chairman of the City Planning Commission, expressed their discouragement most accurately as the Depression deepened in 1930: "The crux of the problem of mass transportation is finance—Who shall pay for it?"[91]

Although transit plans for Los Angeles were presented occasionally during the 1930s, the debate over the 1925 Kelker plan was the high-water mark for local interest in fixed-rail lines before World War II.[92] By the late 1920s local planners and traffic engineers generally believed that the future was in rubberized rather than in rail transit, and they devoted most of their attention to major street and regional highway development. Once committed to the automobile, few local planners indulged in backward glances toward the "old-fashioned" technology of rail lines; they were too busy forming a new urban environment that would take advantage of the freedom promised by the newer invention.[93]

The experiences of those urging construction of rapid transit in other large American cities essentially paralleled those of their contemporaries in Detroit and Los Angeles. During the decade, governments of nearly every large city either prepared their own transit plans or hired outside consultants to prepare them. The pattern of decisionmaking revealed remarkable consistency among the various cities: exacerbation of local traffic problems, preparation of a plan, intense debate, then conscious rejection of the plan.

One may partially understand the failure of rapid transit proposals on the basis of their declining attraction for many urbanites in the 1920s. Fixed-rail lines were very expensive, and their inflexibility was a severe handicap in rapidly changing and expanding cities. In addition, a lingering legacy of hostility and mistrust of public transit companies prohibited some planners from recommending that they operate any proposed new systems. But to fully understand urban America's failure to provide rapid transit systems—at a time when they were still viable possibilities—one must comprehend the contrasting appeal of the motor vehicle solution.

5 The Planners and the Automobile

By the "Jazz Age," the electric trolley was roughly forty years of age, while the automobile was still in its twenties; for many reasons beyond mere youth, the latter proved the more enticing siren. The automobile won both the hearts of most Americans and the minds of most transportation planners, who believed they could control it through innovative engineering and proper methods of traffic control.[1] In the long run, this assumption reinforced the planners' suburban bias. Despite enormous efforts to control mounting downtown congestion, traffic engineers lost ground during the 1920s. In contrast, outlying and suburban areas appeared to be ideal laboratories for experimenting with major street and superhighway building. Traffic engineers may have preferred the latter projects to subway planning partly because they were novel and more experimental; and in the 1920s there did not yet exist a legacy of highway building that failed to relieve congestion.

Highway planning possessed political and economic advantages as well. Unlike rapid transit lines, highways accommodated both private and public transportation. Highways appeared to be more within the tradition of American individualism, because users provided their own means of transportation. And in the American tradition of fair play, taxes on gasoline, tires, and other accessories appeared to mean that only those who used the roads would pay for them. Highways and streets also seemed cheaper than rapid transit, at least in the short run. By promoting streets and highways, traffic planners offered urban politicians a chance to provide prompt, tangible "solutions" to transportation problems in each ward or district. Supporters of rapid transit could not match that appeal. As Blaine Brownell has observed, "the automobile thus became an excellent vehicle for transporting planners into a new, more widely recognized professional status."[2] In addition, highway planning appeared more in harmony with such suburban experimentation of the 1920s as Garden City and New

Town proposals. Highway advocates deftly converted complaints of mounting traffic fatalities into appeals for safer, more modern roads. At the same time, a majority of planners believed that automotive solutions enhanced the urban environment. All these factors contributed to the automobile's domination of transportation planning thought during the 1920s.

To many transportation experts, a major issue of the 1920s was deciding what part of the American landscape most needed improved roads. Almost all agreed that downtown traffic congestion in many American cities had reached crisis proportions. British planner Raymond Unwin observed in 1923 that crowding in central areas of American cities was so bad that any time-saving capacity of the automobile in urban traffic had been very nearly eliminated.[3] Rural interests, however, had traditionally received a lion's share of highway building funds from governmental bodies, and they had no intention of sharing limited resources with their urban brethren.

A number of urban planners believed that they could effectively accommodate the automobile if cities received their fair share of road tax funds. They argued that although getting farmers "out of the mud" might have been an appropriate priority prior to 1920, state and local highway departments had gone overboard in building and maintaining rural roads at the expense of city streets.[4] Detroit planner Sidney D. Waldon, who by 1930 was willing to sponsor any program for public *or* private transportation that promised to speed up urban traffic, urged extension of federal and state highways through cities. According to Waldon, federal and state governments had "built the world's greatest system of highways up to the gates of our cities, and there they stop."[5]

Rural interests countered that many state and federal highways also served interurban traffic, and that farm-to-market roads aided cities by lowering production costs of agricultural products. In addition to permitting lower produce prices for city dwellers, most state and national highways encouraged urbanites to visit the countryside for recreation and leisure.[6] The American Automobile Association (AAA) took no sides on the issue. Club publications diplomatically observed that road building efforts had fallen far behind the needs of both country and city. In the minds of AAA officials, the roads and highway systems of the future had not yet even been conceived.[7]

Whether or not they sympathized with rural highway needs, urban planners realized that prompt solutions to mounting downtown congestion problems were imperative. Some planners, encouraged by those in the automobile business, argued that solving downtown congestion was primarily an engineering problem.[8] They realized, however, that engineering solutions of past years would not suffice. Just as a majority of planners had lost faith in the ability of expensive rapid transit facilities to provide viable urban transportation, a large number abandoned hope that repairing or rebuilding old streets would result in efficient movement of automobiles. Certainly many traffic engineers gave up on widening existing streets. Chicago spent the staggering sum of $340 million over a thirty-year period on street widening alone, to little avail. That was more than twice the estimated cost of a comprehensive subway system at 1923 prices.[9]

Traffic engineers were determined to control the mounting numbers of automobiles in central districts, and they actively experimented with a variety of concepts of street design and traffic control. Before the 1920s planners had believed that minor improvements in streets and highways could permit movement of many more vehicles within the same corridors. Before 1920, they emphasized such advances as grade-crossing improvements and viaducts over railroad yards and major traffic intersections. During the 1920s, while continuing to promote these earlier advances, traffic engineers embarked on an extensive series of improvements in highway design, such as improved all-weather surfaces; more scientific, safer lighting; elimination of cross-traffic with under- and overpasses; and banking of curves to permit faster traffic flow.

While many of the new design concepts for traffic control included rapid transit, their primary purpose was to facilitate the movement of automobiles. A number of innovations affected traffic in congested areas. Some experts emphasized moving all traffic more rapidly through surface streets by means of improved street design, uniform traffic signals, and synchronized lights. A frequent suggestion was that automobiles should traverse downtown areas according to a fundamental principle of rapid transit: movement along more than one horizontal plane. Urban architects such as Harvey W. Corbett designed elaborate plans, including double-decked streets, that completely separated rail and automobile traffic. Corbett's design was actually triple-decked, since he included a third level for pedestrians.[10] Arthur S. Tuttle, chief engineer of New York's Board of Estimate, generally opposed double-decked streets; yet he advocated a three-level elevated expressway to facilitate traffic flow along the Hudson River. He also advanced the idea of arcaded sidewalks recessed under downtown buildings so that the entire width of streets might be devoted to automobiles.[11] Double-decked streets and arcaded sidewalks did not win unanimous approval within the planning profession. Harland Bartholomew of St. Louis believed that multi-level streets would experience the same fate as wider streets or rapid transit systems: they would simply attract more people and become as congested as existing facilities. The result would be a large expenditure of public funds with no effective solution.[12]

Other ideas for downtown traffic relief seemed inspired by

science fiction writers. One planner scientifically proved that the most effective means of easing traffic flow was to rebuild entire central districts in identical, hexagonal blocks; he offered no clue as to who would finance such a project.[13] Although several practical double-decked streets were under construction during the 1920s—most notably Chicago's Wacker Drive—enthusiasts imagined far more elaborate schemes. Angus S. Hibbard seriously proposed eliminating shipping from the Chicago River and paving over its entire width! He suggested that this would make the Loop area immeasurably more accessible from three sides.[14] Drawings for four-, even six-layered downtown street projects were common during the 1920s.[15] While devoid of spectacular drawings, San Francisco planner Stephen Child's proposal for eliminating downtown traffic jams was no less startling. Rather than controlling motor vehicle traffic in congested areas, he proposed eliminating all motor buses and trolleys![16]

Despite uncertainties in other facets of city building, planners were initially confident of their ability to solve congestion problems. A major reason for optimism was the rapid changes in traffic control since the turn of the century. Pittsburgh Traffic Engineer Burton Marsh recalled that in 1900 traffic control consisted of informal police supervision of parades, occasional mediation in disputes between teamsters, and assistance of disabled vehicles.[17] Relatively few advances took place in the first two decades of the new century. Until World War I, vehicle movement was governed only by mounted police or officers on foot operating manual traffic signals.[18] But by the early 1920s, advances in street traffic control were well underway. Cities experimented with manual and mechanical signals, traffic lights, and synchronization of lights to ease the flow of traffic.[19] By the late 1920s experimentation had reached sophisticated levels. Harold M. Lewis of New York talked reassuringly of achieving continuous movement of vehicles through such methods as "progressive," "platoon," or "automatic synchronized" traffic signals. Rather than force all traffic to funnel directly into the crowded central core, major streets would follow the "whirlpool principle," allowing traffic headed downtown to reach its destination quickly, but also permitting through traffic to bypass the core.[20]

Other experts believed that the key to overcoming chaotic traffic conditions, particularly in downtown areas, was to establish standardized nationwide systems of traffic control. William P. Eno, an influential safety expert, argued that once uniform restraints were adopted in every city, effective vehicular control would automatically follow. He believed that effective traffic regulation was 95 percent public education and only 5 percent enforcement, stating in 1920 that "it is easy to control a trained army, but next to impossible to control a mob."[21] Private organizations and public agencies supported these views. The AAA and the American Association of State Highway Officials (AASHO) were but two of the prestigious groups promoting standardization in their official publications. In a similar vein, a Southern California Automobile Club study estimated that once motorists learned to obey new traffic regulations, the average intersection could handle 300 percent more traffic.[22]

A handful of urban observers assumed that all it would take to improve traffic flow in central areas was application of Yankee knowhow. Miller McClintock, perhaps the nation's most widely known traffic consultant, listed the challenges surmounted by applications of engineering expertise, and concluded: "That the traffic problem is susceptible to a similar treatment is not to be doubted."[23] Others echoed McClintock's optimism. In 1925 John C. Long of the AAA admitted that congestion was bad, but he insisted that there was little cause for worry: "It is the American temperament to wait until a situation has become intolerable and then go out and lick it in short order."[24]

9. An example of the typical suburban "response" in Louisville, Kentucky, during the 1920s. Many urban observers emphasized that even these dreary bungalows were distinct improvements over the crowded inner-city flats occupied by many blue-collar families before the popularization of the flivver. Caufield and Shook Collection, University of Louisville, Photographic Archives.

10. Oak Park, Illinois, in 1925. Many urban planners sincerely believed that the automobile would eventually permit the majority of urban residents to "escape" to surroundings like these. Courtesy of the Chicago Historical Society.

11. "Dezendorf's Delightful Dwellings," Queens, New York, around 1920. Monotony and conformity typified many suburban developments long before post–World-War-II critics made them social issues. Courtesy of the Library of Congress, Washington, D.C.

12. Beverly Hills, California, one of America's most famous "automobile suburbs," in 1924. In many sections of the country, wide, modern streets and highways made possible beautiful suburban developments. Courtesy of the Los Angeles County Regional Plan Commission.

11

12

13. Many conventional urban highway and street-widening projects merely created miles of ugly, unplanned strip development. This 1924 view of Whittier Boulevard in Los Angeles suggests why some planners advocated limited-access freeways during the 1930s: they believed freeways could beautify the environment, as well as enhance the functional movement of motor vehicles. Courtesy of the Los Angeles County Museum of Natural History. 14. An example of the unplanned mixture of commercial and residential land use in Louisville, Kentucky, during the 1920s. Caufield and Shook Collection, University of Louisville, Photographic Archives.

13

14

EMORY & HENRY LIBRARY

15. Aerial view of Letchworth, a
famous British experiment in Garden
City planning, complete with generous Greenbelt allocations. Courtesy
of the Harvard Graduate School of
Design.

Although many knowledgeable traffic planners believed that applied engineering could solve downtown congestion, others were not so sure. John Ihlder, a housing and transportation expert, expressed the opinion in 1924 that had turn-of-the-century Americans realized how drastically the automobile would affect cities, they would have crusaded against it.[25] George A. Damon, a Southern California planner, voiced disillusionment with the results of physical planning for downtown areas, including street widening, grade-crossing elimination, and double-decked streets. In his view, "the cure was worse than the disease."[26] Even McClintock, generally the optimist when discussing relief of downtown congestion, evidenced some discouragement as automobile ownership escalated toward the end of the decade. In 1928 he expressed fear that there was no magic cure for the traffic problem, that in fact there was only a series of stopgap measures that provided short-lived remedies for the worst aspects of downtown congestion.[27] Significantly, none of these observers so much as hinted that solutions to central area congestion were beyond the scope of future generations of engineers.

In facing the growing difficulty of dealing with central area problems by arguing that the future of metropolitan regions was in outlying areas, planners greatly expanded the optimistic visions of their turn-of-the-century predecessors. With a handful of exceptions, early planners had conceived of limited suburban development, usually within a few miles of downtown and a few blocks of trolley or steam railway lines, while planners of the 1920s dreamed of gradually filling in huge tracts of land twenty and thirty miles from central districts. This was decentralization on a scale inconceivable twenty years earlier. Los Angeles planner Clarence A. Dykstra spoke of a "natural reaction" of people everywhere to spread out into suburbs and to "get the advantages of a city without its very apparent disadvantages."[28] Many planners believed that the automobile would lead them to the "promised land." As one contributor to *American City* viewed it, it was the highway engineer's duty to employ "daring imagination" in designing roads and streets to effectively scatter people "far and wide out into the outlying open country."[29] He argued that, in addition to creating a beneficial social impact, such a strategy would generally relieve traffic congestion in American cities.

A few demured. Real estate developer Jesse C. Nichols warned that careless planning and overly rapid development could ruin a splendid opportunity to create humane metropolitan environments and relieve congestion. Nichols urged painstaking design of suburban street systems; unless they had generous widths, congestion would quickly emerge even in the outlying areas.[30] Even in the 1920s, Nichols perceived dire consequences for any such shortcomings in street or highway planning. In his travels around America, he had visited numerous regions where haphazard and ugly "strip" development had already created suburban chaos. According to Nichols, small countryside markets first appeared at seemingly unimportant crossroads. Later, a few more substantial buildings appeared. By 1920 many of these seemingly inconsequential subcenters peppered regional landscapes. As these centers grew, they frequently merged with one another, often along the same old narrow roads. "As a result," concluded Nichols in 1929, "throughout the land the present-day congestion problem of our central business areas is being repeated in scores of outlying places throughout every large city."[31] Nichols himself provided a splendid example of careful advance planning of commercial and residential subcenters during the early twentieth century. His Country Club Plaza in Kansas City achieved international acclaim.

Just as they believed they could control automobiles, so many planners believed they could effectively guide the suburban movement. America already possessed a tradition of planning towns and cities from the very beginning (Chapter 2). Perhaps in part a response to urban crises, some planners believed that totally new towns, some distance from downtown areas, would provide the best possible living environments for disaffected urban dwellers.

Because of growing problems in central districts and a continued fascination with the suburban ideal, American planners had a keen interest in Garden City experiments during the 1920s. During World War I the federal government, through the United States Housing Corporation, had embarked upon an ambitious program of community building. Although federal funds for these New Town experiments were terminated almost immediately after the war, some planners hoped that the government would one day re-enter the field.[32] In the meantime, a handful of large corporations continued their first tentative trials in town planning.[33]

No American planner was more fascinated by the New Town concept than John Nolen. During the 1920s his architectural firm developed plans for dozens of proposed New Towns, most of which were never built. One of his best known plans was for Mariemont, Ohio. At the behest of private philanthropist Mrs. Thomas J. Emery, Nolen designed a New Town to accommodate between five and ten thousand residents, located ten miles east of Cincinnati, well above the Ohio River. Nolen hoped to attract small industries, so that the town would be largely independent of Cincinnati, and so that residents could be spared burdensome commuting to their jobs.[34] Nolen's dream was only partially realized. By the mid-1930s Mariemont had failed to attract any significant industries, and breadwinners among its 1,600 residents generally commuted by automobile to jobs in Cincinnati. Of the 700 subdivided lots, some 444 remained undeveloped in 1936.[35]

The American New Towns conceived during the 1920s were

16. Aerial view of Mariemont, Ohio, in 1929. This New Town, planned by John Nolen, was one of America's better-known efforts to match the British experiments, Welwyn and Letchworth. Justin R. Hartzog Papers, Department of Manuscripts and University Archives, Olin Library, Cornell University.

16

17. Regional planners did not plan exclusively for suburban development and decentralization during the years before World War II, as this ambitious proposal to redevelope a five-square-block slum area in New York during the 1920s reveals. *Regional Survey of New York and Its Environs, Vol. VII: Neighborhood and Community Planning (New York, 1929), fig. 13, p. 108.*

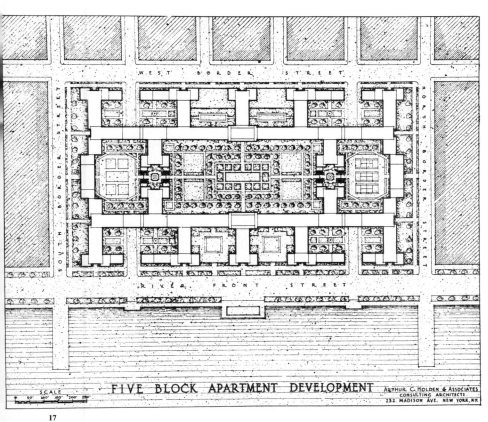

17

distinctly different in both design and function from the planned industrial suburbs of earlier years.[36] Unlike such communities as Pullman, Illinois, or Roland Park, Maryland, which depended upon the electric trolley and steam railway, New Towns such as Mariemont were frankly designed with the needs of the automobile-oriented resident in mind. Perhaps the most famous New Town experiment in the United States during the 1920s was Radburn, New Jersey. In part because it opened just before the stock market crash of 1929, Radburn never attracted many residents. Its design nevertheless received international acclaim. With unique super-blocks and homes facing grassy play areas, there was little risk of automobile injury to children at play. Yet the innovative cul-de-sac design permitted automobile owners convenient access to their living quarters.[37] During the 1920s New Towns housed only a tiny fraction of America's new suburbanites. However, the new design concepts they introduced, particularly in how best to accommodate the automobile, profoundly influenced less renowned urban land developers across the nation.

Meanwhile, the evolution of modern highway building reinforced planners' emphasis upon developing outlying areas. Perhaps planner L. Deming Tilton of St. Louis best expressed the hope of those who envisioned the effective coordination of suburbs and superhighway planning. Tilton's 1927 plan for the regional development of Washington, D.C., foresaw enormous potential for "model suburban communities" within easy commuting distance of the capital. "The basis of such new development is the regional highway plan, putting these communities and outlying centers closely in touch with the city. A first-class system of wide, straight highways in the metropolitan district will do as much as anything else to counteract the tenement building and overcrowding of land in the heart of Washington."[38] As the tech-

nical ability of engineers to build more and better public highways grew rapidly in the 1920s, such sentiments were voiced
with increased frequency.

In retrospect, the regional planners' fascination with superhighway design is easy to understand. For a number of reasons,
they concentrated highway building efforts in outlying rather than
downtown areas. Street widening had proven expensive, even
more costly in terms of traffic relief "yield" per dollar spent than
rapid transit.[39] While city councils were seldom enthusiastic
about the expense of hacking multi-lane expressways through expensive rights of way in central districts, the comparatively small
costs of acquiring rights of way for highways in outlying areas
held considerable appeal. Even more important, the state often
shared road building costs in outlying areas, while inner-city
street improvements were usually paid for entirely by municipalities. Earlier city builders had failed to anticipate the need for
wide streets in central districts, and those areas had suffered the
consequences for years. Planners of the 1920s did not want the
blame for repeating such an oversight in outlying areas.

Planners sensed that failure to construct wide streets and highways, or at least gain the necessary rights of way, would cost
them any chance to shape the suburban landscape according to
their convictions. At the height of the local real estate boom in
Southern California in 1924, the president of the Los Angeles
Regional Planning Commission explained the urgent need for
advanced highway planning in that metropolitan area. "When we
faced the matter of subdivisions in the County of Los Angeles,
. . . subdivisions which were coming like a sea wave rolling over
us . . . , we reached the conclusion that it would be absolutely
necessary to go out into the country and try to beat the subdivider
to it by laying out adequate systems of major and secondary
highways at least, thus obtaining from the subdivider the necessary area for highways and boulevards."[40] Most planning experts

were confident of their ability to control the automobile, at least in outlying areas. As previously noted (Chapter 4), Detroit's ambitious 204-foot-wide superhighway plan was one of the nation's most celebrated attempts to provide a comprehensive solution for urban transportation needs. New York traffic planner Daniel Turner, a key consultant in Detroit's superhighway planning deliberations, admitted that a 1,100 percent increase in motor vehicles in Detroit had enormously complicated its traffic problem. He claimed, however, that the superhighway was a possible solution and argued that Detroit, the "automobile city of the world, should lead the way in accommodating the automobile, both in the present and future."[41]

Traffic engineers in many cities praised and copied the Detroit superhighway plan, yet they made their own contributions to suburban highway planning thought. With numbers of automobiles multiplying rapidly in virtually every city and town, planners and traffic engineers unquestionably felt societal pressure to accommodate the motor vehicle. The public was clearly enchanted with the automobile, and planning commissions would have risked their very existence had they opposed highway development. Planners in larger cities and regions naturally tended to promote the larger, more grandiose designs. In 1928, a planning subcommittee for the Chicago City Council recommended a system of double-decked highways not only downtown, but throughout the entire city.[42] Nevertheless, it would be misleading to argue that planners in every city succumbed helplessly before the automobile. Major street and highway plans for many small and medium-sized cities emphasized making maximum use of existing streets.[43]

Advocates of superhighways and elevated roads also promoted them as conducive to economic redevelopment and social reorganization. Fifty years later such a perspective appears startling, but the Chicago Motor Club insisted in 1929 that elevated highways would "vastly rejuvenate" the slum areas they traversed. The so-called "badlands" area of the west side would be "transformed into a district of apartment buildings and hotels."[44] These sentiments were not simply the blandishments of self-seeking auto interests, as some of the most respected planners in America shared them. On occasion, landscape architects and planners still promoted regional highways as environmentally sound, in language reminiscent of that of City Beautiful advocates twenty years earlier. In a widely studied park plan for Los Angeles, a nationally renowned planning firm argued in 1930 that "Los Angeles may continue to grow as a metropolis of automobile users, living pleasantly in detached houses with plenty of room, with a minor percentage of apartment dwellers, but *only* if it provides motorways (of which the pleasure parkway is one type) on a truly modern scale undreamed of."[45] Sidney Waldon insisted that Detroit's superhighway plan would help create "a new kind of city, with magnificent buildings acquiring a special dignity by reason of such settings as only a tree-ornamented super-highway can give."[46]

Although there was some concern even in the 1920s over pollution caused by exhaust emissions, there was no crusade against it. One reason was that the most obvious source of air pollution was industrial plants, whose smoke darkened skies above many cities; this distracted the attention of scientists who might otherwise have addressed problems of automobile pollution much earlier. Perhaps the most obvious reason for the lack of concern was that there were not enough automobiles to create the brown clouds so prevalent in many metropolitan areas today. There were 24 million registered automobiles in 1929; today there are roughly five times as many. Another apparent reason for the lack of deep concern was that some observers believed that the gasoline-powered internal combustion engine would follow the path of so many other technical innovations by becoming obsolete. John Beeler, an influential consultant from New York who created transportation plans for many of the nation's largest cities, believed that the next half-century would bring solar-powered automobiles, remote-control rapid transit, and airships carrying commuters one hundred miles in the time it took them to travel ten miles in 1925.[47] Suggestive of the futuristic orientation of planners was Edward M. Bassett's coining of the term "free-way" and many of its modern principles, including the expectation that, by moving traffic at uninterrupted, moderate speeds, there would be great savings of both fuel and driving time, and less wear and tear on vehicles and their operators.[48] Technological advances and innovations in highway design would solve any short-term environmental problems caused by the automobile, or so many leading transportation experts believed.

Naturally, automobile interests also urged actions favoring concerns of motorists, as they had done from the turn of the century. In the early years, motor clubs sponsored speed races, coast-to-coast endurance runs, and automobile touring. They also aided the good roads movement. In the early years, automobile clubs had often acted irresponsibly. For example, the Chicago Motor Club complained in 1912 that laws forcing speeding automobiles to slow down when passing schools were designed primarily to harass motorists needlessly.[49] Its monthly publication devoted large amounts of space to complaints that country judges habitually discriminated against even sober, cautious motorists by levying large fines for minor infractions against the law.[50]

Once the automobile's future seemed assured, industry publications presented the image of a business conscientiously pursuing the public interest. Although automobile manufacturers naturally attempted to present the industry in its most attractive light, there is little evidence to indict them for maliciously twisting the truth. From the very beginning, automobile spokesmen worked closely with city planners. Paul G. Hoffman, then vice president of Studebaker Motors, bluntly stated his industry's primary motive for concern with city planning in 1930. "The automobile industry is intensely interested in the progress of city planning—for the very sound reason that a continued increase in motor car sales in the United States of America depends largely upon developing more efficient traffic accommodations in metropolitan areas."[51] Before the anti-automobile crusade of recent years, there seemed to be little reason for motor vehicle manufacturers to camouflage their self-interest.

One apparent threat to the automobile industry and to its campaign for better highways was the clearly growing dangers of motor vehicle operation. As evidence of its concern over both growing congestion and the rapidly mounting number of traffic accidents, the industry subsidized the founding of the Erskine Bureau of Traffic Research at Harvard with considerable fanfare. One of the bureau's primary functions was to promote safety. Despite such efforts, traffic fatalities and serious injuries still continued to mount at an alarming rate during the 1920s. Automobile fatalities were not officially recorded until 1906; between 1913 and 1917 they averaged 6,700 per year, and over the next five years they rose to an average annual toll of 12,500 lives. By 1930 they had climbed to a yearly figure of nearly 32,500.[52] An important public relations concern of industry officials was that as Detroit produced vehicles capable of ever higher cruising speeds, accidents became grislier. During the 1920s one could scarcely pick up a popular magazine without sensing the depth of public anger over the carnage on the highways.

Automobile industry officials worried about this, prompted no doubt by a mixture of genuine public concern and an instinct for self-preservation. Industry spokesmen did voice anguish over the steadily mounting toll. The president of the AAA stated in 1928 that 25,000 people died on public roads the previous year and called it "the great national problem today."[53] In addition, motor clubs organized and assisted safety campaigns and driver-education programs. Still, the responses of those sympathetic to the industry occasionally appeared callous and self-serving. One defender figured that between 1904 and 1929, traffic fatalities had multiplied fifty times, but the number of automobiles had grown five hundred times. "In spite of the doubling of speed and the more-hours-per-day use of autos, the number of fatal accidents per car has decreased ninety per cent."[54]

Even more important for the future of urban transportation, industry spokesmen, whether motivated by concern over human lives, auto sales, or both, used the safety issue as leverage to promote construction of more advanced highways. They urged state and local highway departments to construct roads with more level, wider shoulders, better lighting, more gradual turns, and fewer grade crossings. Arguments favoring sophisticated concepts of highway design, from new types of street paving to the most advanced freeways, consistently emphasized their admirable safety features as well as the belief that they would speed up traffic flow.[55]

However, a vocal, persistent minority of planners viewed accommodation of the automobile with suspicion. Some suggested that superhighways converging on downtown districts would be just as futile in effecting traffic relief as centralized rapid transit systems.[56] Others questioned not so much the practical utility of elevated roads and superhighways as their environmental impact. According to planner Edward Bennett, the lower levels of elevated roads were unsightly front yards for all buildings in their path, and most of the buildings near them would soon become obsolete. "The result would ride rough-shod through the area."[57] James H. Nygren, a Detroit consulting engineer, also criticized the concept of two-tiered highways. While admitting that they wouldn't generate as much noise as elevated railways, he pointed out that noise and gas fumes made them undesirable. In addition, the darkening effect of solid floors and the dangers to lower-level traffic caused by massive concrete supporting columns were also drawbacks.[58] Significantly, most criticism focused on the comparatively rare double-decked highway, rather than more common grade-level urban highways.

The specter of superhighways cutting through not only core-city areas but also sylvan woodlands and quiet residential areas occasionally aroused negative feeling even in the 1920s. No less a friend of superhighway building than Thomas H. MacDonald, chief of the Bureau of Public Roads, anticipated in 1924 the anger that conversion of former "pleasure parkways" to functional movement of automobiles might generate. Such a "strictly utilitarian purpose" would "invade violently" the original purposes of parkways.[59] When Seattle's Department of Streets and Sewers proposed widening a road through Washington Park in 1930, a group of local citizens protested vigorously. One of its spokesmen wrote: "Are our city officials trying to make life hideous for its citizens? Will our city be so ugly and noisy that none but undesirables will want to live here? Amazement has flashed across the faces of some of our councilmen when we remonstrated against this ruinous highway. . . . We now have one speedway in our district with its ugly filling stations, and we certainly don't want to have another. Taxing the home owners is ridiculous. Make the motors [sic] pay for such highways—they're the ones who want them. . . . The motor car has raced around the country leaving destruction long enough; it's time we woke up, unless we are to be conquered by it."[60]

A handful of observers believed even in the 1920s that the automobile was bringing havoc to the former beauty of country areas near many of America's large cities. Henry Wright, so influential in the New Town movement, observed in 1925 that

"In pursuit of the ideal home people use the automobile to escape beyond the borders of the city and beyond its restrictive building codes . . . the plain man is attracted to the edges by the prospects of an individual home; he wakes up to find himself in the midst of a slum. So development of the city becomes a perpetual game of leap-frog, in which the city consecutively destroys its border developments, leaving a wake of sordid, decaying areas."[61] Benton MacKaye, the noted landscape architect whose concept of the "Townless Highway" stressed the harmonious coexistence of nature and automotive technology, largely deplored what lack of planning for the automobile had done to the landscape. In words nearly identical to Wright's, he lamented in 1930 that "the motor slum in the open country is today as massive a piece of defilement as the worst of the old-fashioned urban industrial slums."[62]

Significantly, none of the critics of the motor vehicle fundamentally challenged automobility during the 1920s. Most urban residents who opposed highways traversing their own neighborhoods still demanded easy automobile access to other parts of their cities. Ironically, influential critics such as Wright and MacKaye, who correctly analyzed some of the unfortunate side effects of careless highway planning during the 1920s, may have inadvertently provided impetus to unfortunate suburban "planning" in the future. In the hands of less conscientious and sensitive land developers, partial application of New Town and Townless Highway principles probably contributed to the ugliness of much suburban development in the 1930s and after.

Aside from occasional hostile voices, planning critics of the automobile remained a small minority throughout the 1920s. Perhaps the planners' faith in the automobile is explained by their conviction that they could control it, at least in outlying areas. Because of the many apparent advances made in street and highway design and traffic control, urban planners may be partly forgiven for their lack of prescience regarding future urban traffic congestion. Planners were unquestionably distracted from urban transportation problems by many other demands upon their time. As downtown-area traffic became increasingly congested, it was natural to seek solutions in decentralization. Also, many planners perceived the automobile's potential for opening up new professional opportunities, just as it opened up more land for urban uses. While critics of the automobile occasionally appeared to anticipate its future impact, their analyses often lacked depth, and they offered no realistic, economically feasible alternatives.[63] Just as opponents of rapid transit frequently labeled subways the sole culprit creating downtown congestion, so opponents of the automobile scored it as the chief villain in desecrating the countryside. Although there was truth in both positions, the conclusions were overly simplistic. In part due to a lack of truly well-conceived and coherent opposition, the automobile would become even more firmly entrenched as an urban mass transportation device in the 1930s.

6 Mass Transit's Continuing Decline

For a variety of reasons, the Depression decade marked mass transit's continued decline. A combination of slowing metropolitan-area growth rates and large-scale layoffs of urban workers contributed to rapidly declining mass transit patronage. Both the automobile and the mass transit industries suffered severe reversals in the early 1930s, but the former showed signs of revival by decade's end, while mass transit continued to lose ground to the automobile. Although many of the causes for the industry's continued decline were beyond the control of mass transit officials, their indecisiveness and confusion unquestionably hurt their cause. Transit officials were unable to agree even about dominant trends within their own industry, let alone formulate an effective strategy for combating the motor vehicle. Mass transit was in desperate straits by the eve of World War II, and industry officials seemed simply to pray for miracles.

After several decades of rampant population increases, American cities experienced a respite in the 1930s as population gains nearly ceased. In fact, their collective rate of increase declined even more sharply than the national population growth rate. During the 1920s, while the nation's population gained 16.1 percent, cities increased 27.5 percent; in the 1930s those figures declined to 7.2 and 8.4 percent, respectively.[1] A few cities actually lost population; for example, Boston's population dropped roughly 10,000 or 1.3 percent. Most cities that grew quickly during the 1920s experienced severe slowdowns during the 1930s. Chicago, which gained 675,000 new residents in the 1920s, added only 20,000 during the 1930s. Detroit, which grew nearly 60 percent during the automobile industry's boom years of the 1920s, gained but 3.5 percent during the 1930s. Los Angeles maintained a moderate growth rate during the 1930s, but it was sharply down from that of the 1920s. The few exceptions to this trend included Denver and Washington, D.C. Both cities experienced steady though unspectacular gains during the 1920s, and in the 1930s their growth rates continued at roughly the same level.[2] The continued population gains in these two cities were due largely to their role as important centers for burgeoning federal government bureaucracies—one of the few growth industries of the 1930s.[3]

Outlying areas continued to gain more rapidly than core cities, but they did not grow as quickly as during the previous decade. The suburbs of Boston increased at a rate of but 3.5 percent during the 1930s,while Chicago's gained at a rate of 11.5 percent. Even in Los Angeles, where suburban development had been spectacular during the 1920s, growth was far more modest in the 1930s.[4] Demographer Leo F. Schnore observed that, on a nationwide scale, the average growth rate in metropolitan "ring" areas declined from 33.2 percent in the 1920s to 13.4 during the following decade.[5] Thus, the suburban movement slowed, although inner cities continued to experience very significant patterns of out-migration.

These slowing growth rates had significant effects upon the evolution of urban transportation. During the 1930s, mass transit ridership continued to decline. In 1930 just over 15.5 billion rides were taken on all forms of public transportation; a decade later the figure had declined to 13.1 billion. There were, however, intriguing variations in the trends of specific forms of transit. The decline of street railway patronage, which began in the 1920s, became steeper in the 1930s. Between 1930 and 1940 trolley ridership dropped from 13.1 to 8.3 billion patrons. Yet mass transit officials did possess causes for optimism, since the serious losses in streetcar patrons were partially offset by increases in motor bus and trackless trolley users. Bus patronage rose 20 percent during the 1930s. While it carried a small percentage of mass transit users, the trackless trolley also demonstrated promise as a flexible response to urban America's transportation needs. Trackless trolley ridership jumped from a mere 16 million in 1930 to 534 million ten years later. In addition, spokesmen for public transportation derived some comfort from the fact that by 1940 total patronage on all forms had recovered somewhat from its low point in 1933.[6]

The Depression decade also brought hard times to the automobile industry. If one considers only total registration figures between 1930 and 1940, its straits are not so apparent. From a peak of 23.1 million in 1929, registered automobiles declined to 20.7 million in 1933, before resuming their climb to 27.5 million by 1940. But new-car sales figures fully revealed distress in the industry during the Depression. From 4.5 million sales in 1929— a record the industry would not exceed for twenty years—new car sales plummeted to 1.1 million four years later. Between 1933 and the end of the decade the industry struggled to regain the prosperity of 1929; in 1940 sales recovered to 3.7 million units.[7]

Americans continued to drive their automobiles, although hard times apparently induced them to make fewer daily journeys. Automobile registrations increased in almost every city during the 1930s, albeit at a much slower rate than during the previous decade. Urban residents continued to prefer the motor vehicle to mass transit. In Boston and Detroit, the percentages of individuals entering central districts via mass transit declined 9 and 8 percent respectively during the 1930s.[8] However, business in Detroit was very depressed, and traffic studies revealed that, even with larger proportions of visitors using automobiles, there were actually fewer motor vehicles going downtown. Between 1930 and 1936 the average number of automobiles entering Detroit's central district each day declined 10 percent.[9] Such trends in Detroit, Boston, and other cities, along with the razing of many older buildings in central districts so that space could be used for off-street parking, brought short-term relief of traffic congestion. However, since parking lots yielded far less in taxes than office buildings and warehouses, this brought little cheer for municipal officials. Declining property values and lower tax bases were combined with mounting unemployment and insistent demands for social services. To public officials dealing with starving, dispossessed citizens and municipal employees who frequently went unpaid for weeks, urban transportation issues assumed a low priority.

Although visible signs of decay were nearly everywhere, a sizable minority of trolley company officials, including some of the most influential men in the field, insisted that all was well— or at least improving. Amazingly, many argued even in the early 1930s that the future of the industry was bright. During the 1930s, however, their reasoning and optimism appeared increasingly forced. Some sought comfort in the fact that the trolley was not suffering as badly as many industries. Paul Shoup, president of both the American Electric Railway Association and Los Angeles's Pacific Electric Railway, claimed in July 1930 that the Depression had exerted a very slight effect on patronage, and that such a record was hardly the mark of a nonessential or fading industry.[10] Other trolley officials assumed that hard times would send people back to the cheapest form of urban transportation. If cost of transportation had not been a key determining factor in the prosperous 1920s, things were surely different in the Depression, or so they believed. In an almost classic case of misreading public attitudes, trolley industry officials emphasized that the automobile could never match the streetcar on that score. Figuring the average cost of a five-mile automobile trip at 6.5 cents per mile, Detroit transit official John P. Hallihan argued that use of the motor vehicle was at least three times as expensive as the trolley, exclusive of parking. He also observed that increased traffic density reduced the competitive edge of the automobile in terms of comfort and speed. The result, claimed Hallihan, was that automobile use became "an inconvenience and a waste of time."[11]

The Depression bottomed out in 1933; although millions remained unemployed and some businesses went bankrupt, most industries, including public transit, showed signs of recovery. Optimists within the transit business grasped even the smallest straws to persuade themselves that all was well. Hawley S. Simpson, a research engineer for the American Transit Association, presented an array of statistics in 1937 to prove that the trolley was not soon to be "as dead as the dodo bird." While acknowledging that use of the trolley had declined 19 percent from its mid-1920s peak, he pointed out that patronage was, in fact, on the upswing from its 1933 trough.[12] Yet another industry spokesman proved in 1940 that the trolley was not losing ground to the automobile. First, more Americans rode the trolley in 1940 than before the advent of the automobile. Second, surveys taken in a single city between 1930 and 1938 showed that traffic into the downtown area had actually increased. Auto use grew 17 percent, while transit use gained 25 percent. In light of increased parking space available in torn-down sections of Depression-ridden cities, this trend might have been significant. However, the author went too far in claiming that "the trend, in this city, has been definitely turned toward transit vehicles."[13]

Such arguments suggested that, by the 1930s, many street railway executives perceived their industry with tunnel vision. While a few die-hards may have believed their own rhetoric, it is likely that many officials voiced optimism in desperate attempts to attract investment capital and boost sagging employee morale. Thinly reasoned optimistic statements may have convinced the public at large, and even some planners, but it is unlikely that they fooled many persons within the industry. The observation that more people used the trolley in 1940 than in 1900, while technically valid, totally ignored disturbing recent trends. Trolley patronage had declined steadily both in absolute numbers and rides per capita since the mid-1920s.[14] Even more important, arguments such as the frequent contention that trolleys were holding their own in transporting patrons into downtown areas disregarded changes in intracity patterns of movement. As more people chose suburban sites for their businesses and houses, crosstown traffic became increasingly important, and fewer urbanites wished to commute over the older radial lines of movement served by trolleys.

Continuing to grasp at straws, some trolley officials argued that automobile ownership had reached its apex. In 1933 the president of Oakland's East Bay Street Railway Company predicted that the per capita number of automobiles purchased would not increase in the next few years, and that the automobile industry would be doing well simply to replace older units.[15] There was some support for this view from outside of the trolley industry. In 1935 the California Railroad Commission suggested that even in Los Angeles the competitive impact of the automobile had reached its peak, and that future increases in urban traffic movement would accrue to the public carriers.[16] Given the mentality of most Depression-era observers, their failure to anticipate the 100-million-automobile registration figures of the 1960s is not too surprising. Most optimists thought merely in terms of recapturing the prosperity of the 1920s; they could hardly have conceived of the rapidly multiplying Gross National Product figures of the 1950s and 1960s.[17] Three- and four-car families were probably beyond the imagination of even the most bullish automobile executives.

A few street railway officials were convinced they could offer competitive service through technological advances and more up-to-date equipment. During the 1930s they pinned much of their hope for improved service on the new trackless trolley, or electric bus. Two advocates of public transit from Seattle who conducted a national survey in 1930 noted that, where installed, the trackless trolley had proven very satisfactory. With rubber tires, it provided a ride much quieter than that of steel-wheeled trolleys, making it comparable in "luxury" to the automobile.[18] The engineers from Seattle eloquently praised the "cinderella-like transformation" of the trackless trolley since its introduction in 1928, concluding that it was "the acme of traction vehicles in comfort, silence, profits, and efficiency."[19] Some trolley industry engineers pinned their hopes on new types of fixed-rail equipment. The new President's Conference Committee car promised larger seating capacities, more convenient and rapid loading and unloading, and improved comfort for streetcar patrons. Other supporters of public transit argued that they could significantly improve their service simply through more judicious use of existing equipment. New York's Beeler Organization, a noted transportation consulting firm, estimated that the Seattle transit system could cut commuting time from outlying areas to downtown by 50 percent by converting older buses from feeder service for the electric trolleys to direct, nonstop service.[20] The chief time savings would come from the elimination of transfers.

A final frequently voiced optimistic view from within the transit industry was the continued belief that it would be unthinkable for trolleys to go out of existence. In 1931, Charles Gordon, then president of the American Electric Railway Association, insisted that "to solve the growing problem of traffic congestion in cities it seems hardly conceivable that the enormous economic advantage of collective transportation by electric power will not be used to a much greater degree in the future than in the present."[21] A number of planning organizations were no more prescient regarding the future of streetcars. The Denver Planning Commission concluded in 1931 that mass transit was a vital necessity, and that cities would have to retain it in some form.[22] Although the Denver report was vaguely worded, it assumed a continued dependence on local trolley lines. Even the National Resources Planning Board (NRPB) paid homage to the trolley, observing in 1937 that mass transit, mostly streetcars, still carried up to three-fourths of all patrons to and from central areas of American cities.[23] Significantly, even some of the most sophisticated planners did not fully envision the threat to mass transit in general—and the street railway in particular—posed by the automobile. Most important, they did not deal adequately with major new patterns of urban movement, especially between outlying areas.

Despite persistent optimism among some in the transit industry, many street railway officials were deeply worried over their future by the 1930s. Few voiced such concerns publicly, but some feared the beloved trolley's imminent demise. Cold-eyed realists viewed declining patronage figures as a sign of difficult times, both for the present and the future. While optimists believed the Depression would force people out of their cars and into the trolleys, pessimists sensed that trolley riders were generally more marginally employed than automobile owners, hence more likely to lose their jobs. They correctly anticipated that patronage gains of former automobile owners would be more than offset by losses of unemployed former riders who could no longer afford any form of transportation.[24]

A number of tough-minded trolley company officials were very much aware that their industry provided decreasingly competitive service. An editorial in the *Electric Traction and Bus Journal* admitted that twenty- and thirty-year-old trolley cars could not compete with new 1934-model cars. The writer frankly wondered why streetcars managed to retain *any* patrons, and conceded that "the public certainly does not ride streetcars due to preference over the automobile."[25] Other street railway officials pleaded for public understanding, arguing that financial returns were insufficient to attract the capital necessary for large-scale upgrading of equipment.[26] Yet riders grew increasingly restive during the 1930s. In Detroit they complained of stifling cars during the summer, and drafty, freezing cars in the winter.[27] Noise was another gripe, both from patrons and nearby residents. When Detroit streetcar operators struck in the spring of 1939, one citizen jeered: "What a break for Detroiters who have been forced to listen to the flat-wheeled, noise-making contraptions. Thursday morning, with no cars on the tracks, I had such a good sleep that I have already taken a fresh, wide-awake lease on life."[28] But the most frequent complaints related to lack of speed. A 1937 Chicago study showed that surface trolleys averaged only 9.69 miles per hour throughout the Chicago area, and concluded that, under such conditions, almost everyone preferred to use automobiles. For long trips by way of indirect routes, many urbanites used transit only as a last resort.[29]

These unpleasant realities convinced most electric railway officials that the automobile was indeed a formidable competitor. In 1933 A. B. Patterson, president of New Orleans's street railway, admitted that the automobile provided more versatile service than that offered by streetcars. Patterson noted that the entire family could be transported without the multiple fares required by the trolley.[30] The automobile permitted Americans to exercise their penchant for easy mobility, as they were not restricted by fixed schedules, predetermined routes, or time-wasting delays. In a similar vein, a 1933 American Transit Association study suggested that the automobile challenged even the trolley's ultimate appeal, economy. With greater numbers of used cars on the market, and increasing numbers of families pooling resources to purchase one vehicle, automobile costs were cut to the bone.[31] The automobile thus threatened all forms of public transportation, and transit spokesmen frequently voiced their discouragement. *Mass Transportation* reported a case of a local transit company arranging free bus service to a Works Progress Administration (WPA) job site near a large city. Less than half of the workers took advantage of the offer; the majority arrived by automobile. The account sadly concluded that even workers on relief found money to buy gas and oil.[32] William Reilly, a transit official from New York, studied the depressing patronage figures and drew this parallel: "It is possible to take a healthy frog, so I am told, set him in a pan of water at room temperature, increase the temperature of the water very slowly until it reaches the boiling point, and Mr. Frog will not jump out. Unaware that any change is taking place he is gradually lulled into peaceful unconsciousness."[33] The mass transit industry was the gullible frog being boiled alive by the automobile.

Public transit officials attempted to counter the effect of the inexpensive automobile ride, but their strategies revealed inconsistencies, even desperation. Although they complained of the numbers of automobiles crowding streets, particularly in downtown areas, they often opposed practices that would have reduced automobile flow, however slightly. In sharp contrast to the 1970s, during the 1930s mass transit officials actively campaigned against car pooling and tried to persuade motorists not to give rides to hitchhikers. One public transit spokesman criticized the commuter "who shares the cost of gasoline and oil with a few friends on regular trips to the city or place of employment, thus depriving the local carriers of rightful revenue."[34] Particularly during the worst years of the Depression, mass transit executives argued that car pooling threatened the economy. In Corning, New York, in 1933, a local bus company advertisement observed that automobilists giving rides to hitchhikers robbed bus lines of patrons, reduced revenues, and threatened the jobs of bus drivers.[35]

As the plight of mass transportation, particularly the street railway, grew increasingly serious during the 1930s, industry spokesmen placed greater emphasis upon aggressive public relations campaigns. Although some hard-pressed public transit companies cut publicity appropriations because they produced no direct revenue, others placed even greater emphasis on self-promotion. Reflecting on the industry's past, a 1938 *Mass Transportation* editorial pointed out the need to expand public relations departments beyond the efforts of one or two "ex-newspaper men or broken-down advertising writers."[36] Some public transit firms waged extensive campaigns to win back patrons, but few exceeded the aggressive tactics of the Boston Elevated Railway. That line offered free parking adjacent to its stations, promoted holiday "special" trains, and sponsored special radio performances designed to present its view of the urban transportation situation.[37]

During this period, relations between mass transit and automobile interests were far more complex than the simple adversary relationship that some modern observers take for granted. Pessimistic trolley officials vacillated between blaming themselves and blaming the automobile industry for their troubles. They did level occasional blasts at their chief competitor. A transit industry publication charged in 1937 that "well organized groups" had initiated efforts to "unpopularize" streetcars and drive them off congested downtown streets. In particular, the article criticized automobile clubs for selfishly promoting the alleged "rights" of motorists, regardless of social cost.[38] A more frequently voiced theme was trolley officials' admiration and envy of the automobile industry's success. This sentiment appeared even in the early 1930s, when automobile sales were plummeting. A 1931 *Electric Traction* editorial stated that "the time has passed when the electric railway industry can lay the blame for its troubles to the automobile competition, the radio, and other outside influences. Honestly, has the automobile become popular by sales efforts based on criticism of the streetcar and its frailties? . . . The automobile became popular on its own merits, and not through criticism of another mode of transportation."[39] Charles Gordon, president of the AERA, paid similar homage to the inventiveness of his industry's competitors in observing that, while street railway engineers sought utility and efficiency, automobile designers had pursued the more "modern" aesthetic values of speed, attractiveness, and even luxury. "As a result," Gordon concluded, "the public likes and wants the automobile, and will not be deterred by cost alone from providing facilities for its use."[40]

In marked contrast to trolley industry representatives, automobile executives gave little evidence of concern over competition from mass transit. If anything, they profited to a modest extent because of new trends in the transit industry. As more street railway operators began converting to buses, automobile manufacturers produced buses. There appeared to be little reason for automobile executives to sabotage street railways consciously; by generally ignoring them and simply working for legislation beneficial to their own interests, they were winning control of urban transportation.[41] Just as important, as fixed-rail lines became less prominent in the future plans of mass transit operators, there were fewer causes for disagreements over uses and design of city streets. Since efficient bus operations were enhanced by wide streets and urban highways, from the 1930s on automobile and mass transit interests occasionally combined efforts to promote better facilities for all forms of rubberized transit.[42]

There seemed little question in the minds of a wide range of Americans that the automobile was rightfully king of the road. As President Roosevelt publicly stated in 1938, it had become not only a flexible means of transportation and a vital industry, but an integral part of the daily lives of millions of ordinary American families.[43] Other endorsements of the automobile were even more reverential. Chicago's Department of Highways rhapsodized that not only was the motor car considered a necessity by most families, but it was "one of the marvels of modern civilization."[44] In 1935 Detroit Mayor Frank Couzens, rejecting the Rapid Transit Commission's plea for political support for yet another subway proposal, informed Sidney Waldon that no form of rapid transit service could possibly be as satisfactory as driving one's own automobile, for the latter involved no timetable and no transfers.[45]

Proponents of the automobile missed few opportunities to boost their product, and before the Depression they were hardly reticent about stretching their claims. Yet the 1930s brought a distinct reduction of extravagant automobile promotion. Advertisements emphasizing the status appeals of expensive cars were far less flamboyant than during the 1920s. For equally obvious reasons, advertisers did not emphasize the fact that the automobile permitted riders to avoid physical contact with persons from other racial and ethnic groups. It seems curious, however, that industry publications did not emphasize one of the automobile's enormous advantages over the trolley, namely that it was much more convenient for errands. The family breadwinner found the automobile far superior as he stopped at the grocer, the cleaners, and the newsstand on his way home from work. The automobile was especially convenient for carrying packages. Drivers had no waiting time or multiple fares, no packages crushed by fellow trolley patrons, and no four-block walk from a neighborhood shopping center to the nearest car line. As widely separated shopping centers sprouted with greater frequency, the automobile became more and more a necessity. Only a few urban critics sensed the automobile's potential for creating inconvenience even in suburban districts.

In yet another key respect, the Depression decade was the age of innocence regarding public acceptance of the automobile. Virtually nobody predicted an energy shortage. In fact, even a public-transit-oriented journal editorial claimed in 1939 that America possessed sufficient petroleum resources for the next 2,000 years![46] Such blind faith symbolized the failure of even experts within the transportation industry to anticipate the potential magnitude of future problems—and challenges.

Despite widespread public acceptance of the automobile, there was considerable concern within the industry over the motor vehicle's future during the 1930s. The sanguine estimates of future petroleum reserves offered little comfort to automobile salesmen watching their sales plummet. Actually, much of their competition came from their own products; people simply kept their clunkers running.[47] As industry managers desperately sought new markets, they directed attention to the fact that per capita automobile ownership was far lower in most urban areas than in the country.[48] In New York in 1930, there was but one automobile for every twelve residents; Chicago and Boston boasted but one automobile for every eight residents.[49] Automobile industry representatives hence became increasingly aware of the huge potential urban market for their products.

Before the industry could fully exploit that market, cities would have to accommodate the automobile on a far greater scale. Paul Hoffman, president of Studebaker Motor Company, argued in 1934 that urban markets for automobiles were saturated not because potential buyers lacked purchasing power, but because of poorly conceived street systems and inadequate traffic regulation.[50] Despite his unofficial position as "captain" of pro-transit forces in Detroit, Sidney Waldon complained that for years most government funds aided rural highways and neglected the needs of urban America. Waldon argued in 1930 that most American farmers had long since been dragged up out of the mud, and that rural favoritism in allocation of road funds had gone far enough.[51] Austin F. Bement, vice president of the Lincoln Highway Association, concurred, stating that "in the field of

city planning and adequate construction of municipal arteries—
lies the greatest opportunity for immediately beneficial construc-
tive effort."[52] The prestigious American Automobile Association
(AAA), which in the 1920s had even-handedly promoted both
city and country road building, urged greater attention to urban
streets and highways in the 1930s.[53]

Yet even as the automobile was assuming greater control of
urban arteries during the 1930s, a slowly emerging minority of
thinkers challenged its dominance. Not surprisingly, some of the
negative views came from Los Angeles, where automobiles encouraged a new urban lifestyle. Ed Ainsworth, a feature writer
for the *Los Angeles Times,* perceived the automobile as already
beyond control in 1938. "Frankenstein is thundering across the
map of America today, spouting exhaust smoke and reeking of
burnt gasoline fumes. . . . The automobile, designed to be the
emancipator of man, to give man freedom in his movements so
that he might live where he pleases and work where he chooses,
is defeating its own purpose. Man is becoming enslaved again by
the servant he created. The emancipation is becoming a mockery
and a memory."[54] Ainsworth concluded that only by preserving a
balanced urban transportation system, integrating freeways for
autos with special bus lanes and fixed-rail lines, could Los
Angeles retain its unique attraction as a new type of twentieth-
century city. No less a supporter of the automobile than the chief
engineer of the Southern California Automobile Club essentially
agreed with Ainsworth. According to E. E. East, as long as street
railways ruled city streets, metropolitan areas had possessed form
and character, because the transportation systems exerted a controlling influence on land-use patterns. However, this all changed
when the popularity of the automobile damaged the ability of the
street railway to control land uses. "The result is the present day
American city, sprawling, nonconformist, ugly, and inefficient."

East concluded that without adequate public transit systems, the "fluid state" of most American cities could not be controlled or stabilized. Los Angeles, according to East, provided the best example of uncontrolled urban growth.[55]

Mounting motor traffic drew occasional fire from other quarters, and for other reasons. Denver Lions Club President Richard Ossenbaugh nostalgically lamented the decline of the slower-paced life of the olden-day city, where those passing through its streets allegedly took the time to extend courtesy and consideration to others.[56] In the same vein, a writer for *Fortune* observed in 1936 that just as the automobile had damaged the urban landscape by promoting blighted areas and cheap architecture, it had also ravaged the psyches of urbanites with smashups, killings, and increasingly unpleasant traffic jams.[57] But regardless of these forceful observations, automobile critics remained a tiny minority during the 1930s.

The 1930s brought the continued decline of the public transit industry in general and the street railway in particular. Obviously, the most important factor behind this decline was the public's preference for individualized mass transit. However, mass transit industry officials must bear some of the blame. Despite growing numbers of pessimists within the industry, too many mass transit executives still deluded the public about the health of America's trolley systems. Partly for this reason, they failed to develop a consensus about the industry's weaknesses and effectively dramatize their requirements. Had either public officials or transportation engineers foreseen mass transit's bleak future, they might have taken more effective steps. In retrospect, the country may have lost its last real chance to preserve or develop viable public transportation systems at reasonable cost during the Depression. However, few planners or traffic engineers perceived or regretted that lost opportunity at the time.

7 The New Deal and Urban Planning

It would be comforting to argue that the Depression exerted a positive effect upon urban America, in that limited physical changes gave planners a brief respite, an opportunity to develop new maturity and bring fresh perspectives to their work. However, the crises of the 1930s did not provide an atmosphere conducive to quiet, productive contemplation. Rather, they demanded quick, pragmatic responses to immediate needs. By the end of the 1930s the planners' challenge was significantly different from what it had been in 1929. In earlier years they had been hard pressed to control exuberant, rampant urban growth. By 1940 they were challenged to revive a very sick patient. It was a rare planner who did not prefer the former task.

The 1930s brought profound changes to the planning profession. Planners enjoyed greatly expanded opportunities by decade's end, but their responsibilities appeared far more formidable and complex than ever before. Important shifts in relationships between local, state, and federal bureaucracies forced planners to develop entirely new strategies. Private planning firms generated fewer, less lucrative consulting jobs with land developers, and city planning commissions faced sharply curtailed budgets. As the government injected millions of dollars into social welfare programs through a variety of New Deal programs, local planners often found it a matter of survival to establish working ties with federal agencies.

The New Deal programs profoundly influenced the rise of national planning. Unfortunately from the standpoint of urban needs in general and mass transit in particular, national planners emphasized rural rather than urban programs. While city and country dwellers shared most social welfare services on a roughly equal basis, large-scale physical planning concentrated on rural and regional projects. New Deal thinkers pioneered important innovations in public housing and Greenbelt towns, but they devoted little energy to most inner-city needs and almost none to

132

rapid transit.[1] They had little interest in expensive mass transit proposals. This reflected neither a plot against public transit nor a spineless sellout to automobile interests, as some recent critics have implied. Rather, the immediate needs of vast numbers of Americans, both rural and urban, demanded major relief efforts and shunted mass transit requirements to a low priority in the minds of almost all planners.

It is difficult to accurately assess the changing status of planners during the 1930s.[2] Their horizons broadened significantly, and the profession itself became considerably more institutionalized. By decade's end, city planners who thirty years earlier had thought chiefly in terms of civic centers and public monuments routinely deliberated the opportunities and challenges of influencing the development of entire regions, at least in theory.

This does not mean that all planners thought simply on a larger scale. There was, significantly, a reawakened interest in former areas of planning activity. Conscientious thinkers fostered a new sense of responsibility for all parts of metropolitan regions, including the inner city. By the late 1930s, at least a few planners realized the need to save the core city, if for no other reason than to spare other areas from the cancer of urban blight.

It was clear early in the Depression that the severe economic jolt profoundly affected the planners' challenge. Until the Depression, planners had often been forced to respond to rapidly changing physical environments. But the 1930s brought the very different problem of inertia caused by economic stagnation. A few initially welcomed the slowdown in physical urban evolution. According to Harland Bartholomew, the Depression offered planners an "opportunity . . . to consider and study fundamental problems which were ignored in the rush of individual planning movements."[3] Bryant Hall, a regional planner from Los Angeles, concurred, but observed that the Depression was no time for a letdown. In fact, hard times brought an even greater need for creative thinking, as planners were required to do more with less money.[4]

In terms of sheer volume of work, American planners compiled a seemingly impressive growth record during the 1930s. Much of the growth was along very traditional lines. Zoning remained the chief responsibility of most planning groups; a 1939 survey revealed that planners played a role in creating zoning ordinances in nearly 1,200 cities. The next most frequently achieved planning function was preparation of "comprehensive" city plans, and 217 of those cities surveyed possessed such documents. The relative importance of public transit compared to the automobile, at least in the minds of civic leaders, may be reflected in the fact that, while there were 205 thoroughfare plans in 1939, there were but 86 transit plans.[5]

American planners performed their daily tasks in the midst of continuing efforts to gain professional recognition. In preparation and training, the majority of planners remained amateurs. Many possessed a deep knowledge of their urban environments and their needs, gained through years of practical experience. Yet even by the end of the decade, very few had any significant formal training. The concept of a formalized critical core of knowledge, essential for effective interaction between planners, remained foreign to most.[6] Harvard University, which had pioneered the first course in city planning principles, founded the first school of city planning in 1929. By the end of the 1930s, only four universities offered full-scale planning programs.[7]

This was at least partly because many planners remained unconvinced of the need for academic training. A special committee of the American City Planning Institute, formed in 1937 to examine the need for university training, took a casual view of the whole question. While the report noted that the planning departments then operating were poorly endowed, it denied a need to open up large numbers of schools and hastily train a new generation of planners. The report emphasized a need for quality rather than quantity.[8] Some planners challenged the need for any academic training at all. Lawrence M. Orton of New York's Regional Planning Commission may have reflected many of his contemporaries' contempt for, or at least suspicion of, planning education when he stated in 1941 that "instruction on a theoretical and academic plane is almost worse than useless. Students must be taught in terms of actual problems and at all cost avoid academic 'lingo.' Unless a subject can be presented in plain English, it is a liability rather than an asset."[9] Clearly the heavy demand for formally trained city planners was some distance in the future; it would not become evident until well after World War II.[10]

During the 1930s, most planning efforts were consistent with the chief impulses of New Deal reform in emphasizing pragmatic programs and downplaying elaborate theories.[11] Considering the nonacademic composition of the typical planning commission, this was predictable. A 1939 study revealed that over half of the members of planning commissions in thirty-one of the nation's largest cities were businessmen or realtors. Lawyers comprised 11.1 percent; architects and engineers followed with 10.1 and 7.7 percent respectively. A mere 1 percent had any university affiliation. The study concluded that in their composition and basic value systems, planning commissions were, like most public advisory groups, "conservative in their political and social outlook."[12] As planning historian Blaine Brownell has observed, "By the 1930s, audacity and promise had lost considerable ground to the more modest and accepted goals of practicality and narrow problem-solving."[13]

Although many planners disdained academically trained theoreticians, they urged greater "professionalization," at least to the extent of hiring full-time staff for planning commissions.

During the 1930s, a conviction developed that planning commissions run by part-time amateurs volunteering a few hours a month were incapable of coming to grips with increasingly complex urban problems. By the time amateurs understood the issues, their terms were frequently near completion.[14] Since part-time volunteers rarely possessed the reservoir of skills needed to perform in-depth technical studies of urban problems, cities had in the past frequently commissioned out-of-town consultants. By the late 1930s many planners realized that such tactics contributed to their lack of political clout. Opponents of specific proposals could simply criticize them as ideas imposed by "outsiders," rather than firm convictions of those with a direct stake in the outcome. Hugh R. Pomeroy of the American Society of Planning Officials (ASPO) observed in 1939 that, as a result of such suspicions, "all over the country [one finds] the corpses of consultant-made plans."[15]

Without question, many local planners grew discouraged during the Depression decade. Though many sensed the need for greater professionalism and more recognition, they also realized that city departments remained suspicious of any infringements upon their "territory." New York planning chief Rexford G. Tugwell complained of constant harassment from imperious Park Commissioner Robert Moses and the irrepressible Mayor Fiorello La Guardia.[16] Detroit planner Herbert L. Russell worried in 1933 that the mayor and city council considered planners "busybodies or snoopers."[17] Charles H. Bennett, then a Milwaukee planner, perhaps best articulated the truth when he observed in 1941 that "nothing offends other public officials more than having a new municipal activity receive all the newspaper ink, while departments of long standing have to beg for space."[18]

Some planners felt that the shoe was on the other foot. They stressed that most of their work consisted of such thankless but necessary drudgery as processing zoning variance requests. As

Southern California planner L. Deming Tilton viewed it, "many city planning commissions have discovered . . . the proposals which call for large expenditures get fire-whistle headlines, but the quiet, money-saving, preventive work which goes on from day to day does not receive a measure of acclaim in proportion to its importance."[19] From Tilton's perspective, politicians did not give planners enough credit. Yet a few planners realized that the tenuous position of local planners was at least partly their own fault. Robert A. Walker's 1939 nationwide survey of local planning concluded that too many planners simply distrusted politicians as a matter of course. The report urged planners to upgrade both their understanding of public administrators' needs and their skills in public relations.[20] These views suggested the frequent tensions between politicians and planners during the 1930s.

Given these strained relations, and the much higher priorities of providing relief and maintaining basic services, it is hardly surprising that planning departments were among the first to feel budgetary constrictions during Depression-era belt-tightening.[21] This had little direct effect upon planning commissions in many cities and towns; a 1937 survey revealed that, of 1,178 commissions in the United States, 904 received no appropriation at all. Another 158 received appropriations of $500 or less annually. At the top of the scale, only nine commissions boasted annual budgets in excess of $20,000.[22] However, specific figures on budget cuts in some large cities underscore the dramatic impact of hard times. In Boston, the commission budget was halved in three years, declining from $34,276 to $16,750 between 1931 and 1934. Detroit's commission suffered even larger cuts; its budget dropped from $53,055 in 1930 to $8,413 in 1934. But Chicago planners suffered the largest proportional cut. Somewhat surprisingly, as late as 1932 the commission prospered on an annual budget of $40,000. In both 1934 and 1935 it received a pittance of $1,000 each year.[23] Chicago Plan Commission Chair-

man Albert A. Sprague believed no other comparable organization experienced as great a diminution of income; he pointed out
the obvious when he observed that it could not continue to function on $1,000 per year.[24] In Detroit, the City Plan Commission
struggled along despite severe budget cuts. Its 1934 annual report
pointed out that most work was being done by part-time Federal
Emergency Relief Administration (FERA) workers, who averaged a mere nine hours each week. Few of these workers were
experienced in planning; the commission undoubtedly under-
stated its case in pointing out that, considering the technical
nature of the work, much inefficiency must be expected.[25]

Severely limited budgets during the 1930s were one symptom
of simmering suspicion between city administrators and planners.
Also worrisome was the commissions' very limited legal authority. As in earlier periods, planning bodies remained purely advisory in function.[26] While some planners pushed for more authority, optimists persistently emphasized the virtue of limited power
for local groups. Charles W. Eliot, a member of both the National Resources Committee (NRC) and the National Capital Park
and Planning Commission (NCPPC), provided a contemporary
twist to an old argument by observing in 1936 that if planners
gained legal authority they would experience increasing difficulty
avoiding administrative paper shuffling.[27]

Despite such headaches, local planners occasionally developed
cordial working relations with existing government agencies. A
national planning survey in 1939 praised the work of the Los
Angeles County Regional Planning Commission. According to
the survey, Los Angeles planners had been extremely sensitive to
political realities and had assiduously cultivated friendly working
relationships with other county and city departments. In formu-
lating long-range plans, regional planners invariably consulted
any existing agencies that might be affected.[28] Unfortunately,
even in this purportedly "ideal" working relationship between

planners and local governing bodies, public officials in Los Angeles followed planning recommendations only when they conveniently served short-term, obvious needs.

Since the founding of the Republic, federal assistance for roads, canals, harbor improvements, and railroads had promoted regional and national commerce. Conservation of natural resources was firmly established as a legitimate federal concern early in the twentieth century. There had been discussion of a national plan as early as 1900, but not even limited progress occurred until the inauguration of Franklin Roosevelt in 1933.[29] Even then, despite the enthusiasm of some New Dealers, progress was slow. In the early months of the Roosevelt presidency, the concept was discussed, but short-term emergencies assumed top priority.[30] The NRC and the National Resources Planning Board (NRPB), created late in Roosevelt's first term, suggested progress, but, like earlier planning efforts, they generated more reports than concrete action.

The reasons for the modest initial progress of broad-based national planning are complex. Historian Otis L. Graham, Jr., suggested that the NRPB possessed few friends either within or outside of government. Like their counterparts at the local level, national planners resisted either framing or lobbying for enabling legislation.[31] In addition, planners realized that other matters were more urgent; the New Deal emphasized relief and recovery first, reform second. National planners promoting long-range projects that included large-scale physical building had to compete for federal funds with a large number of agencies providing immediate social welfare services. Politicians, whether motivated by humanitarian concerns or self-interest, usually preferred the immediate benefits of social welfare.

The massive construction projects sponsored by the Tennessee Valley Authority (TVA) appeared to be a notable exception to this trend. Nevertheless, promoters of TVA projects emphasized not only reclamation and conservation objectives but also the inestimable social benefits to local residents of irrigation, flood control, and electrification. Several other New Deal programs seemed within the tradition of national planning, including the Public Works Administration (PWA) and the Rural Electrification Administration (REA). Sponsors of both programs—particularly the former—envisioned massive building programs. In practice, disposition of most funds earmarked for the two agencies was heavily influenced by local administrators; these officials preferred small-scale local building projects.[32] By and large, projects of a national scale, such as the St. Lawrence Seaway and the interstate highway system, would come only after World War II.

The concept of comprehensive national planning made little impact in the 1930s in terms of practical results, and Depression-era planners had no way to fully perceive its promising future. The dominant mood within the profession seemed to be one of discouragement. In 1940 planner Russell V. Black charged that even the NRPB had bowed to political expediency by approving many public works despite the absence of an overall plan.[33] The NRPB itself was hardly blind to planners' difficulties; it observed in 1939 that resistance to planning might even be an inherent facet of the American character.

Planning by government, whether national, state, or local, is a relatively new and little understood concept, for this nation of traditional individualists. At heart, we are still a rural pioneering people, each the lord of his own domain . . . not yet are we generally convinced that some degree of conscious direction and regulation of both public and private activities on the land is essential to a reasonable amount of freedom and satisfaction in community living.[34]

Another widely circulated study of the entire planning movement observed that what passed for national planning at the end of the 1930s was "piecemeal, pluralistic, ... uncoordinated, and dispersive in character."[35]

At the national level, planning thought consistently emphasized rural rather than urban concerns. The reasons were at least partly political. Early in 1933 the nation's farmers appeared close to organized revolt, and they were as firmly entrenched politically as almost any interest group. In response to farm lobby pressures, and perhaps some genuine conviction, New Deal legislators emphasized salvation of the rural sector first.[36] Influential planner Jacob L. Crane anticipated lean pickings from the pile of New Deal legislation for those interested in urban rebuilding. After the famous first one hundred days of Roosevelt's administration in 1933, Crane observed that "the cities must take care of their own rebuilding with such help as they can get in credit and housing and public works."[37] He likewise sensed that, to the extent national legislators considered physical rebuilding at all, they were primarily interested in funding rural and regional programs like TVA. Such projects crossed new frontiers of their own and seemed more fashionable to many than rebuilding dilapidated old urban cores.

First the NRC and then the NRPB appeared almost studiously to ignore the physical rebuilding requirements of large cities. The Roosevelt administration did not officially recognize a need to develop a discrete urban policy until deep into its first term. Even then the NRPB produced more studies than specific proposals. In 1936 the Research Committee on Urbanism, a subcommittee of the NRPB, presented its first "interim report," which recognized some of the hitherto ignored needs of the cities: "Recently we have been shocked into a recognition of our ignorance of urban life by a host of problems. . . . Even the most cursory sampling of a few specific problems that are currently encountered will make evident the regrettable consequences of our past neglect of the urban scene in the information services of the government."[38] Not until the beginning of Roosevelt's second term in 1937 did an NRPB report raise the question of why it was more difficult and controversial to develop concrete programs for rehabilitation of cities than for conservation of rural areas. After all, urban poverty was just as real as rural. The answer, suggested the report, was that "the country had a uniform base of agriculture, the farm and the farmer, while the city had no such common symbol or group to characterize it."[39] This insight was nearly offset by federal planners' almost startlingly naive faith in their ability to effect meaningful improvements in the urban environment. In 1939 the NRPB Committee on Local Planning insisted that "the form of cities may be considerably molded and always much improved through planning and replanning processes."[40]

This faith may have been based on the undeniable fact that the New Deal brought enormous benefits to most urban residents in the 1930s. After all, the Federal Emergency Relief Administration (FERA), section 7A of the National Industrial Recovery Act (NIRA), PWA, WPA, and other legislative acts provided crucial assistance and at times even the basic life-sustaining necessities to millions of urban residents.[41] And the National Housing Act, however limited its completed projects, firmly established the principle of government involvement in urban renewal. It was not without good reason that the basis of huge Democratic majorities in American cities between the 1930s and 1960s rested largely on the foundation of urban support wrought by New Deal programs. Without the epochal initiatives of the Roosevelt years, the urban rebuilding portions of Truman's Fair Deal and Johnson's Great Society programs might have been impossible. Present-day urban critics deplore the shortcomings in both theory and implementation of urban renewal programs, but they should remember that forty or fifty years ago, sensitive, thoughtful urban liberals had high hopes for these programs.[42]

But even as energetic New Dealers injected exciting new concepts into some phases of the planning movement, the debate over urban decentralization followed largely traditional lines at both the national and local levels. Those favoring decentralization promoted several new devices to achieve their goals, including active federal participation, and pursued their objective with unmistakable sincerity and enthusiasm. But the 1930s also brought a marked increase in the vocal and articulate minority of thinkers who foresaw direful future effects of overly rapid horizontal growth.

On the side of those promoting the further spreading of population were some highly influential voices. President Roosevelt expressed his belief in 1939 that decentralization would create some disadvantages in "manufacturing efficiency," but these would be more than offset by reductions in costs of governing and providing urban services.[43] The President's generalizations about administrative costs of government and providing utilities could be challenged, but his preference for spreading urban growth was shared by other influential thinkers. Cambridge planner John Nolen endorsed decentralization unequivocally in 1931. "The future city will be spread out, it will be regional, it will be the natural product of the automobile, the good road, electricity, the telephone, and the radio, combined with the growing desire to live a more natural, biological life under pleasanter and more natural conditions."[44] The New England branch of the NRC echoed this sentiment in 1939, arguing that decentralization made possible sunny, healthy industrial villages, "unmarred by the worst features of the overjammed industrial cities."[45] Such views suggested both the ambiguity and the complexity of planning thought in the 1930s. Despite disarray and discouragement within the profession over many Depression developments, there remained a fairly persistent faith among many that they could control the evolution of entire metropolitan areas as long as they cooperated with administrators in suburban municipalities.[46] Generalizations about planning are risky, but optimism regarding the ability of the federal government to guide certain facets of American development was central to American planning thought during the 1930s.[47] Some federal planners at least shared the optimistic pragmatism typical of New Deal bureaucrats.

Others endorsed decentralization for more specific, down-to-earth reasons. Some regional planners emphasized condemnation of land and acquisition of park space in outlying areas not on the basis of present need but because immediate action would yield immense financial savings in the long run.[48] At the other extreme, a handful of planners believed that the decay of the older portions of many cities was so advanced as to be terminal and that all life-support systems should be cut immediately. Carol Aronovici's extreme view, although not new in 1932, is worth quoting at some length.

> Let the old cities perish so that we may have great and beautiful cities. . . . What is needed is a thorough emancipation of the suburban communities from the metropolis. As long as New York, Boston, Chicago or Los Angeles can depend upon the outlying communities to pay them tribute, as long as business and cultural parasitism is encouraged and planned for by the metropolitan center, there is little hope of social, cultural, and economic integration of the smaller suburban places. They will remain mere bedrooms for the advantage of which their people will have to pay tribute until such time as the metropo-

lis, hydra-like, will suck their very physical existence into the body politic of decayed and corrupted political organization.[49]

From a contemporary perspective, such a statement appears startling. Yet suburban fears over annexation remained strong, and the typical urban core, besieged by Hoovervilles and boarded-up businesses in the fall of 1932, may well have appeared beyond salvation to scores of urban planners.

One additional factor may have motivated some planners' preference for decentralization. As many urban governments cut planning department funding in the 1930s, planners sensed that increased use of metropolitan space might lead to more professional opportunities, either at the regional or state levels, or with suburban administrative agencies. Greater use of space would create both a need for more physical plans and the formation of more suburbs—which might in turn generate additional openings for planners.[50]

As pointed out earlier (Chapter 6), outlying areas continued to experience larger population increases than central districts. The federal government had briefly engaged in community building through its World War I housing programs. In commencing the Greenbelt town movement in the 1930s, the federal government for the first time consciously promoted both decentralization and subsidized suburban housing. In immediate, practical terms, the Greenbelt town program achieved little. Federal planner Rexford Tugwell, who sponsored the idea originally, hoped 3,000 brand new towns could be developed; in 1935 the Resettlement Administration selected 25 town sites. Only three Greenbelt towns were actually built; together they resettled only a few thousand people.[51] Yet social historian Paul K. Conkin suggested that, in worldwide influence, the Greenbelt program was one of the most important New Deal achievements, "hardly excelled, even by the

Tennessee Valley Authority, in imagination, in breaking with precedents, and in broad social objectives."[52] Conceptually, the stage was set for massive FHA subsidies for suburban housing during the post–World-War-II period.

Despite the publicity surrounding federal experiments in suburban planning, there was actually more partial implementation of Ebenezer Howard's Greenbelt concepts by private entrepreneurs than by the government. No private developer designed a town as complete and self-contained as the federally sponsored experiment of Greenbelt, Maryland; and some private efforts were dreary, even repressive company towns. Nevertheless, private entrepreneurs provided innovative ideas for new community structures in outlying regions, including the widely acclaimed Baldwin Hills development near Los Angeles.[53] A 1936 report by the NRC counted 68 functioning experimental towns in the nation, most developed by private enterprise.[54]

However, a slowly growing number of planners and other observers were articulating decentralization's potentially deleterious effects. Some argued that abandoning the central city was short-sighted expediency that would have disastrous long-term effects. An Urban Land Institute study pointed out in 1940 that migration from city to suburb had already left vacant nearly one-third of all privately owned lots within city limits; future development of the lots seemed doubtful. The report stated categorically that if uncontrolled decentralization continued, cities would face financial ruin.[55] A study committee of the United States Chamber of Commerce agreed that abandoning the central districts would be foolish from an economic standpoint, since it would require reorganization of the entire machinery of production and distribution.[56]

Even more significant was the conversion of some noted planners who had earlier championed horizontal development. Nobody probed the effects of decentralization more deeply than St. Louis planner Harland Bartholomew. In the 1920s he had enthusiastically advocated that pattern of growth, arguing that spreading the population could solve urban problems almost automatically.[57] But a decade of hard experience, plus witnessing the devastation of the Depression upon the core cities, changed his mind. By 1932 his conversion was complete, and he argued that decentralization, as currently practiced, was economically unsound, destructive of fundamental urban character, and likely in the long run to produce enormous social disadvantages.[58] The same year, he urged "a real effort to prevent endless spread of population with its concomitant disintegration of the larger central areas of cities."[59]

As Bartholomew saw it, unplanned decentralization took a frightful toll in both economic and human terms. Abandonment of core cities by businesses, either by choice or because they went broke, removed vital sources of tax revenue and directly contributed to spreading blight in areas between core cities and suburbs.[60] Even more to the point, Bartholomew challenged Aronovici's contention that central cities fed off of suburban largesse. In fact, argued Bartholomew, suburbanites more often played the role of parasite, as they increasingly made use of urban services without paying their proportionate share of the cost.[61] Perhaps most important in human terms, decentralization shattered the dreams of many urban residents. As the more successful members of early immigrant groups joined the movement to suburbs, new immigrants and the poor and aged members of older groups were left to fend for themselves in what some perceived as an increasingly inhuman environment.[62] Occasionally the suburban "drift" even brought tragedy to those able to join the movement. Bartholomew related the sad tale of a family maid and her husband who lived happily and healthfully for two years in modest quarters in one of the central areas of St. Louis. They were persuaded one day to buy a small lot in a suburban tract that had inadequate water and sewage facilities. The couple was sold on the advantages of the great open spaces and lived in a ramshackle garage until they could afford to build a real home on the front of the lot. Six months later the maid was dead from exposure and pneumonia, leaving her husband and small baby behind. This melodramatic tragedy, according to Bartholomew, was no isolated case. Similar cases could be found repeatedly, in one form or another, on the outskirts of many cities.[63]

Another influential planner, Clarence A. Dykstra, became a critic of decentralization at about the same time. As recently as 1926 Dykstra, then with the Los Angeles Water Board, had been an enthusiastic advocate of suburban growth.[64] By 1934 his thinking had changed dramatically. He admitted to American Transit Association members at their annual convention that expansion had turned into uncontrolled sprawl, and one of the prices was over-speculation and overbuilding of transit facilities.[65] In an article published the same year, Dykstra argued that decentralization was no answer at all to inner-city decay. Abandoned urban cores, and the problems they generated, would not magically disappear.[66]

Perhaps Homer Hoyt, a noted expert on urban land use, best explained why increasing numbers of planners were growing critical of decentralization in the 1930s. Up until World War I and even through the 1920s, few planners worried about the core city, because conversion of its space was almost invariably to a "higher and better use." In the core city, larger and more imposing office buildings (which often yielded more tax revenues) replaced their more modest predecessors. This orthodox view held that, as industrial districts expanded, the workers who were driven out of their cheap wooden duplexes frequently moved out to better residential areas immediately beyond the zone of workingmen's homes. "Under this beneficient process, there was a constant expectation that a succession of higher land uses moving from the center in the form of concentric circles would take up any slack and prevent any decay in the urban structure."[67] The crash of 1929 shattered this illusion and cast in sharp relief some of the negative facets of decentralization. When central districts continued to lose commercial establishments to outlying areas, when multi-story office buildings advertised hundreds of vacancies, and when industrial-zone businesses closed their doors, blight invariably appeared.[68]

Some social critics, including Lewis Mumford, believed that much decentralization was a result of city builders simply following the line of least resistance.[69] This view received support elsewhere. The president of the Denver Planning Commission charged that this attitude permeated decisionmaking at all levels, from those of individual citizens to the most sophisticated business and governmental groups. "It was easier to travel long distances to and from work, easier to build a new home amid cleaner surroundings than to put forth the effort to bring old neighborhoods up to the rising standards of American residential requirements. So the vicious circle of blight spread."[70] By the late 1930s, it was clear that decentralization was already creating problems even for some portions of metropolitan districts that had recently prospered. Echoing Ralph Hare's and J. C. Nichols's warnings of a decade earlier, Henry Babcock, a Los Angeles civil engineer, observed in 1937 that in some areas, "each of the *outlying* centers, whether large or small, also had its little ring of blight or potential blight."[71]

All told, planning thought remained highly fragmented. American planners were at last beginning to have second thoughts about the hitherto assumed benefits of decentralization. Nevertheless, they generally failed to clearly articulate realistic long-range options for future directions of urban growth, and they obviously achieved no consensus regarding preferred patterns of development. The consequences of these failures would be even more evident in later years; in the post–World-War-II era, planners would be only slightly better prepared to state clear alternatives than were their predecessors.

American planning experienced unparalleled change in the 1930s. Many city planning commissions were in the doldrums, but the decade brought the rapid growth of regional planning and some hopeful first steps in national planning. Many planners were overwhelmed by the growing challenges they faced, along with the rapidly expanding administrative mazes through which they had to shepherd their proposals. Other planners were frustrated over the inconsistencies of their missions. Theoretically, they were to design long-range projects with enormous, if distant, benefits. They soon learned that survival necessitated short-term practical proposals with immediate payoffs. Nevertheless, the rise of regional and national planning convinced some that their profession had finally achieved permanence.

The Depression brought a new sense of maturity to planning thought by destroying once and for all the blind faith that urban problems could be easily overcome. However, continued confusion within the profession, and the growing complexity of urban and regional issues, hampered efforts to provide adequate mass transit. During the 1930s, pressures for automotive solutions to urban mass transit needs were building. Yet, given their implicit faith in the motor vehicle, it seems unlikely that traffic planners would have favored major commitments to public transportation systems in any event.

8 Transit Planning versus Automobile Planning

American city planners devoted comparatively little thought to urban transportation during the Depression, but those who did generally persisted in favoring the automobile over mass transit. Planners and traffic engineers remained fascinated by the promise of new technology, and mass transit seemed dated compared to the automobile. There were a handful of innovations in public transit, but no great breakthroughs. In contrast, the 1930s marked important advances in street and highway design. Perhaps lulled by a leveling off of motor-vehicle registrations, planners and traffic engineers remained confident that they could always control the impact of the automobile upon the urban environment through careful application of new technologies.

There were other compelling reasons why planners favored the automobile. At least in the short run, accommodating the motor vehicle was far less expensive than new rapid transit systems, and cost was probably *the* critical consideration during the Depression. Present-day critics of automotive planning should also bear in mind that half a century ago, streets and superhighways appeared to be a democratic response to urban transportation needs. Unlike the turn-of-the-century parkway that transported the carriages of the rich, the urban highway of the 1930s carried not only the automobile of the middle classes, but buses for those unable to afford private transportation. In a similar vein, the federal government encouraged highway building, both to revive America's single largest industry and as a means of directly employing thousands of jobless victims of the Depression. Highway engineers undoubtedly stretched the truth in promoting highways for safety and environmental reasons, but most planners believed their automobile-oriented response to urban transportation needs was tough-minded, pragmatic, and compassionate.[1]

Most urban streets and highways built in the 1930s eased traffic more effectively in the suburbs than in central districts. One reason was that proponents of both rapid transit and inner-city highways frequently drew up hastily conceived plans, more appropriate for attracting suddenly available federal grants than for solving real transportation needs. By the end of the decade, the two camps had largely stymied each others' efforts to gain the upper hand. Unfortunately, core-city transportation plans frequently became mired in local politics, or they conflicted with New Deal–inspired proposals for slum clearance and other public works. Finally, since virtually nobody challenged the dominance of the automobile in outlying areas, a large proportion of the traffic planning effort of the 1930s was devoted to suburban superhighway construction. After all, poorly planned transportation routes were much more obvious downtown than in more remote suburbs. Federal planners, supported by millions of dollars, reinforced the generally pro-automobile bias of local planners throughout the 1930s. By the end of the decade, the triumph of the automobile seemed inevitable.

The proposals of the few Depression-era rapid transit enthusiasts reflected neither originality nor realism during hard times. A serious shortcoming was a lack of flair and enthusiasm. However sound the reasoning of rapid transit supporters, most arguments for subways and elevateds could have been copied directly from proposals of twenty years earlier. Robert H. Whitten, a Washington, D.C., planner, sounded a familiar note by arguing in 1932 that the automobile could never rival the mass carrying ability of elevated trains and subways, at least along the most heavily traveled corridors.[2] Another idea dating from World War I was that automobiles were reaching their "saturation point" in terms of use inside urban areas. John Nolen, Jr., of the National Capital Park and Planning Commission (NCPPC) articulated this view, and suggested that future remedies must emphasize "the more efficient movement" of mass transit.[3] Perhaps succumbing to wishful thinking, in 1938 Oakland planner I. S. Shattuck predicted a de-emphasis on individualized transportation facilities, along with a new focus on public transit.[4] Shattuck presented no evidence to back up this expectation.

Surprisingly, optimism about the competitive attractiveness of rapid transit persisted in some quarters. The American Society of Planning Officials (ASPO) insisted that people abandoned mass transit for their automobiles only in areas possessing inferior transit systems. As late as 1940 an ASPO newsletter argued that where rapid, comfortable, and inexpensive mass transit systems existed, people could be induced to use them instead of automobiles.[5] The newsletter did not comment upon the prospects of actually building new, updated rapid transit systems or refurbishing older ones. Some of those who doubted the survival capabilities of the snail-paced street-level trolley believed that former streetcar users could be "won back" from their automobiles by rapid transit subways. For example, Chicago transit consultant Charles E. de Leuw urged Detroit to build a subway along Woodward Avenue. He believed that it would yield an average speed of 24 miles per hour, which would be even higher than that achieved by automobiles during non-rush hours.[6] This suggestion, like so many earlier rapid transit proposals for Detroit, fell on deaf ears.

Support for some type of rail rapid transit came occasionally from unexpected sources. Although the Los Angeles Transportation Engineering Board was even then much better known for its imaginative and far-reaching freeway proposals, it nevertheless stated flatly in 1939 that "the ultimate solution in areas of high density is found only in rail transit."[7] And Norman Bel Geddes, whose 1939 portrayal of "Cities of Tomorrow" so stimulated public thinking in favor of massive urban freeway building, saw a place for a futuristic subway to carry "the great masses of the future metropolis" on most of their daily journeys.[8] But what little innovation existed in rapid transit thought was usually tied to larger projects. In the few major cities that developed rapid transit proposals during the 1930s, planners laid out basic super-highway or freeway systems with space reserved for future rail rapid transit lines.[9] Even in these few instances, creative thinking about rapid transit was quite limited, since the major concepts dated back at least to Detroit's plan of 1923.

Those advocating rapid transit during the Depression also insisted that it was the most democratic response urban governments could make. Charles Gordon, managing director of the American Transit Association, argued that other facets of city planning, including public housing and park development, directed attention to the needs of those in lower-income brackets. As Gordon saw the situation, by directing most of their attention to facilitating automobile movement, many planners ignored the transportation needs of the poor.[10] Detroit planner Sidney D. Waldon concurred in a letter to Mayor Richard W. Reading in 1939. "When you fight for better transportation you are fighting for those who fill the entire base of the social pyramid. . . . These people are the wage earners in overalls and white collars. They are the students going to school and the housewives going to market. They are the great mass of our people who live close to the edge of bare necessity. They cannot own a car for every member of the family. . . . They *must* use public transportation *and like it.*"[11]

A few planners urged immediate rapid transit construction on strictly pragmatic grounds. First, some municipal experts viewed any such construction projects as excellent means of hiring the unemployed and, incidentally, easing local relief burdens. An advisory committee in Detroit informed the mayor that going ahead with plans to build a twenty-mile subway system would directly employ 9,000 men and create another 16,000 jobs in related industries.[12] Second, planners occasionally urged local governments to take advantage of Depression-level prices by

commencing rapid transit construction immediately. John P. Hallihan, another proponent of rapid transit development in Detroit,
estimated that the city could save roughly 25 percent in total
construction costs by starting subway construction in 1932.[13] After Roosevelt's inauguration, and the mushrooming of various
New Deal programs, planners in some cities urged urban governments to pursue federal grants for rapid transit construction.
Finally, a few planners insisted that construction of rapid transit
systems would benefit virtually all urban residents. Henry C.
Koch pointed out that a primary reason for building rapid transit
systems was the "community-at-large" benefit of checking inner-
city decay. In addition, insisted Koch, "the motorist like-wise
benefits through the removal from street surfaces of many millions of passenger miles, clearing traffic ways for greater freedom of movement and safety."[14]

Notwithstanding these arguments, efforts to place rail rapid
transit systems in large American cities during the 1930s almost
invariably failed; only Chicago initiated a subway system. There
were many reasons for this. Los Angeles transit expert Donald
M. Baker pointed out that automobile registrations in that city,
which paralleled trends in other cities, may have stifled enthusiasm for such projects. According to Baker, the leveling off of
automobile ownership and inner-city traffic in Los Angeles convinced some that the worst traffic problems were in the past.
Evidently, they perceived temporary relief as a permanent
trend.[15] In Detroit, Waldon had for years urged construction of
rapid transit in order to induce patrons to return to public transportation. According to Waldon's figures, if per capita patronage
could be raised to its peak levels of 1916, rapid transit construction costs could be more than realized from increased passenger
revenues.[16] Opponents sensed that this perspective was essentially negative: patronage figures evidenced a declining industry;
"artificial stimulants" for public transportation would simply de-

lay the "inevitable" collapse of rail transit.[17] Oakland planner I. S. Shattuck had been sanguine about the prospects of mass transit in 1938, but in 1940 he voiced discouragement over the prospects of innovative rapid transit. He specifically scored the New Dealers' lack of a discrete urban policy; despite the relief programs and the isolated rebuilding projects taking place under a variety of government programs, there was almost no support for comprehensive rapid transit.[18]

Some urban observers objected to rapid transit in principle; ironically, most of their criticisms were just as dated as pro-transit arguments. No planner opposed subways more consistently than John Nolen of Cambridge, who observed in 1931: "Subways are evidence of an unsuccessfully planned city. They may be a necessary evil, but they represent the failure of planning."[19] Edward M. Bassett of New York once again insisted that subways created cities with crowded, dark, and "evil" buildings.[20] Frederick A. Delano of the NCPPC argued in 1940 that downtown-oriented subways or elevated systems were demonstrably costly, but had "proved to be only a palliative and not a cure for the disease of congestion and blight."[21] John Ihlder of Washington took this argument one step further, repeating the long-standing view in 1935 that subways exacerbated rather than relieved urban congestion. "Instead," claimed Ihlder, "they concentrated the working population both in shop and dwelling."[22] When Vermont Senator Ernest W. Gibson proposed a subway for the District of Columbia, the *Washington Post* stood firmly against it for much the same reason.[23]

Other arguments opposing rapid transit stressed economy. Although similar views had been expressed for at least three decades, they took a new twist during the Depression. A 1933 Boston Municipal Research Bureau study stated unequivocally that limited federal grants available to the city should not be squandered for "relief" of the floundering Boston Elevated Railway, which had lost more than 20 percent of its patronage in just six years: "This is the worst possible time for new commitments which will still further increase the cost of service."[24] Chicago banker John A. Carroll, a frequent critic of subway plans that fed all lines into the downtown Loop, expressed a similar view. In an unsuccessful attempt to persuade Secretary of the Interior Harold Ickes to oppose a PWA grant for subway construction in Chicago, Carroll charged that enormous expenditures for subways would be a waste of money in a city near bankruptcy.[25] Citing cost estimates varying from $2.5 to $5 million per mile, the *Washington Post* editorialized that, before any local subway was built, "there should be proof that it would be sufficiently convenient and cheap to induce workers to use it."[26]

By the 1930s, the support remaining for rail rapid transit was frequently half-hearted. The Los Angeles Transportation Engineering Board approved rail rapid transit lines in principle, but its 1939 report stated that "the high cost of the most approved rail arrangements tends to defer into the indefinite future the time when they can be financed."[27] As further evidence of its lack of conviction about the urgency of such a project, the board declined to provide even a cost estimate to accompany its elaborate rapid transit map. Similarly, Detroit transit planners Sidney Waldon and John P. Hallihan anticipated even as they proposed rail lines in the middle of that city's superhighways that their vision would probably never be realized. In 1932 they candidly pointed out that "it is not impossible that the central reservation on some of the superhighway may be put to still other uses than those now mentioned."[28] Apparently they anticipated that the reserved space would be paved over for automobiles to use.

The failure of rapid transit enthusiasts to revise their arguments in the face of rapidly changing conditions is curious. By the 1930s, traffic counts clearly revealed the increasing importance of crosstown and intersuburban commuting. Yet Depression-era rapid transit proposals, just like those presented decades earlier, still emphasized the superiority of subways for moving the masses into urban cores. One factor was the continued support of downtown commercial interests, which often sponsored core-city–oriented rapid transit proposals in last ditch efforts to make their businesses more accessible to vanishing patrons.[29] Their efforts were largely unsuccessful, and as businesses boarded up and many others either set up branches or moved entirely to suburban locations, the influence of downtown interests inevitably waned.[30] Another contributing factor nay have been the dependence of local planning departments upon city council funding: few pro-transit local planners had the temerity to explicitly downgrade core-city accessibility. Even so, most city councils cut local planning departments' share of annual budgets during the 1930s, and pressure for downtown-oriented rapid transit probably lessened even further. Neither factor adequately explains their lack of creative thinking, but the growing realization of diminished chances for subways may partly explain why the few remaining pro-transit planners appeared to be simply going through the motions during the Depression.

Urban planners' responses to new rail rapid transit proposals unquestionably reflected the inexorable shift of public preference toward the automobile for urban transportation during the 1930s. Many planners' perceptions of ideal urban forms continued to assume the automobile's central role. John Ihlder stated in 1935 that the automobile was crucial in permitting settlement of urban land at the lowest possible density. He did not question decentralization as a social benefit, and he concluded that, "second only to the shank's mare [walking], the private passenger car is the best means of transit now available."[31]

Few remained who stressed that accommodating the auto-

mobile ignored the needs of the less fortunate in American society. While a handful of pro-transit planners insisted on subways
for the masses, others observed that automobile ownership extended downward through almost every level of society. Planners
from the latter group argued that providing facilities for the automobile was not only non-elitist, but enlightened and democratic.
Milwaukee planner Charles B. Whitnall praised the automobile
in lavish terms in 1937. "The automobile has taught people that
they can live as comfortably beyond the city's confines, with all
the coveted city conveniences and do so with less expense and
greater benefits to themselves and their children."[32]

Public agencies frequently supported these contentions of private planners. The New England branch of the National Resources Committee insisted in 1939 that the automobile, priced
within reach of the blue-collar worker, enabled him to live in a
pleasant suburban house rather than in a hovel next to a factory.[33]
This view very nearly assumed the character of official government policy. When federal officials constructed Greenbelt,
Maryland, they made no effort to provide public transportation.
Although steam railway and street railway lines indirectly served
the area, the nearest access was three or four miles distant. A
report on the transportation situation labeled the automobile the
"most economical and convenient" solution to its needs; although
many Greenbelt residents would earn low incomes, most families
would own an automobile and provide their own transportation.
After all, "second hand cars can be obtained very cheaply and
people of even very low incomes seem able to tinker with them
and keep them running."[34] In certain respects, public policy
seemed based on the realization that even the "Okies" drove cars
to California.

Tangible evidence of American planners' and traffic engineers' ongoing shift of thinking in favor of the automobile was

their efforts to facilitate its use. In contrast to the lack of progress in rapid transit development, the 1930s marked enormous strides in modern superhighway planning. In a 1937 speech to the leaders of the American Automobile Association, Miller McClintock articulated a central question confronting urban transportation planners. "Shall we subsidize, at great and continuing expense to the public treasury, rapid transit rail facilities affording comparatively low-grade and unprofitable mass transportation? Or shall we, out of public funds made available by the generous contributions of street users themselves, provide adequate, safe, efficient, and modern traffic facilities so that automobile users will provide their own transportation of a high character at their own operating costs?"[35] Although obviously tailored for the audience, his speech was consistent with his views expressed elsewhere.[36] McClintock's assumptions were fascinating, particularly in light of the future evolution of urban transportation; he was remarkably prescient on some points, spectacularly wrong on others. He was on the mark in predicting that nearly everyone wanted and would soon be able to own an automobile. In addition, he sensed that providing highways was more consistent with the spirit of personal responsibility, as Americans supplied their own vehicles. It was unfortunate, in the long run, that McClintock and many other planners dismissed mass transit because it was unprofitable. Had they fully perceived its contributions to regional stability, they might at least have supported government subsidies to save existing systems, if not to build new ones. McClintock was not amiss in his belief that automobiles could handle the bulk of urban transportation, nor in his view that highway planning was initially less expensive than rail rapid transit. But McClintock and many planners too often measured success according to a single inflexible standard: short-term definitions of who would benefit.[37] This concept by its very nature favored highways over rapid transit in all but the most densely populated urban areas.

Other planners shared McClintock's enthusiasm for automobile planning, and many encouraged construction of better roads and highways for related economic reasons. Sidney Waldon, who possessed a remarkable talent for arguing both sides of the issue of public versus private transportation, pointed out that in cities such as New York, per capita automobile ownership figures were extremely low. Adequate urban highways would constitute a boon to the automobile companies by creating a huge new demand for their product. Waldon argued in 1932, during the depths of the Depression, that if the automobile industry was to resume a healthy growth rate, obsolete street systems in all large American cities had to be "gradually reshaped."[38] In a 1933 report urging a new plan for "limited ways" in Chicago, the City Council Committee on Traffic and Public Safety stressed a slightly different rationalization for improved highways. In its view, automobile owners suffered direct economic losses when traffic delays forced them to operate their vehicles at but a fraction of their potential speeds. More superhighways would permit urbanites to operate their vehicles at efficient speeds, which would greatly reduce their costs per mile of operation.[39]

In addition to economic reasons for favoring the automobile over rail rapid transit, many traffic engineers believed the automobile provided long-term answers to urban transportation problems. As they had during the 1920s and earlier, many influential experts continued to believe that simple application of American ingenuity would bring lasting solutions. Perhaps Philadelphia traffic engineer Burton W. Marsh best reflected the spirit of technocracy; he admitted in 1931 the need for far more scientific inquiry on traffic movement, but clearly implied that solutions were merely a matter of applied research.[40] Suggestive of the widespread faith in traffic engineering in the 1930s, McClintock optimistically claimed that "if it were possible to apply everything we know about traffic control, we could eliminate 98 percent of all accidents and practically all congestion."[41] It fell upon later urban critics to point out that the fallacy lay in the difficulty and expense of applying engineering knowledge.

As American planners and traffic engineers focused their primary attention on superhighway design, historical "lessons" supported highway building before needs became critical. Earlier city builders had failed to anticipate problems associated with advances in transportation technology, and the price for overcoming their mistakes had been high. They had likewise failed to anticipate the impact of individual vehicles in densely built-up areas; consequently, cities had been forced to spend millions of dollars on street widening. The planners of the 1930s feared being caught short once again by failing to anticipate and control the impact of the automobile in outlying areas. After all, streets and highways were the most permanent facets of the cityscape; thus, they should be planned at the earliest opportunity. Nor were American planners alone in their fascination with highways. Construction of the autobahn in Germany impressed them profoundly. A Washington, D.C., highway engineer noted the impact of this and similar foreign achievements in 1937, and he cautioned American planners against waiting until the traffic situation became intolerable before confronting the problem.[42] Given this variety of pro-automobile stimuli, it is not surprising that American city planners emphasized highway design during the 1930s.

Without question, the 1930s marked a dynamic period in the evolution of more sophisticated highway design. By the late 1920s it was obvious that traditional methods of street widening were losing the contest with the rising tide of automobiles in downtown areas. Reflecting back upon the early faith in street widening, McClintock observed in 1937 that most planners finally realized that widening existing streets was a false hope.[43] Norman Bel Geddes urged planners and transportation system cesigners to think in far bigger terms in 1940. "Because we today move more freely than our ancestors, we have a tendency to overlook the fact that we should be able to move ten times more freely."[44] Specifically, highway engineers believed that limited access superhighways with superior lighting, wide radius curves, and other innovations could greatly speed up automobile movement.

Americans' faith in technology, symbolized by futuristic exhibits at Chicago's 1933 Century of Progress Exposition and the 1939 New York World's Fair, was clearly reflected in their perceptions of how the automobile might serve them in the years ahead. Unrealistic expectations were clearly encouraged by the media. A 1938 article in *Life* portrayed a widely accepted vision of future urban traffic.

> In 1958 the New York City commuter will be able to drive 50 miles to his office in an hour without ever doing more than 55 miles per hour. From his home he will head for the nearest limited highway. As he gets into the city this road will become an elevated highway. Four blocks from his office he will follow a ramp down to the street level, park his car in a basement, and walk into his building. There will be no more red lights, congested crossings, or cars parked on the street, and accidents will be reduced to a minimum. The car of the future will all but ride on railroad tracks.[45]

Significantly, such visionary expectations were not limited to imaginative writers; to a degree, they were shared by pragmatic traffic engineers. John S. Crandell, a noted professor of highway engineering at the University of Illinois, suggested that the dream had become reality, at least for users of New York's West Side highway. Crandell claimed that an automobile journey from his former office in the city, which used to take between 55 and 90 minutes, had been reduced to only twelve minutes by the new highway.[46]

Urban planners and traffic engineers believed in the efficacy of advanced highway design for several reasons. In addition to moving increased numbers of automobiles more rapidly within the same space, limited access highways or freeways would reduce the frightening toll of traffic accidents. New York engineer Charles M. Noble argued in 1937 that "correct design methods" could increase both safety and speed of highway travel.[47] Burton W. Marsh admitted that hundred-mile-per-hour freeways were out of the question, but he argued that conscientious application of the most advanced concepts in highway design would allow automobiles to move in a continuous flow at sixty to seventy miles per hour with a far higher degree of safety.[48]

Perhaps most fascinating in retrospect is the conviction of many planners that freeways were aesthetically highly desirable. Such a view appears naive today, but Justin R. Hartzog, a noted protege of John Nolen, argued in 1933 that modern parkways "provide a pleasant and quick channel of traffic from the country or suburbs to the town—between home and work for millions of automobile owners, rich and poor."[49] In 1939 Flavel A. Shurtleff, longtime secretary of the National Conference on City Planning, praised New York's system of parkways as a genuine contribution to the whole region's beautification.[50] At a dedication speech at the grand opening of Los Angeles's Arroyo-Seco Parkway in December 1940, Director of California's Department of Public Works Frank W. Clark stressed the advantages of freeway design over old-fashioned, unrestricted highway development. Older highways, noted Clark, led to "string towns" or "ribbon cities," along which service stations, hot dog stands, motels, fruit stands, junkyards, and other ramshackle commercial establishments were thrown up "with utter disregard for aesthetics."[51] The new freeway would enhance its setting by preventing unsightly commercial developments.

Some arguments citing environmental advantages of highway building were far-fetched indeed. For instance, some planners argued that elevated highways enhanced the desirability of heavily built-up areas they traversed. Chicago planners promoting local transportation improvements in 1939 praised the concept of elevated highways that by "segregating large masses of motor vehicles, with their exhaust gases and noises, from surrounding property would not only cost no more in the long run, but [might] actually be a benefit to the area traversed."[52] Charles H. Alden, chairman of the Seattle Plan Commission, went even farther, stating that property fronting on a freeway had little business potential on account of limited access. Alden's astonishing "solution" was to retain abutting property for residential use, with houses facing parallel streets. With the freeway providing "open space" at the rear of residential lots, property values would increase.[53]

Chicago, alone among American cities, constructed a subway during the 1930s; meanwhile, dozens of cities enthusiastically commenced development of comprehensive new highway systems. Los Angeles's commitment to future freeway building was unmatched, but other cities made significant strides in that direction during the 1930s. Although designed as much for regional traffic flow as for expediting commuter traffic, New York's Westchester Parkway system achieved worldwide fame during the 1930s. While Detroit planners also urged construction of a subway, far more actual activity on behalf of freeway construction took place.[54] Chicago transit historian Paul Barrett concluded that, despite subway construction, the city made an equal commitment to the superhighway during this period.[55]

Despite New Dealers' preoccupation with improving the quality of rural life and providing basic relief for all citizens, it is unlikely that urban transportation planning would have swung so heavily in favor of the automobile over mass transit without the active support of the federal government. A variety of New Deal agencies poured millions of dollars into street and highway projects, but provided comparatively little assistance to mass transit. The Works Progress Administration (WPA) and the Public Works Administration (PWA) were the chief New Deal agencies providing assistance for transportation. Through mid-1939 the WPA expended 38.3 percent of all its funds on roads, streets, and highways, and only 2.6 percent on all other forms of transportation. While spending a far smaller part of its total budget on transportation, the WPA provided ten times as much assistance to street and highway projects as it did to mass transit.[56] Enthusiasts promoted highway construction as an effective means of unemployment relief. In 1931, the chief of the Automotive Division of the United States Chamber of Commerce claimed that over 75 percent of the road building dollar went to labor, directly or indirectly. Hence "the IMMEDIATE result of larger road programs would be a rapid increase in employment." Still another inducement was that "more roads would create more sales for automobiles, in turn giving more men jobs."[57] Federal officials evidently endorsed these arguments. Of a grand total of 2,070,000 workers on WPA rolls at the end of 1939, over 900,000 were engaged in street or highway building projects.[58]

Perhaps an overriding reason for this commitment to improved streets and highways by New Deal planners and politicians was that increasing automobility was one of the few objectives shared by rural and urban factions. Congressmen from sparsely populated, comparatively non-urbanized southern and western states had little reason to support subway plans, but they could agree with representatives from urban areas upon at least the principle of improved highways. Nevertheless, just as they competed over federal funding for social programs in general, so did rural and urban factions fight over road-building grants. Rural groups still pushed farm-to-market roads, and urban interests promoted improved street and highway networks.

18. Manhattan's West Side Highway, 1937. Such automotive "solutions" clearly detracted from the environment, though perhaps not to the same extent as elevated railways.

New York Regional Plan Association Records, Department of Manuscripts and University Archives, Olin Library, Cornell University.

18

19. The Bronx River Valley in 1907. This view reveals the environment characteristic of unplanned regional development. Courtesy of the Harvard Graduate School of Design.
20. The same general area in 1922. Properly planned urban highways could improve the areas they traversed, although highway reports seldom mentioned what became of the residents who were displaced. Reprinted from Norman T. Newton, *Design on the Land: The Development of Landscape Architecture* (Cambridge, Mass., 1971). Courtesy of the Westchester County Park Commission. Photo in the Harvard Graduate School of Design Library.

19

20

21. This 1933 view of the Taconic State Parkway appears to support the belief of many highway engineers in the modern superhighway's ability to open out the urban environment. Reprinted from Norman T. Newton, *Design on the Land: The Development of Landscape Architecture* (Cambridge, Mass., 1971). Courtesy of the Taconic State Parkway Commission. Photo in the Harvard Graduate School of Design Library.

21

22. The Westchester Parkway during the 1930s. Planners had some basis for assuming that properly designed limited-access highways could enhance their surroundings while moving traffic more efficiently than conventional highways. Reprinted from Norman T. Newton, *Design on the Land: The Development of Landscape Architecture* (Cambridge, Mass., 1971). Courtesy of Gilmore D. Clarke.

22

That highway and road building was highly politicized was evident to anybody close to the situation. As Secretary of the Interior Harold L. Ickes noted at the 1933 National Conference of City Planners, "heretofore highways have been more or less a crazy quilt affair. The politician with the strongest pull has been able to entice a concrete road into his community or past his farm even although [sic] from an engineering and social standpoint the road should have run elsewhere."[59] Despite the past successes of farm interests in promoting rural roads, urban planners were at last ready to push for a larger share of the pie. Between the 1890s and the 1930s, rural legislators had aggressively pursued state and federal funds for road building; clearly they possessed the edge in experience over their urban counterparts.[60] But qualification for federal grants under the New Deal required new tactics, and each interest group appeared to start from the same place in the race for funds. In 1935 Chicago Chief Engineer Hugh E. Young observed that, due to the lure of hundreds of millions of dollars of available aid, both city and state governments had too often hastily drawn up poorly conceived proposals.[61] Whatever the merits of competing rural and urban proposals, Detroit planner Walter H. Blucher argued in 1936 that it was the cities' turn to profit from federal handouts. "It has been frankly admitted by certain highway officials that the outlying sections of counties and states have received approximately all of the improved roads that are required for some time . . . it appears logical that a considerable portion of these funds should be spent on the improvement of highways within the limits of municipalities."[62] Three years later, Thomas H. MacDonald, influential chief of the Bureau of Public Roads and a longtime advocate of rural road building efforts, pointed out the need for greater concentration upon the highway needs of urban areas.[63]

It is difficult to assess the success of urban interests during the 1930s in correcting the imbalance formerly favoring rural road building. Figures alone present a fuzzy picture. Of the 38.3 percent of all WPA funds spent on road building through fiscal 1939, 12 percent was spent on farm-to-market roads, 9.2 percent on urban street and highway projects. This would suggest a continued, if modest, imbalance favoring rural interests. However, the impact of the remaining 17.1 percent is difficult to analyze. Much of the money was spent on state and trunk roads, which served the needs of both country and city traffic.[64] By another measure, namely the complaining tone of correspondence from rural legislators to federal officials, it appeared that urban administrators were learning their lessons.[65] In Detroit, John P. Hallihan revealed himself as a planner in the pragmatic New Deal mold. Thwarted in a time-consuming bid for subway funds for his city, he urged Waldon to push plans for superhighways. Hallihan argued that superhighways were used by buses and thus facilitated mass transit as well as the automobile.[66] Despite the emerging political savvy of some urban planners, a 1941 NRPB study suggested that urban interests had not eliminated the imbalance in road building expenditures, and that urban traffic problems were far from being solved. "Major emphasis in future highway development must be directed to the provision of express highways and off-street parking in urban areas."[67]

Occasionally, highway advocates' enthusiasm and narrow vision drove them to excesses. If proponents of expensive rapid transit proposals often ignored more basic urban needs during the Depression, highway promoters were equally derelict. While few transportation planners directly opposed federal aid to the unemployed, they frequently fought advocates of federal slum-clearance proposals.[68] In Chicago, the Department of Superhighways was in direct conflict with advocates of urban renewal. Highway interests perceived slum-clearance proposals as not only competing for large federal grants, but also for valuable urban space needed for access routes. The Chicago agency argued that although slum clearance "heralded a better urban future," the agency should attempt to beat housing interests in the race to acquire valuable property needed for trans-city connections and express highways.[69] This view was shared by powerful highway interests at the national level. A Bureau of Public Roads (BPR) report stated in 1939 that "there is a growing danger that the more compact developments by the government in its slum-clearance projects will block the logical projection of the needed arteries into the city center."[70] Ironically, present-day critics of urban renewal might conceivably argue that urban highway interests unwittingly achieved an admirable social result in pursuing the lesser of two evils! These actions presaged an attitude held by advocates of private transportation that would become even more apparent following the Second World War: unlimited movement of motor vehicles should be encouraged at virtually any social cost.

But the general approval of the principle of highway building was not universal. Some urban observers noted that major street and highway proposals frequently disrupted existing land-use patterns. Two such critics writing in 1936 argued that busy streets through good residential areas often produced lower property values and premature obsolescence.[71] Others complained that sophisticated superhighway plans chewed up far greater amounts of urban space than their proponents acknowledged. A New York realtor voiced a telling argument before the Regional Plan Association in 1936: "I often wonder if the engineers who plan the parkways realize that in addition to the land taken for the roadway, they really need about 300 feet on either side as one must live at least that distance from the traveled part to get away from the terrific noise."[72] Yet the toll on usable space was even greater in congested areas. Consulting engineer P. S. Coombs scored the system of freeways designed for Los Angeles in 1939, particularly the construction proposed for the downtown area. He was appalled at the prospect of 250-foot swaths, some of which diagonally traversed entire city blocks and would have entailed enormous costs in condemned property.[73]

Ironically, some of the most advanced concepts in highway planning received criticism even from friends of the automobile. Perhaps no single urban planner did more to promote massive urban parkway systems than New York's Robert Moses. Yet Moses had little but contempt for such futuristic design concepts as those of Norman Bel Geddes, which he viewed as utterly impractical. "It is all right for Norman Bel Geddes to make entertaining models of sixteen ply motor roads with four or five speed levels, radio beam robot control of cars, elimination of the human element, single cable bridges flung lightly from peak to peak and other figments of the imagination. He is a scene painter and publicity man and no one will ask him to make good in 1960."[74] Moses had little fear that sophisticated traffic engineers would swallow Bel Geddes's vision. The problem, as Moses saw it, was that such projections created overly sanguine expectations among not only the general public, but some influential policymakers. Yet some of the most "advanced" highways actually built during the 1930s also received criticism. Victor Scales, director of the American Petroleum Institute, criticized Moses's own highway network in Westchester County. He acknowledged the beauty of the system, but argued that narrow lanes and constant tight curves made them "tireing [sic] and nerve-wracking" to drive on.[75] Perhaps most important, some automobile enthusiasts themselves acknowledged that advances in traffic control and highway design alone could not solve the problems of urban automobile congestion. Washington Cleveland, manager of the District of Columbia branch of the AAA, admitted in 1937 that recent experience showed that expanded highway facilities invariably attracted more traffic.[76] This perspective would not gain widespread acceptance until freeway opponents more forcefully advanced similar views in the 1960s and 1970s.[77] In retrospect, urban freeway enthusiasts' most critical mistake was failing to perceive how much new traffic their roads would generate. Their mistakes would be more obvious with the postwar return to prosperity. After the war, registrations far outpaced roadbuilding, which was often delayed by rising expenses and increased competition for funds. Unfortunately, most planners only perceived immediate needs to catch up with the automobile.

During the 1930s, however, planners seemed almost to be looking backward, as if hoping congestion would disappear if ignored. Cincinnati planner Ladislas Segoe foresaw few problems in the future and flatly stated that there were no unusual difficulties in traffic management in his city.[78] Boston's response to the automobile was, perhaps, uniquely casual. While city planners argued for a central artery through the downtown area, nothing was accomplished before the Second World War. Apart from street-widening projects, comparing city maps from 1900 and 1940 reveals very little effort to accommodate the automobile. Granted, Boston's early street system, featuring twisting narrow avenues through heavily settled and traveled areas, would have made a large-scale commitment to facilitating automobile flow extremely difficult and expensive. In all likelihood, the effect of anything other than a massive commitment to vehicular movement would have been slight. Nevertheless, Bostonians appeared to take an almost perverse delight in ignoring the automobile. City Planning Commission Secretary Elizabeth Herlihy defended the original settlers' crooked streets as "cherished by posterity," at the same time quoting with approval the words of Oliver Wendell Holmes: "Boston has opened and kept open more turnpikes that led straight to free thought and free speech and free deeds than any other city of live men or dead men."[79]

While the fate of the trolley was increasingly evident to many, the alternative of fixed-rail rapid transit attracted little support. In contrast, superhighways could accommodate both buses and automobiles. With millions of motorists on the road from almost every level of society, traffic engineers believed the superhighway was a democratic response to urban transportation needs. Superhighways were unquestionably cheaper than rapid transit, at least in the short run, and this was a critical consideration in the 1930s.

Planners' and traffic engineers' range of options became increasingly narrow in the 1930s and after. For obvious reasons, the massive human misery wrought by the Depression assumed top priority with government officials at all levels. They possessed little energy and fewer resources to deal with urban transportation needs. In addition to creating enormous physical and social upheaval in America's cities, the demands of World War II once again relegated comprehensive mass transit proposals to a very low priority. When the war ended, cities seemed farther from viable solutions to urban transportation needs than ever before.

Conclusion

Contemporary critics of the automobile culture have been guilty of presentism in condemning early planners and traffic engineers for the decline of urban mass transportation, for failing to build rapid transit systems, and for "irresponsible" horizontal growth. I believe the early-twentieth-century planners deserve more praise, or at least understanding, than condemnation. Some critics perceive planners' support of suburbanization and automobility as either naiveté or as evidence of a conspiracy of realtors, automobile producers, and government officials to fleece the general public. In fact, the majority of planners enthusiastically endorsed both automobility and the suburban movement out of conviction, not greed.

In any case, conditions in 1900 were such that rapid horizontal development certainly would have occurred with or without the blessing of city planners. Almost unimaginable core-city crowding had sharpened the demand for livable urban space. Such technological advances as structural steel, the elevator, the suspension bridge, electric traction, and the automobile provided urban decisionmakers the tools to alter profoundly the turn-of-the-century cityscape. The challenge to use intelligently so many new inventions was extraordinary and unprecedented, and there were few guidelines to help planners coordinate these changes and direct them toward optimum social benefit. Hindsight reveals mistakes, but given the challenges planners faced and the constraints under which they worked, it is remarkable that they performed as well as they did.

However, present-day urban critics are justified in asking why the planners did not do better. A key to understanding the motives of early planners lies in their evolution within society. Planners were part of a broad reform movement, and while other reformers tried to rationalize taxation, political systems, or factory working conditions, planners pursued their own visions of order in the urban environment. To their credit, planners' suggestions made suburban development somewhat less haphazard than it would have been otherwise. That they did not have a greater impact on metropolitan America is due more to the timing of the emergence of the planning profession than to a lack of insight or courage. Planners received little recognition until World War I, when recent technological advances had already exerted significant impacts upon the urban environment. The suburban movement was in full gear, the automobile was gaining widespread acceptance, and mass transit was showing signs of decay. Planners sensed that, although they could do little to solve long-entrenched core-city problems, they might influence the initial development of outlying areas. They lacked the political clout to effect real cooperation between local government units on regional issues, but their perceptive reports induced some conscientious officials to begin thinking in metropolitan terms by the 1920s, if not earlier. Partly as a result of these efforts, planners were in a position by the 1930s to extract from federal officials at least a modest commitment to local, state, and national planning.

It is also important to remember that urban transportation was but one of many challenges facing American planners. The urgent priorities of piloting America through the Depression and World War II distracted public officials from urban transportation, which they considered a lower-priority, local problem. Even so, the war appeared to create the miracle that mass transit officials had prayed for, as patrons returned to trolleys and buses by the millions. Severe rubber and petroleum shortages and interrupted automobile production created a quick fix for the public transit industry. Although the war years marked the construction of hundreds of new plants in outlying areas; curtailment of new housing construction delayed resumption of rapid residential decentralization. This probably worked to the short-term advantage of mass transit companies, as patrons were hemmed in relatively close to existing routes. In the long run, of course, wartime restrictions only delayed the suburban housing boom that rendered mass transit service increasingly inconvenient. As in previous periods of high profits, too many mass transit officials simply basked in the luxury of good times and hoped the prosperity would never end.

For a variety of reasons, the wartime prosperity probably hurt mass transit more than it helped. During transit's temporary revival, government officials were even less inclined than before to provide the massive subsidies needed to ensure its survival. The war years and those immediately following brought an enormous expansion of federal government commitments to a wide range of social welfare programs. As federal subsidies for highways, education, housing, and many other programs multiplied rapidly, urban transportation systems were virtually ignored. The emergence after the war of sprawling automobile suburbs coincided with the deaths of countless electric railway systems, deaths that government officials at all levels did little to prevent. Few voiced concern at the time, since the prosperity of the 1950s and 1960s permitted virtually every American family to own at least one automobile. By the time transportation planners made any significant effort to save mass transit systems, many were either defunct or beyond financial salvation. With the escalation of regional sprawl by the 1970s, the challenge of providing viable public transit, even with enormous federal subsidies, became increasingly complex.

This study ends in 1940, however, because a number of scholars and urban critics have already analyzed the postwar evolution of suburbs and recent trends in urban transportation. Many scholars agree that the automobile enjoyed its golden age between 1945 and 1970, when federal policies and public preference enshrined the motor vehicle and left urban mass transit on the verge of extinction. It is just as obvious that the 1970s marked severe strains in America's long-lived romance with the automobile.

Yet it is too soon to predict the imminent demise of individualized urban mass transportation. Americans are too used to personal mobility, and they have too great an economic stake in the preservation of a mobile population, to tolerate immediate radical changes in urban transportation. One can imagine scenarios where they would have no choice; and home computer terminals, wholly automated retail delivery systems, and other technological innovations may remove much of the present need for high degrees of personal mobility. The only certainty today is that the entire urban transportation situation is extremely volatile. The 1970s marked the opening of several new subway systems and the upgrading of older core systems, both in America and abroad. The responses to two recent subway/rapid transit experiments in San Francisco and Washington, D.C., are very mixed, but they do not change what experts have long known: even the most sophisticated, expensive subway systems cannot serve more than a fraction of all urban transportation needs.

Americans possess a tradition of rapid adjustments to technological innovations; hence, it seems ironic that the 1980s are likely to bring widespread experimentation with less expensive, seemingly more traditional urban mass transit systems. The so-called "light rail" trolley, in many respects similar to the trolley of eighty years ago, will appear on the streets of a number of American cities in the near future. San Diego's light rail system is scheduled to open soon. Buffalo, New York, has commenced construction of a light rail system, and work on a similar system will begin in Portland, Oregon, in 1981. Residents of other cities will soon vote on light rail referendums. In addition, several cities that never completely abandoned old trolley lines are renovating their tracks and buying new equipment. Finally, bus service, to make either entire mass transit systems or feeder lines, appears destined to grow at a healthy rate.

If scientists develop a cheap and readily available synthetic fuel for motor vehicles, these projections for future mass transit lines could become obsolete overnight. But even the most optimistic projections for synthetic fuels see no possibility of their having widespread impact upon urban transportation before the 1990s. Thus the final chapter in the history of public transportation, seemingly so near completion in the 1950s, now seems to be years, decades, or even centuries away. Perhaps the ultimate irony is that, despite their impressive educational credentials, sophisticated analytical tools, and high degree of public acceptance, the position of planners today is little different—and little better—than that of their professional ancestors.

Notes

Introduction

1. Perhaps the best-known critique of the American city is Jane Jacobs, *The Death and Life of Great American Cities* (New York, 1957). More recent, and also more controversial, is E. C. Banfield, *The Unheavenly City: The Nature and Future of Our Urban Crisis* (Boston, 1968). Other incisive commentaries include Lewis Mumford, *The City in History: Its Origins, Its Transformations, and Its Prospects* (New York, 1961); Zane L. Miller, *The Urbanization of Modern America: A Brief History* (New York, 1973); and Sam Bass Warner, Jr., *The Urban Wilderness: A History of the American City* (New York, 1972). The best recent text on urban America is Blaine A. Brownell and David R. Goldfield, *Urban America: From Downtown to No Town* (Boston, 1979).

2. John Keats, *The Insolent Chariots* (Philadelphia, 1958), pp. 12–13.

3. Mumford, *The City in History*, pp. 508, 510. Significantly, even recent scholars of urban transportation have supported the conspiracy view. See Robert B. Carson, *What Ever Happened to the Trolley?* (Washington, D.C., 1978), pp. 92–95; and James V. Cornehls and Delbert A. Taebel, *The Politics of Urban Transportation* (Port Washington, N.Y., 1977), p. 23 and appendix.

4. B. Bruce-Briggs, *The War against the Automobile* (New York, 1975), pp. 188–189.

5. There is, however, a significant body of literature touching certain facets of this subject. See Blaine A. Brownell, "A Symbol of Modernity: Attitudes toward the Automobile in Three Southern Cities during the 1920s," *American Quarterly* 24, no. 1 (March 1972): 20–44, and his *The Urban Ethos in the South, 1920–1930* (Baton Rouge, La., 1975); James J. Flink, "Three Stages of Automobile Consciousness," *American Quarterly* 24, no. 3 (October 1972): 451–473, and his *The Car Culture* (Cambridge, Mass., 1975); Mark S. Foster, "City Planners and Urban Transportation: The American Response, 1900–1940," *Journal of Urban History* 5, no. 3 (May 1979): 365–396; John Hancock, "Planners in the Changing American City, 1900–1940," *Journal of the American Institute of Planners* 33, no. 5 (September 1967): 290–304; Glen E. Holt, "The Changing Perception of Urban Pathology: An Essay on the Development of Mass Transit in the United States," in Kenneth T. Jackson and Stanley K. Schultz, eds., *Cities in American History* (New York, 1972), pp. 324–343; Clay McShane, "American Cities and the Coming of the Automobile, 1890–1915" (Ph.D. diss., University of Wisconsin, Madison, 1975); Howard L. Preston, *Automobile Age Atlanta: The Making of a Southern Metropolis, 1900–1935* (Athens, Ga., 1979); John B. Rae, *The Road and Car in American Life* (Cambridge, Mass., 1971); Mark H. Rose, *Interstate: Express Highway Poli-*

tics, 1941–1956 (Lawrence, Kans., 1979); Joel A. Tarr, "From City to Suburb: The 'Moral' Influence of Transportation Technology," in Alexander B. Callow, Jr., ed., *American Urban History: An Interpretive Reader with Commentaries,* 2nd ed. (New York, 1973), pp. 202–212; Warner, *The Urban Wilderness*; William H. Wilson, *Coming of Age: Urban America, 1915–1945* (New York, 1974).

6. See John G. Clark and Mark H. Rose, "Light, Heat, and Power Energy Choices in Kansas City, Wichita, and Denver, 1900–1935," *Journal of Urban History* 5, no. 3 (May 1979): 340–364.

7. The planning profession evolved so rapidly between 1900 and 1940 that it would be very misleading to offer a fixed definition of "planner." Instead, I have chosen to discuss significant developments within the profession at appropriate places in the text. For an analysis of this problem of defining planners, see Blaine A. Brownell, "Urban Planning and the Motor Vehicle in the United States in the Early Twentieth Century" (paper presented at the First International Conference on the History of Urban and Regional Planning, University of London, September 1977).

8. Flink, *The Car Culture,* p. 40. Unfortunately, according to Flink, by the 1920s automobility had ceased to be a progressive force and was "beginning to petrify into a complacent maturity" (p. 166).

9. Several books demonstrate the popularity of the automobile and its impact upon American society and culture. Among the best are James J. Flink, *America Adopts the Automobile, 1895–1910* (Cambridge, Mass., 1970), and his *The Car Culture*; and Rae, *The Road and Car*.

10. According to John C. Burnham, automobile interests began seriously organizing only in the 1930s, and their attention focused primarily on fighting diversion of gasoline taxes to nonautomotive uses, such as welfare, schools, and general government expenses. See Burnham, "The Gasoline Tax and the Automobile Revolution," *Mississippi Valley Historical Review* 68 (December 1961): 435–459. For details of the argument that automobile interests attempted to sabotage mass transit, particularly between the 1930s and the 1950s, see Bradford C. Snell, "American Ground Transport: A Proposal for Restructuring Automobile, Truck, Bus, and Rail Industries, February 1974," in U.S., Congress, Senate, Subcommittee on Antitrust and Monopoly, Hearing on Bill 1167, 93rd Cong., 2nd sess., 1974, pt. 4, pp. A1–A103.

Chapter 1

1. Robert Fishman, *Urban Utopias in the Twentieth Century: Ebenezer Howard, Frank Lloyd Wright, and Le Corbusier* (New York, 1977), pp. 10–11.

2. Stephen Crane, *Maggie and Other Stories* (New York: Airmont, 1968), pp. 163–164.

3. Jacob Riis, *How the Other Half Lives: Studies among the Tenements of New York* (New York, 1890), p. 8; U.S., Bureau of the Census, *Abstract of the 1930 Census* (Washington, D.C., 1933), p. 77. It is risky to generalize about inner-city population trends from raw data because census tract boundaries changed frequently and cities annexed varying amounts of new territory. Nevertheless, it is safe to conclude that, during the early twentieth century, population densities in the most crowded portions of most large American cities declined gradually. See Harlan P. Douglass, *The Suburban Trend* (New York and London, 1925); and Homer E. Hoyt, *The Structure and Growth of Residential Neighborhoods in American Cities* (Washington, D.C., 1939).

4. This unfavorable picture at least partly reflects present-day biases. David Ward has aptly pointed out that some late-nineteenth-century urbanites perceived the propinquity of such services as an advantage. See his *Cities and Immigrants: A Geography of Change in Nineteenth Century America* (New York, 1971), pp. 117–118.

5. James J. Flink, *The Car Culture* (Cambridge, Mass., 1975), p. 34; see also Otto Bettman, *The Good Old Days: They Were Terrible* (New York, 1974), pp. 7–9.

6. For an excellent account of nineteenth-century urban transportation, see George R. Taylor, "The Beginnings of Mass Transportation in Urban America," pts. 1 and 2, *Smithsonian Journal of History* 1 (summer and fall 1966): 31–50.

7. U.S., Bureau of the Census, *Abstract of the Twelfth Census, 1900*, 3rd ed. (Washington, D.C., 1904), p. 387; U.S., Bureau of the Census, *Historical Statistics of the United States, Colonial Times to 1970* (Washington, D.C., 1975), 2: 721. For a good study of mass transit in three cities, see Charles W. Cheape, *Moving the Masses: Urban Public Transportation in New York, Boston, and Philadelphia, 1880–1912* (Cambridge, Mass., 1980); see also Harold Barger, *The Transportation Industries, 1889–1946* (Washington, D.C., 1952).

8. William S. Rossiter, *Increased Population of the U.S., 1910–1920*, Census Monograph 1 (Washington, D.C., n.d.), pp. 19, 22.

9. John A. Beeler, "Planning Transportation for the City of the Future," *Electric Railway Journal* 66, no. 13 (September 26, 1925): 526. New York boasted the highest per capita ridership on all forms of local transportation—444 rides annually.

10. Rossiter, *Increased Population*, pp. 19, 22.

11. U.S., Bureau of the Census, *Sixteenth Census of the U.S., 1940: Population* (Washington, D.C., 1942), 1: 63–64.

12. The standard sources on suburban emergence before World War II include Douglass, *The Suburban Trend*; Hoyt, *The Structure and Growth*; and President's Commission on Recent Social Trends, *Report* (Washington, D.C., 1933).

13. *Sixteenth Census: Population*, 1: 63–64. Recent studies document the difficulties of measuring inner-city versus suburban growth. Most studies suggest that annexations have obscured rates of decentralization, which were in fact much greater than statistics alone would show. See John D. Kasarda and George V. Redfearn, "Differential Patterns of City and Suburban Growth in the United States," *Journal of Urban History* 2 (November 1975): 43–66; Warren S. Thompson, *The Growth of Metropolitan Districts in the United States, 1900–1940* (Washington, D.C., 1947); Donald J. Bogue, *Population Growth in Standard Metropolitan Areas, 1900–1950* (Washington, D.C., 1953); and Amos H. Hawley, *The Changing Shape of Metropolitan America: Deconcentration since 1920* (Glencoe, Ill., 1956).

14. The literature on this topic is massive. Good starting points are Joel A. Tarr, "From City to Suburb: The 'Moral' Influence of Transportation Technology," in A. B. Callow, ed., *American Urban History: An Interpretive Reader with Commentaries*, 2nd ed. (New York, 1973), pp. 202–212; and Kenneth T. Jackson, "The Crabgrass Frontier: 150 Years of Suburban Growth," in Raymond A. Mohl and James F. Richardson, eds., *The Urban Experience: Themes in American History* (Belmont, Cal., 1973), pp. 196–221.

15. Sam Bass Warner, Jr., *Streetcar Suburbs: The Process of Growth in Boston, 1870–1900* (Cambridge, Mass., 1962), pp. 25–29; Taylor, "The Beginnings of Mass Transportation," pt. 2, pp. 39–50; Jackson, "The Crabgrass Frontier," pp. 196–221.

16. Many books and articles provide insight into the minds of late-nineteenth-century urbanites. A good starting point is Richard Sennett, *Families against the City: Middle Class Homes in Industrial Chicago, 1872–1890* (Cambridge, Mass., 1972). A sharp critique of Sennett's book is Mark Haller, "Family Fictions," *Reviews in American History* 1, no. 1 (March 1973): 112–119. See also Warner, *The Private City: Philadelphia in Three Stages of Its Growth* (Philadelphia, 1968).

17. Joel Tarr has suggested that the electric railway did not actually enable the poor to escape the central city (Tarr, "From City to Suburb," pp. 202–212). Yet the trolley benefited nearly everybody. As the middle classes moved away, the pressure on living space for the poor was at least temporarily eased (see Jackson, "The Crabgrass Frontier," pp. 196–221). Warner points out that many nineteenth-century Bostonians did move in response to ethnic "invasions," but

they more often sought economic rather than ethnic homogeneity in their new neighborhoods (Warner, *Streetcar Suburbs,* pp. 52–66).

18. Warner, *Streetcar Suburbs,* pp. 35–45. On the other hand, Joel Tarr found that for cities as a whole it was clear early in the twentieth century that the electric trolley had permitted suburbanization of only the wealthy and the middle class. Slum dwellers were largely left behind. See his "From City to Suburb," p. 209.

19. A number of late-nineteenth- and early-twentieth-century observers of urban life praised suburbs as potential outlets for working-class residents and documented the progress to date. See Adna F. Weber, *The Growth of Cities in the Nineteenth Century* (New York, 1899); and Graham R. Taylor, *Satellite Cities* (New York, 1915).

20. Stanley Buder, *Pullman: An Experiment in Industrial Order and Community Building, 1880–1930* (New York, 1967).

21. Paul Barrett, "Mass Transit, the Automobile, and Public Policy in Chicago, 1900–1930" (Ph.D diss., University of Illinois, Chicago Circle, 1976), p. 4.

22. George M. Smerk, "The Streetcar: Shaper of American Cities," *Traffic Quarterly* 21 (October 1967): 569–584.

23. For a charming account of the rise and fall of this system, see Spencer A. Crump, *Ride the Big Red Cars: How the Trolley Helped Build Southern California* (Los Angeles, 1962).

24. Charles N. Glaab and A. Theodore Brown, *A History of Urban America,* 2nd ed. (New York, 1976), pp. 256–257.

25. In the early days of the trolley, before some of its abuses of trust became evident, city governments routinely awarded valuable franchises without reserving protective clauses sufficient to guarantee, for example, adequate service. After 1900, as reform groups became increasingly critical of long-term franchises, provisions were generally tightened, and franchises, when awarded, were far less favorable to private transit interests. George Hilton and John Due, *The Electric Railway Industry* (Palo Alto, Cal., 1960), pp. 208–212, 230; see also Padraic Burke, "The City Beautiful Movement in Seattle" (M.A. thesis, University of Washington, 1973), p. 34; and Cheape, *Moving the Masses.* John G. Clark and Mark H. Rose are studying the effect of public utility growth upon the physical, social, and spatial development of several cities. For a preliminary report on their findings, see "Light, Heat, and Power: Producers and Users in Denver, Kansas City, and Wichita, 1900–1935," *Journal of Urban History* 5 (May 1979): 340–364.

26. Massachusetts Street Railway Association, *Agreement of Everett W.*

Burdette, Esq. and Report on Relations of Street Railway and Municipal Corporation, 1897–1898 (Boston, 1898), p. 23. Historian Carl Condit observed that in the early twentieth century many urban governments urged steam railway companies to electrify their urban operations to protect the environment. Electric operation would eliminate some fumes from coal-burning engines in the city air. Condit, "The Pioneer Stage of Railroad Electrification," *Transactions of the American Philosophical Society, Held at Philadelphia, November 1977* (Philadelphia: American Philosophical Society), vol. 67, pt. 7, pp. 38–43.

27. "Relief of Street Traffic in Boston," *Municipal Engineering* 20, no. 1 (January 1901): 2.

28. The literature on the nature and roots of progressivism is too voluminous to be fully discussed or even listed here. Three of the most articulate and differing analyses of the origins of progressivism are Richard Hofstadter, *The Age of Reform: From Bryan to F.D.R.* (New York, 1955); Robert H. Wiebe, *The Search for Order, 1877–1920* (New York, 1965); and Gabriel Kolko, *The Triumph of Conservatism* (New York, 1963). For a more recent contribution to the debate, see John C. Burnham, "Essay," in John D. Buenker, John C. Burnham, and Robert M. Crunden, eds., *Progressivism* (Cambridge, Mass., 1977), pp. 3–29.

29. The inherent structural weaknesses in the milieu in which many cities developed their street railway systems are discussed at length in Chapter 2.

30. An excellent biography of Pingree is Melvin G. Holli, *Reform in Detroit: Hazen S. Pingree and Urban Politics* (New York, 1969). In Cleveland, Mayor Tom L. Johnson battled the local street railway "trust" for eight years for a three-cent fare (Wiebe, *The Search for Order*, p. 172). For an excellent overview of the early troubles of the street railway industry, see Stanley Mallach, "The Origins of the Decline of Urban Mass Transportation in the United States, 1890–1930," *Urbanism Past and Present* 8 (spring and summer, 1979): 1–17.

31. Hazen S. Pingree, "3¢ Fares" (pamphlet dated July 14, 1899, box 1, Ralph Stone Papers, University of Michigan Transportation Library, Ann Arbor, Mich.).

32. Frederick C. Howe, "The City as a Socializing Agency," *The American Journal of Sociology* 17 (March 1912): 597. Reformers such as Howe received support from disinterested scholars. See, for example, Ralph E. Heilman, *Chicago Traction: A Study of the Efforts of the Public to Secure Good Service* (Princeton, N.J., 1908); and James B. Walker, *Fifty Years of Rapid Transit, 1864–1917* (New York, 1918).

33. Nelson P. Lewis, Speech before St. John's Church Club, Waterbury, Conn., February 3, 1908 (mimeographed ms., box 1, Nelson P. Lewis Papers,

Olin Library, Cornell University). A good account of the career and influence of Lewis is Jeffrey K. Stine, "Nelson P. Lewis and the City Efficient: The Rise of the Municipal Engineer in City Planning" (unpublished paper).

34. Clay McShane, "Transforming the Use of Urban Space: A Look at the Revolution in Street Pavements, 1880–1924," *Journal of Urban History* 5 (May 1979): 291–296.

35. Few topics have received as much attention from historians as the early years of the automobile industry. Published works are legion. An excellent starting point is John B. Rae, *The Road and Car in American Life* (Cambridge, Mass., 1971). See also James J. Flink, *America Adopts the Automobile, 1895–1915* (Cambridge, Mass., 1970).

36. *Automobile Facts and Figures* (New York, 1941), p. 15. This perception has changed. See James J. Flink, "Three Stages of Automobile Consciousness," *American Quarterly* 24, no. 3 (October 1972): 451–473.

37. Michael L. Berger reports that farmers and small-town residents tended to be hostile to automobilists until they perceived the commercial advantages of promoting tourism and the social benefits it could bring to their lives. Berger, *The Devil Wagon in God's Country: The Automobile and Social Change in Rural America, 1893–1929* (Hamden, Conn., 1979). For a superb account of the early days of automobile touring, see Warren J. Belasco, *Americans on the Road: From Autocamp to Motel, 1910–1945* (Cambridge, Mass., 1979).

38. Ray S. Baker, "The Automobile in Common Use: What It Costs, How It Is Operated, What It Will Do," *McClure's Magazine* 13, no. 3 (July 1899): 195–197.

39. Cleveland Moffett, "Automobiles for the Average Man," *Review of Reviews* 21, no. 6 (June 1900): 710. See also William Baxter, Jr., "Gasoline Automobiles," *Popular Science Monthly* 57 (October 1900): 593–604.

40. W. A. Whittlesey, in Behalf of an Association Investigating Motor Vehicles, "The Motor Vehicle Industry" (pamphlet dated 1900, AAA Headquarters Library, Falls Church, Va.), p. 43. Scholars have observed that bicyclists and sportsmen exerted early pressure for good roads. See Philip P. Mason, *The League of American Wheelmen and the Good Roads Movement, 1880–1905* (Ann Arbor, Mich., 1958); Ballard Campbell, "The Good Roads Movement in Wisconsin, 1890–1911," *Wisconsin Magazine of History* 49, no. 4 (summer 1966): 273–293.

41. William F. Dix, "The Automobile as a Vacation Agent," *Independent* 56 (June 2, 1904): 1260.

42. Winthrop E. Scarritt, "The Low-Priced Automobile," *Munsey's Magazine* 29, no. 2 (May 1903): 179.

43. Flink, *America Adopts the Automobile*, p. 112.

44. One of Them, "The Automobile Suburbanite," *American Motorist* 1, no. 1 (April 1909): 16.

45. Two studies showing the contrast between effects of suburbanization wrought by trolleys and automobiles are Warner, *Streetcar Suburbs*, and Mark S. Foster, "The Model-T, the 'Hard Sell,' and Los Angeles' Urban Growth: The Decentralization of Los Angeles during the 1920s," *Pacific Historical Review* 44, no. 4 (November 1975): 459–484.

46. Daniel H. Burnham, *Plan of Chicago* (Chicago, 1909), p. 42.

Chapter 2

1. John Hancock, "Planners in the Changing American City, 1900–1940," *Journal of the American Institute of Planners* 33, no. 5 (September 1967): 290–304; Norman J. Johnston, "Harland Bartholomew: His Comprehensive Plans and Science of Planning" (Ph.D. diss., University of Pennsylvania, 1964); Blaine A. Brownell, "Urban Planning and the Motor Vehicle in the United States in the Early Twentieth Century" (paper presented at the First International Conference on the History of Urban and Regional Planning, University of London, September 1977); and David R. Goldfield, "Planning History in the United States" (paper presented at the convention of the American Historical Association, San Francisco, December 1978).

2. This basic point of view is set forth in several analyses of the evolution of late-nineteenth-century American society. While the literature is enormous in scope, one might start with Robert H. Wiebe, *The Search for Order, 1877–1920* (New York, 1965), pp. 168–170; and Samuel P. Hays, *The Response to Industrialism, 1885–1914* (Chicago, 1959), pp. 104, 109.

3. Brownell, "Urban Planning and the Motor Vehicle." Brownell has done pioneering work on the early efforts of planners to achieve professional recognition, and I am deeply indebted to him for generously sharing his insights. See also Stanley K. Schultz and Clay McShane, "To Engineer the Metropolis: Sewers, Sanitation, and City Planning in Late-Nineteenth-Century America," *Journal of American History* 65, no. 2 (September 1978): 389–401. Schultz and McShane argue that city planners possessed somewhat more authority than I suggest here (see pp. 407–409).

4. Schultz and McShane, "To Engineer the Metropolis," pp. 398–411. For additional insights into the early years of the planning profession, see Hancock, "Planners," pp. 290–304; Jon A. Peterson, "The City Beautiful Movement:

Forgotten Origins and Lost Meanings," *Journal of Urban History* 2, no. 4 (August 1976): 415–434; Mel Scott, *American City Planning since 1890* (Berkeley, Cal., 1969), chs. 1, 2; Mark S. Foster, "City Planners and Urban Transportation: The American Response, 1900–1940," *Journal of Urban History* 5, no. 3 (May 1979): 365–396. The literature on planning is enormous. Interested readers might begin with Lewis Mumford's classic, *The City in History: Its Origins, Its Transformations, and Its Prospects* (New York, 1961).

5. For a variety of reasons, planners virtually ignored housing. See Peter Marcuse, "Housing in Early City Planning," *Journal of Urban History* 6 (February 1980): 153–176.

6. Two general histories of city planning are Scott, *American City Planning*; and John W. Reps, *The Making of Urban America: A History of American City Planning* (Princeton, N.J., 1965). An exemplary account of planning in Washington, D.C., is Frederick Gutheim, *Worthy of the Nation: The History of Planning for the National Capital* (Washington, D.C., 1977).

7. The literature describing the surrender of the urban landscape to private interests is too voluminous to discuss, or even fully list here. For general accounts of the process, see Charles N. Glaab and A. Theodore Brown, *A History of Urban America*, 2nd ed. (New York, 1976); and Blake McKelvy, *The Urbanization of America, 1860–1915* (New Brunswick, N.J., 1963).

8. From the Michigan Pioneer Collections: "Judge Woodward's Protest against the Sale of Certain Lands in Detroit, June 1, 1918" (ms., box 2, Sidney D. Waldon Papers, Detroit Public Library).

9. Boston Tercentenary Committee, Subcommittee on Memorial History, *Fifty Years of Boston: A Memorial Volume Issued in Commemoration of the Tercentenary* (Boston, 1930), pp. 44–46.

10. Schultz and McShane, "To Engineer the Metropólis," pp. 389–411. Glaab and Brown, *A History of Urban America*, pp. 218–219, 233–235. McShane, "American Cities and the Coming of the Automobile, 1870–1915" (Ph.D. diss., University of Wisconsin, Madison, 1975), points out that even as early as the Civil War period, urban thinkers actively promoted suburbanization as a way to alleviate the American city's most egregious social ills. Technical aids included suspension bridges, improved thoroughfares and parkways, upgraded streets in proposed new subdivisions, as well as large-scale expansion of public services (see especially pp. 111–113).

11. Schultz and McShane, "To Engineer the Metropolis," pp. 389–411; Peterson, "The Impact of Sanitary Reform upon American Urban Planning, 1840–1890," *Journal of Social History* 13 (fall 1979): 83–103.

12. Mumford, *The City in History*; Mason Hammond, *The City in the Ancient World* (New York, 1972); A. E. J. Morris, *History of Urban Form before the Industrial Revolutions,* 2nd ed. (New York, 1979).

13. Ebenezer Howard, *Garden Cities of Tomorrow* (London, 1902).

14. See Mumford's critique of the American response to Howard in Howard, *Garden Cities of Tomorrow,* ed. F. J. Osborn (Cambridge, Mass., 1965), pp. 30–34; see also Robert Fishman, *Urban Utopias in the Twentieth Century: Ebenezer Howard, Frank Lloyd Wright, and Le Corbusier* (New York, 1977).

15. Scott, *American City Planning,* p. 80.

16. *Ibid.,* p. 163. Studies that suggest the diverse characters of city planners in the early twentieth century include Roy Lubove, *The Progressives and the Slums: Tenement House Reform in New York City, 1890–1917* (Pittsburgh, 1962), pp. 217–245; Lubove, *The Urban Community: Housing and Planning in the Progressive Era* (Englewood Cliffs, N.J., 1967), pp. 1–22; Scott, *American City Planning,* ch. 1; Hancock, "Planners," pp. 292–294.

17. John Hancock, "John Nolen—The Background of a Pioneer Planner," *Journal of the American Institute of Planners* 26, no. 4 (November 1960): 308; Hancock to author, October 26, 1979.

18. Career profiles from *Who's Who in America, 1934–35* (New York, 1935), 18: 1780–1781; *Who Was Who in America* (Chicago, 1942), 1: 905; and *Who's Who in America, 1940–1941* (New York, 1941), 21: 321.

19. A brief overview of their early training is Frederick J. Adams and Gerald Hodge, "City Planning Instruction in the United States, 1900–1930," *Journal of the American Institute of Planners* 31, no. 1 (February 1965): 43–51.

20. "City Planning at Harvard University," *Journal of the American Institute of Architects* 1, no. 10 (October 1913): 449.

21. I refer to formal planning organizations, separate and distinct from engineering, architectural, and related organizations. For a careful analysis of these distinctions, see Brownell, "Urban Planning and the Motor Vehicle," pp. 2–5.

22. Nolen to Thomas Adams, February 15, 1911 (box 8, John Nolen Papers, Olin Library, Cornell University).

23. This statement is challenged directly by Park D. Goist, who wrote that by 1916 "the city planning movement had come to maturity in this country" (*From Main Street to State Street: Town, City, and Community in America* [Port Washington, N.Y., 1977], p. 127). Goist is correct in emphasizing planners' rapid progress, but my evidence strongly suggests that they were some years away from maturity.

24. Walter D. Moody, "The New Profession—City Planning," *Journal of the American Institute of Architects* 4, no. 3 (March 1916): 119.

25. Boston City Planning Commission, *Annual Report, 1940* (Boston, 1941).

26. Los Angeles Department of City Planning, "City Planning in Los Angeles: A History" (pamphlet dated 1964, in Municipal Reference Library, City Hall, Los Angeles). Perusal of the minutes of early meetings of the Los Angeles City Planning Commission revealed that when the commission consisted of fifty-one voluntary members, attendance seldom amounted to a 50-percent quorum.

27. *Commercial Club of Chicago Yearbook, 1919–1920* (Chicago, 1920), p. 293.

28. Scott, *American City Planning*, p. 169.

29. Quoted in Charles H. Wacker, "Address to Chicago Plan Commission, November 4, 1926" (pamphlet, Chicago, 1926), p. 8.

30. John Nolen, "City Making," *The American City* 1, no. 1 (September 1909): 19.

31. Scott, *American City Planning*, p. 251–252; and Brownell, "Urban Planning and the Motor Vehicle," pp. 3, 6–7.

32. Hancock, "Planners," p. 291. Blaine A. Brownell reveals that planners responded to this majority outlook at least through the 1920s. See Brownell, *The Urban Ethos in the South, 1920–1930* (Baton Rouge, La., 1975), pp. 171–189.

33. Massachusetts Metropolitan Plan Commission, *Report of the Metropolitan Plan Commission, January 1, 1912* (Boston, 1912), p. 13.

34. Goldfield, "Planning History in the United States," Paper presented at the American Historical Association Convention, San Francisco, December 1978, p. 6.

35. John Nolen to Winthrop Griffin, January 24, 1912 (box 71, in Nolen Papers). William H. Wilson, who has done extensive research on the City Beautiful Movement, says that many planners, including Nolen, did in fact "agitate" for adoption of plans, particularly in cities where they were well known and respected (Wilson to author, December 2, 1979). See also Wilson, "Harrisburg's Successful City Beautiful Movement, 1900–1915," *Pennsylvania History* 47 (July 1980): 213–233.

36. Seattle Civic Plans Investigation Committee, "The Bogue Plan Question" (Seattle, pamphlet dated 1912), pp. 13–14.

37. Padraic Burke, "The City Beautiful Movement in Seattle" (M.A. thesis, University of Washington, 1973), p. 119.

38. George E. Kessler, "The Plan of Cincinnati," *The American City* 2, no. 1 (January 1910): 3.

39. *Detroit Times,* January 10, 1913.

40. Detroit City Plan Commission, *Annual Report, 1927* (Detroit, 1928), p. 1.

41. Robert A. Walker, *The Planning Function in Local Government: A Report to the Local Planning Committee of the National Resources Board* (Washington, D.C.: National Resources Planning Board, July 28, 1939), pp. 4–13. See also Hancock, "Planners," pp. 290–294; Peterson, "The City Beautiful Movement," pp. 415–434.

42. Theodora K. Hubbard and Henry V. Hubbard, "Our Cities Today and Tomorrow" (mimeographed ms. dated 1919, box 50, Herbert C. Hoover Papers, Stanford University), pp. 5–6.

43. Schultz and McShane, "To Engineer the Metropolis," pp. 389–411; Wiebe, *The Search for Order,* pp. 149, 168, 170.

44. The best expressions of City Beautiful concepts are found in the actual plans of turn-of-the-century landscape consultants such as Charles M. Robinson and Frederick L. Olmsted, Jr. Between 1895 and 1912 they prepared plans for dozens of cities, large and small.

45. Wiebe, *The Search for Order,* p. 149; see also Burke, "The City Beautiful Movement," p. 4. William H. Wilson strongly contests suggestions cf many recent historians that City Beautiful planners were impractical dreamers. See Wilson, "Harrisburg's Successful City Beautiful Movement," pp. 213–233.

46. George B. Ford, "Digging Deeper into City Planning," *The American City* 6, no. 2 (February 1912): 559, 562.

47. Arnold Brunner, "The Meaning of City Planning," *Proceedings of the Fourth National Conference on City Planning* (Boston, May 27–29, 1912), pp. 24, 27. It should be pointed out that the vast majority of planners did not clearly fit the mold of City Beautiful or city practical planners. Their plans usually reflected elements of both perspectives.

48. John Nolen, "City Streets," *The American City* 3, no. 4 (October 1910): 119; Frederick L. Olmsted, Jr., "The Basic Principles of City Planning," *The American City* 3, no. 2 (August 1910): 68.

49. George R. Taylor, "The Beginnings of Mass Transportation in Urban America," pt. 2, *Smithsonian Journal of History* 1 (fall 1966): 39–50.

50. Alfred Bettman, "Rapid Transit in Cities," *The American City* 14, no. 6 (June 1916): 569.

51. Bion J. Arnold, *Report on the Chicago Traction Problem, 1902* (New York, 1905), p. 19.

52. Arnold, "City Transportation: Subways and Railroad Terminals," *Journal of the Western Society of Engineers* 19, no. 4 (April 1914): 20–21. An exhaustively researched account of the development of rapid transit in Chicago is Paul F. Barrett, "Mass Transit, the Automobile, and Public Policy in Chicago, 1900–1930" (Ph.D. diss., University of Illinois, Chicago Circle, 1976).

53. George B. Ford, "The Relation of City Planning to the Municipal Budget," *The American City* 4, no. 2 (February 1911): 68–69. See also John P. Fox, "Subsurface Terminals for Street Cars Open to Criticism," *The American City* 21, no. 5 (November 1919): 419–422.

54. *Proceedings of the Fifth National Conference on City Planning Held at Chicago, May 5–7, 1913* (New York, 1913), p. 125.

55. Barclay, Parsons, and Klapp, *Report on Detroit Street Railway Traffic and Proposed Subway Made to Board of Street Railway Commissioners, City of Detroit* (New York, 1915), p. 52.

56. Mallach, "Origins of the Decline of Urban Mass Transit," pp. 4–5.

57. See, for example, Charles de Leuw, *Report on a Proposed Woodward Avenue Subway to the Rapid Transit Commission, City of Detroit, September 1938* (Detroit, 1938), p. 55; Seattle City Planning Commission, Rapid Transit Committee, *Report on Rapid Transit by William P. Trimble et al.* (Seattle, 1926), pp. 81–82, 89.

58. Harland Bartholomew, *A Major Street Plan for St. Louis* (St. Louis, 1917), p. 14.

59. Los Angeles Department of Public Utilities, *Fourth Annual Report of the Board, July 1, 1912–June 30, 1913* (Los Angeles, 1913), p. 113; and *Fifth Annual Report, 1913–1914* (Los Angeles, 1914), p. 120. One could interpret this as a recommendation *against* rapid transit construction, since Los Angeles would not reach 750,000 residents for another decade.

60. Virgil C. Bogue, *Plan of Seattle: Report of the Municipal Plans Division* (Seattle, 1911), p. 132.

61. Schultz and McShane, "To Engineer the Metropolis," pp. 396–397, 400–402, 408–409.

62. John Nolen, "City Planning Article for *Municipal Encyclopedia*" (typescript dated 1919, box 1, Nolen Papers), p. 40.

63. Alfred J. Roewade to Alderman Francis D. Connery, January 9, 1902 (box 1, Alfred J. Roewade Papers, Chicago Historical Society).

64. Ernest B. Goodrich, reply to Nelson P. Lewis, "The Automobile and the City Plan," *Proceedings of the Eighth National Conference on City Planning* (Cleveland, June 5–7, 1915), p. 75.

65. John Nolen, "City Planning: Abstract of Address Delivered at Greens-

boro, N.C., May 16, 1914" (typescript, Lecture No. 101, box 2, Nolen Papers), p. 41.

66. Unwin quoted by John Nolen in *Christian Science Monitor*, October 10, 1922.

67. Tarr emphasized that "decentralizers" were "as motivated by considerations of social control as by a desire to enable man to lead more comfortable or healthy lives." Joel A. Tarr, "From City to Suburb: The 'Moral' Influence of Transportation Technology," in A. B. Callow, ed., *American Urban History: An Interpretive Reader with Commentaries*, 2nd ed. (New York, 1973), p. 209.

68. See the series of regional highway maps, Daniel H. Burnham, *Plan of Chicago* (Chicago, 1909), appendix A.

69. Bogue quoted in *New York Times*, July 16, 1916.

70. Lewis, "The Automobile and the City Plan," pp. 54–55. For a good overview of Lewis's career, see Jeffrey K. Stine, "Nelson P. Lewis and the City Efficient: The Rise of the Municipal Engineer in City Planning" (unpublished paper in possession of author, Department of History, University of California, Santa Barbara, 1979).

71. John B. Rae, *The Road and Car in American Life* (Cambridge, Mass., 1971), pp. 67–72.

72. Lewis, "The Automobile and the City Plan," p. 41.

73. *Ibid.*, p. 71.

74. Nelson P. Lewis, speech to American Road Builder's Association (typescript dated November 3, 1916, box 1, Nelson P. Lewis Papers, Olin Library, Cornell University).

75. Goodrich, reply to Nelson P. Lewis, *Proceedings of the Eighth National Conference on City Planning*, p. 75, 77. While no figures are available, one may assume that increasing numbers of planners themselves owned automobiles, which may have dulled their ardor in promoting modern rapid transit.

76. See, in particular, Mumford, *The City in History*, pp. 508–510; Robert M. Fogelson, *Fragmented Metropolis: Los Angeles, 1850–1930* (Cambridge, Mass., 1967), pp. 144–145, 245–246, 265.

Chapter 3

1. Several scholars have commented perceptively on nineteenth- and early-twentieth-century suburbanization: Kenneth T. Jackson, "Urban Deconcentration in the Nineteenth Century: A Statistical Inquiry," in Leo F. Schnore, ed., *The New Urban History: Quantitative Explorations by American Historians*

(Princeton, N.J., 1975), pp. 110–142; Sam Bass Warner, Jr., *Streetcar Suburbs: The Process of Growth in Boston, 1870–1900* (Cambridge, Mass., 1962); Schnore, "The Timing of Metropolitan Decentralization: A Contribution to the Debate," in Schnore, ed., *The Urban Scene: Human Ecology and Demography* (New York, 1965), pp. 98–113; and Charles N. Glaab, "Metropolis and Suburb: The Changing American City," in John Braeman and David M. Brody, eds., *Change and Continuity in Twentieth-Century America: The 1920s* (Columbus, O., 1968), pp. 399–437.

2. U.S., Bureau of the Census, *Sixteenth Census of the United States, 1940: Population* (Washington, D.C., 1943), 1: 32–33.

3. Studies probing important facets of the boom years in Detroit and Los Angeles include Melvin G. Holli, *Reform in Detroit: Hazen S. Pingree and Urban Politics* (New York, 1969); Donald F. Davis, "The Decline of the Gasoline Aristocracy: The Struggle for Supremacy in Detroit and the Automobile Industry, 1896–1933" (Ph.D. diss., Harvard University, 1976); Robert M. Fogelson, *Fragmented Metropolis: Los Angeles, 1850–1930* (Cambridge, Mass., 1967); and James J. Findley, "The Economic Boom of the 1920's in Los Angeles" (Ph.D. diss., Claremont Graduate School, 1958).

4. Two scholars doing research on the energy-induced aspects of horizontal growth are John G. Clark and Mark H. Rose. See their essay, "Light, Heat, and Power: Energy Choices in Kansas City, Wichita, and Denver, 1900–1935," *Journal of Urban History* 5, no. 3 (May 1979): 340–364.

5. Schnore suggests that at least 10 of the 99 cities with populations in excess of 100,000 in 1950 began to decentralize prior to 1900 ("Timing," pp. 98–103). Jackson supports Schnore's contention, but suggests that, if one measures decentralization from the standpoint of city boundaries as they existed in the nineteenth century, its origins can be traced back even farther—in one case, to 1790 (Jackson, "Urban Deconcentration," pp. 110, 142). For an update on the decentralization literature, see John D. Kasarda and George V. Redfearn, "Differential Patterns of City and Suburban Growth in the United States," *Journal of Urban History* 2 (November 1975): 43–66.

6. Jackson, "Urban Deconcentration," p. 141. It should be noted that much of the statistical growth of even central cities, particularly during the late nineteenth and early twentieth centuries, resulted from annexations. See especially Glaab, "Metropolis and Suburb," 399–437.

7. In addition to the Schnore and Jackson studies, which confirm this view, see Amos H. Hawley, *The Changing Shape of Metropolitan America: Deconcentration since 1920* (Glencoe, Ill., 1956); and Warren S. Thompson, *The*

Growth of Metropolitan Districts in the United States, 1900–1940 (Washington, D.C., 1947). Kasarda and Redearn take exception to this generalization ("Differential Patterns," pp. 43–66).

8. Schnore, "Metropolitan Growth and Decentralization," in Schnore (ed.), *The Urban Scene*, p. 80.

9. *Ibid.*, p. 82.

10. A good overview of the process is Charles N. Glaab and A. Theodore Brown, *A History of Urban America,* 2nd ed. (New York, 1976), pp. 122–133. Two excellent, probing analyses of the tensions wrought by this transformation are Elliot Rudwick, *Race Riot in East St. Louis, July 2, 1917* (Edwardsville, Ill., 1964); and William M. Tuttle, Jr., *Race Riot: Chicago in the Red Summer of 1919* (New York, 1970).

11. Glaab and Brown, *A History of Urban America,* pp. 262, 267–268. For a deeper contemporary analysis of this trend, see Harlan P. Douglass, *The Suburban Trend* (New York, 1925).

12. Mark S. Foster, "The Model-T, the 'Hard Sell,' and Los Angeles' Urban Growth: The Decentralization of Los Angeles During the 1920s," *Pacific Historical Review* 44, no. 4 (November 1975): 459–484; Fogelson, *Fragmented Metropolis,* pp. 141–148, 154–163; Frank G. Mittelbach, "Dynamic Land Use Patterns in Los Angeles, the Period 1924–1954" (unpublished report, Real Estate Research Institute, University of California, Los Angeles). Two popular writers suggest that Los Angeles's decentralization was due, at least in part, to the fact that large numbers of retired midwestern farmers and small-town people migrated to the region, especially during the 1920s. Their natural inclinations and the region's excellent weather for raising small crops encouraged them to settle in one- and two-acre homesteads. See Morrow Mayo, *Los Angeles* (New York, 1932), p. 327; and Carey McWilliams, *Southern California Country* (New York, 1946), pp. 158–159.

13. Walter V. Woehlke, "How Long Los Angeles? An Examination of the Root System That Fed Los Angeles's Astonishing Growth," *Sunset* 52 (April 1924): 10.

14. Glaab and Brown, *A History of Urban America,* p. 255.

15. U.S., Bureau of the Census, *Historical Statistics of the United States: Colonial Times to 1970* (Washington, D.C., 1975), 2: 721.

16. *Ibid.* A good analysis of the relative advantages of buses and streetcars is Donald N. Dewees, "The Decline of the American Street Railways," *Traffic Quarterly* 24 (October 1970): 563–581.

17. In almost every large city, a check of local newspapers between 1916 and

1922 reveals tension between trolley companies and jitney operators. Fights between the conflicting interest groups were particularly intense in Los Angeles and Chicago. Blaine A. Brownell reports that this was a problem persisting into the 1920s in several southern cities as well (see *The Urban Ethos in the South, 1920–1930* [Baton Rouge, La., 1975], p. 123). Howard L. Preston confirms this for Atlanta. See *Automobile Age Atlanta: The Making of a Southern Metropolis, 1900–1935* (Athens, Ga., 1979), pp. 56–63. Dewees also stresses the adversary relationship between trolley companies and jitney operators in the early years ("America Street Railways," p. 570).

18. This theoretically sound dovetailing of functions seldom worked in practice. Public transit officials soon discovered patrons' resistance to transfers from one form of transit to another. Hence, by the late 1920s or early 1930s, many bus lines connected suburbs directly to central districts. See W. F. Evans, "Ability of the Bus to Handle Mass Transportation," *Bus Transportation* 5, no. 1 (January 1926): 44–45; Beeler Organization, *Report to the City of Seattle on Its Municipal Street Railway System* (New York, 1935), pp. 4, 38.

19. *Bus Transportation* 2, no. 8 (August 1923): 388. Yet it must be noted that many trolley officials continued to stress the trolley's advantage over the bus in tight quarters. Specifically, trolleys contained more seats and they had a higher overload capacity, in that they could accommodate larger numbers of standees. See Dewees, "American Street Railways," p. 570; and Donald F. Davis, "Mass Transit and Private Ownership: Another Perspective on the Case of Toronto, 1891–1920" (unpublished paper). I am indebted to Davis for providing a copy of this paper.

20. Preston, *Automobile Age Atlanta*, p. 68.

21. *Electric Railway Journal* 70, no. 15 (October 8, 1927): 666.

22. John A. Beeler, "Planning Transportation for the City of the Future," *Electric Railway Journal* 66, no. 13 (September 26, 1925): 525–530.

23. "Public Transportation Gaining Steadily in Large Cities," *Electric Railway Journal* 74, no. 3 (March 1930): 125. By contrast, a 1937 study revealed the magnitude of the industry's decline. While there were 1,307 street railway companies operating in 1917, there were only 963 in 1927 and but 487 a decade later. More important, total trackage dropped slightly from 44,835 miles in 1917 to 40,722 miles ten years later. By 1937 it was only 23,770 miles. See U.S., Bureau of the Census, *Street Railways and Trolley Bus and Motor Bus Operations* (Washington, D.C., 1937), p. 8.

24. *Electric Railway Journal* 70, no. 12 (September 17, 1927): 459.

25. Robert F. Kelker, "The Effect of Passenger Automobiles on Mass Trans-

portation Traffic," *American Electric Railway Association Proceedings: Transportation and Traffic Association* (New York, 1928), pp. 50–51. One could argue that, since Kelker was hired to present transit plans in specific cities, his endorsements of street railways reflected only what he was paid to say by city bureaucrats. However, Kelker consistently supported street railways before a variety of audiences, and whether or not he received remuneration.

26. "An Opportunity of a Century," *The Columbian,* April 3, 1925.

27. Sidney D. Waldon to William Mayo, Ross Schram, and Daniel L. Turner, March 5, 1924 (box 1, Detroit Rapid Transit Commission Papers, Burton Historical Collection, Detroit Public Library; hereafter referred to as "Detroit RTC Papers").

28. Lucius Storrs, "The Place of the Street Car in the Modern City Plan," *Annals of the American Academy of Political and Social Science* 133 (September 1927): 190.

29. Quoted in Glen E. Holt, "Urban Mass Transit History: Where We Have Been and Where We Are Going," in Jerome E. Finster, ed., *The National Archives and Urban Research* (Athens, O., 1974), p. 86.

30. "Let's Stop 'Talking Poor,' " *Electric Railway Journal* 64, no. 1 (July 5, 1924): 3.

31. L. R. Nash, "Taxation without Misrepresentation," *Electric Traction* 19, no. 9 (September 1923): 450.

32. D. Emmons, "Coordinating Motor Bus and Electric Railway," *Bus Transportation* 2, no. 5 (May 1923): 288. Emmons's suggestion that automobile owners enjoyed free use of the streets was, of course, inaccurate. They paid at least part of the costs through a variety of taxes on automobile sales, gasoline, and license fees. See John C. Burnham, "The Gasoline Tax and the Automobile Revolution," *Mississippi Valley Historical Review* 68, no. 3 (December 1961): 435–459; and John B. Rae, *The Road and Car in American Life* (Boston, 1971), pp. 62–65, 73–74.

33. Leslie Blanchard, *The Street Railway Era in Seattle: A Chronicle of Six Decades* (Forty Fort, Pa., 1968), p. 107.

34. Owen D. Young, "Facing the Streetcar Problem" (address before the American Electric Railway Association, Cleveland, O., September 25, 1928), p. 3.

35. Raymond Thompkins, "The Troubled Trolley," *American Mercury* 13 (April 1928): 400.

36. *Pacific Electric Magazine* 13 (October 10, 1928): 11. See also John P. Hallihan, "Relation of Rapid Transit to Community Development," *Electric Railway Journal* 73, no. 19 (September 14, 1929): 912.

37. Edwin M. Walker, "What the Private Automobile Has Brought to Transportation," *Electric Railway Journal* 66, no. 13 (September 26, 1925): 488.

38. "Street Cars Coming Back?" *Electric Traction* 21, no. 10 (October 1925): 552.

39. American Electric Railway Association, "Report of the Committee on Movement of the Vehicle," *Proceedings, Transportation and Traffic Association* (New York, 1930), p. 28.

40. James A. Gregg, "The Future of City Transportation," *Electric Traction* 22, no. 9 (September 1926): 468.

41. Thompkins, "The Troubled Trolley," p. 406.

42. Britton I. Budd, "The Present and Future of Electric Railways" (pamphlet, Chicago, ca. 1926), p. 11.

43. H. G. Taylor, "Future of the Industry," *Electric Traction* 23, no. 12 (December 1926): 656. See also Westinghouse Electric and Manufacturing Co., *Report on Seattle Municipal Street Railway* (Seattle, December 30, 1926), p. 8; John A. Beeler, *Report to the City of Atlanta on a Plan of Local Transportation* (Atlanta, 1923); and Howard L. Preston, "A New Kind of Horizontal City: Automobility in Atlanta, 1900–1930" (Ph.D. diss., Emory University, 1974), ch. 3.

44. United States Federal Railway Commission, "Our Electric Railway Problems" (pamphlet, Washington, D.C., 1920), p. 14.

45. "Bus Riders from Car Riders," *Bus Transportation* 4, no. 10 (October 1925): 511.

46. "Industry's Fundamental Problems," *Electric Railway Journal* 74, no. 8 (July 1930): 459.

47. McClellan and Junkersfeld, Inc., *A Summary of the 1925 Transportation Study of the City of Washington, D.C.* (New York, 1925), p. 20.

48. U.S., Bureau of the Census, *Historical Statistics to 1970* 2: 716.

49. "Why We Are Not 'Saturated' with Automobiles," *Literary Digest* 78, no. 13 (September 29, 1923): 62.

50. *Facts and Figures of the Automobile Industry, 1931* (New York, 1931), pp. 20–22.

51. See, for example, Arthur A. Shurtleff, *Future Parks, Playgrounds, and Parkways* (Boston, 1925), p. 6.

52. "Autoists Leave $74,000,000 in California," *Public Works* 49, no. 19 (November 6, 1920): 434. For an excellent study of the national impact of automobile tourism, see Warren J. Belasco, *Americans on the Road: From Autocamp to Motel, 1910–1945* (Cambridge, Mass., 1979). Blaine A. Brownell has shown that while "commercial-civic elites" in southern cities basically

approved of the automobile and welcomed its impact upon the urban eccnomy, they did voice a few reservations, particularly about the cities' ability to adjust rapidly to it (*The Urban Ethos,* pp. 116–124).

53. "The Automobile Peril Twenty-five Years Ago, and Today," *Public Works* 60, no. 11 (November 1929): 437.

54. Sidney D. Waldon to Colonel Robert D. McCormick, July 25, 1924 (box 1, Detroit RTC Papers).

55. A major reason for auto companies' cooperation was that local street railways promised to repay their help with improved service to their plants. See Davis, "Decline," chs. 8–15; and Davis, "The Curious Fate of Automotive Progressivism: The Subway Crusade in Detroit, 1910–1929" (unpublished paper), pp. 1–40.

56. "Our New Colossus of Roads," *Municipal and County Engineering* 63, no. 4 (October 1922): 19.

57. Stanley L. McMichael, "The Influence of the Automobile upon Real Estate," in *Annals of Real Estate Practice* (Chicago, 1928), p. 206.

58. "What Do Folks Use Their Cars For?" *Literary Digest* 9, no. 7 (November 17, 1923): 66. Unfortunately, the study did not provide breakdowns of commuter use in cities, towns, and rural areas.

59. John C. Long, "Motor Cars to Solve Housing Problem," *Motor News* 11, no. 8 (August 1921): 17; and Michigan Super Highway Commission, *First Annual Report* (Lansing, October 1926), p. 9.

60. Lewis Mumford, "The Fourth Migration," *Survey Graphic* 54, no. 3 (May 1, 1925): 132.

61. Blaine A. Brownell, "The Impact of the Motorcar in Southern Urban Areas in the 1920s" (paper read at the Southern Historical Association meeting, November 19, 1971), pp. 3–4. See also James J. Flink, "Three Stages of American Automobile Consciousness," *American Quarterly* 24 (October 1972): 451–473.

62. Flink, *The Car Culture* (Cambridge, Mass., 1975), p. 149. Sociologists Robert and Helen Lynd reported that substantial numbers of working-class families in Muncie, Indiana spent one week's pay each month on their automobiles. *Middletown: A Study in American Culture* (New York, 1929), p. 255.

63. Glen E. Holt, "The Changing Perception of Urban Pathology: An Essay on the Development of Mass Transit in the United States," in Kenneth T. Jackson and Stanley K. Schultz, eds., *Cities in American History* (New York, 1972), p. 338; see also Joel A. Tarr, "From City to Suburb: The 'Moral' Influence of Transportation Technology," in A. B. Callow, Jr., ed., *American*

Urban History: An Interpretive Reader with Commentaries, 2nd ed. (New York, 1973), pp. 202–212.

64. Lewis Atherton, *Main Street on the Middle Border* (Bloomington, Ind., 1954), pp. 234–240.

65. Robert Whitten, "Unchoking Our Congested Streets," *The American City* 13, no. 4 (October 1920): 352.

66. "Discussion," *Proceedings of the American Society of Civil Engineers* 55, no. 1 (January 17, 1929): 574.

67. "Head of Pennsylvania Motor Federation Condemns Parking," *Electric Railway Journal* 70, no. 24 (December 10, 1927): 1051. See also Miller McClintock, *Street Traffic Control* (New York, 1925), p. 4.

68. "Quiet Pavements Near Schools," *Public Works* 51, no. 21 (November 19, 1921): 402.

69. Charles H. Wacker, "Address at the Meeting of the Chicago Plan Commission" (Chicago, pamphlet dated November 4, 1926), p. 20. Yet such protests against declining air quality were very infrequent before World War II.

70. "Discussion: Street Designing for Various Uses," *Proceedings of the American Society of Civil Engineers* 54, no. 11 (November 1928): 2611. For an in-depth discussion of the problems generated by competing approaches to zoning in American cities, see Homer E. Hoyt, *One Hundred Years of Land Values in Chicago* (Chicago, 1933).

71. George S. Wehrwein, "Some Problems of Recreational Land," *Journal of Land and Public Utility Economics* 11 (May 1927): 163.

Chapter 4

1. A sophisticated treatment of the vicissitudes experienced by planners in their search for professional recognition is Blaine A. Brownell, "Urban Planning and the Motor Vehicle in the United States in the Early Twentieth Century" (paper presented at the First International Conference on the History of Urban and Regional Planning, University of London, September 1977). I am indebted to Brownell for generously sharing his insights and research.

2. Throughout this book, I define "rapid transit" as subways, elevated lines, and any other technologies proposed that provided exclusive rights of way for the transit vehicles. Under "mass transit" I include buses, trolleys of all sorts, horse-drawn omnibuses, and so forth. Mass transit vehicles share space with other vehicles and with pedestrians.

3. *Public Works* 55, no. 6 (June 1924): 181.

4. Chicago City Clerk's Office, *Annual Appropriations of the City of Chicago for 1930* (Chicago, 1930), pp. 2225, 2300. Boston City Planning Commission, *Annual Report, 1940* (Boston, 1941), p. 27. Los Angeles County Regional Planning Commission, *Annual Report of the Regional Planning Commission for the Los Angeles County Regional Planning District and the County of Los Angeles, Fiscal Year Ending June 30, 1940* (Los Angeles, 1940), p. 2a. Appropriations for planning are insignificant compared to money spent on other government functions.

5. Boston City Planning Board, *Tenth Annual Report of the City Planning Board for the Year Ending January 31, 1924* (Boston, 1924), p. 47.

6. Detroit Bureau of Government Research, *The Detroit Metropolitan Area: A Report Prepared for the Metropolitan Committee of the Detroit Chamber of Commerce* (Detroit, January 1924), p. 24.

7. *Proceedings of the Sixteenth National Conference of City Planners, April 7–10, 1924, Los Angeles, California* (Baltimore, 1924), p. 10.

8. W. L. Pollard, untitled paper delivered before California Planning Association, October 1932 (mimeographed, Los Angeles City Planning Library).

9. T. B. Eldridge to Jefferson C. Grinnalds, April 28, 1923 (box 1, Jefferson C. Grinnalds Papers, Olin Library, Cornell University).

10. *Boston City Record* 18, no. 1 (January 2, 1926): 28.

11. Mel Scott, *American City Planning since 1890* (Berkeley, Cal., 1969), pp. 251–252.

12. Blaine A. Brownell, *The Urban Ethos in the South, 1920–1930* (Baton Rouge, La., 1975), 171–189; and Brownell, "Urban Planning," pp. 5–7.

13. *Chicago City Plan Commission Proceedings* (October 27, 1925), 5: 1244; in Chicago Municipal Reference Library.

14. National Conference on Highway Safety, "Comments by Non-Members of Committee on Tentative Draft of a Model Traffic Ordinance" (mimeographed, ca. 1928, box 35, John Ihlder Papers, Franklin D. Roosevelt Library, Hyde Park, N.Y.).

15. *Chicago City Plan Commission Proceedings* (October 27, 1925), 5: 1244.

16. "Remarks of Chairman Charles H. Wacker of the Chicago Plan Commission at the Anniversary Meeting of the Chicago Association of Commerce, November 20, 1925" (typescript, box 1, William E. Dever Papers, Chicago Historical Society).

17. Adams to John Nolen, July 7, 1920 (box 8, John Nolen Papers, Olin Library, Cornell University); emphasis in original. Some historians have taken issue with Adams's perspective. Blaine Brownell suggested that many private

planning consultants merely argued what they believed their clients wished to hear (Brownell to author, January 15, 1979). Mark H. Rose pointed out that Adams soon changed his tune; when working with the New York Regional Plan of the late 1920s, Adams was a leader in lining up private funding (Rose to author, January 3, 1979).

18. H. A. Overstreet, "Arousing Public Interest in City Planning," in *Regional Planning Notes*, June 28, 1928 (mimeographed newsletter of the Los Angeles County Regional Planning Commission, Municipal Reference Library, City Hall, Los Angeles).

19. Russell V. Black to John Nolen, April 18, 1924 (box 71, Nolen Papers).

20. John A. Beeler, "Planning Transportation for the City of the Future," *Electric Railway Journal* 66, no. 13 (September 26, 1925): 528. See also Frederick A. Delano, "Regional Planning Next!" *National Municipal Review* 13, no. 3 (March 1924): 141.

21. Robert H. Whitten, "A Method of Adopting and Enforcing a Comprehensive Development Plan for Unbuilt Areas" (typescript dated February 11, 1924, box 10, Grinnalds Papers). Brownell has observed correctly that planners in many cities "desired *both* a strong, vital business core and an expanding periphery—*both* continued centralization . . . and decentralization" ("Urban Planning," p. 11); emphasis in original. Brownell labels this their "urban ethos." My own view is that while many planners desired both results, their actions generally emphasized expansion of the periphery.

22. Beeler, "Planning Transportation," p. 529. See also Jacob L. Crane, Jr., "Statement of Policy and Purpose. Chicago Regional Planning Association" (typescript, ca. 1923, box 1, Chicago Regional Planning Association Papers, Chicago Historical Society).

23. "General Discussion" of O. H. Koch, "City Planning in Small Cities," *Proceedings of the American Society of Civil Engineers* 13, no. 12 (December 1929): 1437.

24. Lewis Mumford, "Climax," *Journal of the American Institute of Architects* 13, no. 12 (December 1925): 455.

25. Gordon Whitnall, untitled (mimeographed paper dated April 7, 1924, in Whitnall Scrapbook, City Planning Commission Library, City Hall, Los Angeles). See also Mark S. Foster, "The Western Response to Urban Transportation: A Tale of Three Cities, 1900–1945," *Journal of the West* 18, no. 3 (July 1979): 31–39.

26. Walden E. Sweet, "The Denver City Plan," *Western City* 6, no. 5 (May 1930): 16.

27. Nelson P. Lewis, *The Planning of the Modern City: A Review of the*

Principles Governing City Planning, 2nd rev. ed. (New York, 1923), p. 55.

28. S. Herbert Hare, discussion of Harold S. Buttenheim and Theodora K. Hubbard, "Trends in Present-Day City Planning," *City Planning* 8, no. 2 (April 1922): 101. Nichols shared his colleague's misgivings. See, for example, Jesse C. Nichols, "The Development of Outlying Shopping Centers," in *Planning Problems of Town, City, and Region: Proceedings of the Twenty-First National Conference on City Planning* (Buffalo and Niagara Falls, N.Y., May 20–23, 1929), pp. 16–31.

29. Louis W. McIntyre, "Improved Traffic Regulation Needed to Reduce Congestion and Prevent Premature Decentralization," *The American City* 39, no. 3 (September 1928): 158.

30. Robert H. Whitten, "Some Limitations," *City Planning* 4, no. 2 (April 1928): 81.

31. Miller McClintock, "Preventive and Palliative Measures for Street Traffic Relief," *City Planning* 6, no. 2 (April 1930): 101–102.

32. John P. Fox, "Subsurface Terminals for Street Cars Open to Criticism," *The American City* 21, no. 5 (November 1919): 421–422.

33. Seattle City Planning Commission, *Annual Report, 1928* (Seattle, January 8, 1929), p. 2.

34. Seattle City Planning Commission, Rapid Transit Committee, *Report on Rapid Transit by William P. Trimble et al.* (Seattle, 1926), p. 94.

35. *Ibid.,* p. 82. For other subway cost projections, see Kelker, de Leuw, and Co., *Report and Recommendations on a Rapid Transit Plan for the City and County of Los Angeles* (Los Angeles, 1925), p. 22; Miller McClintock, *Report of the Chicago Street Traffic Survey* (Chicago, 1926), p. 6; Daniel L. Turner, "Proposed Rapid Transit System for the City of Detroit" (mimeographed, dated June 26, 1923, box 9, Detroit Rapid Transit Commission Papers [hereafter shown as "Detroit RTC Papers"], Burton Historical Collection, Detroit Public Library).

36. Sidney D. Waldon, "Superhighways and Regional Planning," in *Planning Problems of Town, City, and Region: Papers and Discussion at the Nineteenth National Conference on City Planning* (Washington, D.C., May 9–11, 1927), p. 152. See also his comments in Detroit RTC, *Minutes* (April 14, 1927, box 16, Detroit RTC Papers). That such appeals succeeded in aligning important support from Detroit manufacturers for local referendums on rapid transit is borne out by Donald F. Davis, "The Curious Fate of Automotive Progressivism: The Subway Crusade in Detroit, 1910–1929" (unpublished paper).

37. Sidney D. Waldon, "Provide Now for Future Transportation" (mimeo-

graphed address to American Electric Railway Association, dated October 5, 1926).

38. Edward Dana, "Answering the Growing Need for Adequate Rapid Transit," *Electric Railway Journal* 74, no. 7 (June 1930): 391.

39. Henry I. Harriman, "Rapid Transit" (typescript dated 1930, Boston Public Library), p. 20.

40. Waldon to Mayor John C. Lodge, April 3, 1923 (box 17, Detroit RTC Papers).

41. *Charter of the City of Los Angeles, Adopted by the Electors of the City of Los Angeles May 6, 1924, Effective July 1, 1925*, Art. 1, sec. 3, para. 9, p. 11. While not all cities with "official transit plans" actually adopted such regulations during the 1920s, this "comprehensive and complete" system thinking was explicit in virtually every major transit plan published during the decade.

42. Daniel L. Turner, "Is There a Vicious Circle of Transit Development and City Congestion?" *National Municipal Review* 15, no. 6 (June 1926): 322.

43. Clarence Stein, "Dinosaur Cities," *Survey Graphic* 54, no. 3 (May 1, 1925): 138.

44. John Ihlder, "Coordination of Traffic Facilities," *The Annals of the American Academy of Political and Social Sciences* 133 (September 1927): 7.

45. Waldon to Lodge, September 19, 1924 (box 1, Detroit Mayors' Papers, 1924, Burton Historical Collection, Detroit Public Library).

46. Thomson to Rapid Transit Commission of Seattle, November 18, 1925 (box 13, Reginald H. Thomson Papers, Suzzallo Library, University of Washington, Seattle).

47. Bradway to John C. Lodge, February 9, 1923 (box 1, Detroit Mayors' Papers, 1923).

48. George C. Sykes, "The Eternal Traction Question" (typescript dated April 1923, box 1, Dever Papers). See also Paul Barrett, "Mass Transit, the Automobile, and Public Policy in Chicago, 1900–1930" (Ph.D. diss., University of Illinois, Chicago Circle, 1976), p. 411. Barrett's is the definitive analysis of the evolution of transportation in early-twentieth-century Chicago.

49. Evan W. Thomas, "An Analysis of Proposals to Provide Rapid and Adequate Mass Transportation for the Los Angeles Area" (M.A. thesis, University of California, Los Angeles, 1939), p. 103.

50. *Electric Railway Journal* 64, no. 15 (October 25, 1924): 598.

51. Mayo, untitled (typescript dated 1923, box 5, Detroit Mayors' Papers).

52. *Detroit Saturday Night*, September 24, 1927.

53. There were a few additions to and extensions of existing systems. See for example Joel Fischer, "Urban Transportation: Home Rule and the Independent

Subway System in New York City, 1917–1925" (Ph.D diss., St. John's University, N.Y., 1978). During the 1920s, traffic consultants included a wide range of modes of transportation under the general rubric of rapid transit. Most, however, defined rapid transit as fixed rails segregated from other forms of traffic—that is, subways and elevated trains—though a few included express buses and interurban streetcars.

54. Readers desiring a deeper knowledge of the Detroit transit situation should consult Graeme O'Geran, *A History of the Detroit Street Railways* (Detroit, 1931); William H. Henning, ed., *Detroit: Its Trolleys and Interurbans* (Detroit, 1976); and Davis, "The Curious Fate."

55. John C. Lodge to Sidney D. Waldon, December 28, 1922 (box 4, Detroit Mayors' Papers, 1922).

56. See John P. Hallihan to Waldon, May 1, 1923 (box 17, Detroit RTC Papers); and Detroit RTC, *Minutes*, August 8, 1923 (box 9, Detroit RTC Papers).

57. Detroit RTC, *General Plan of Rapid Transit and Surface Line System for the City of Detroit* (Detroit, 1923).

58. Waldon to Fred J. Haynes, April 5, 1924 (box 1, Detroit RTC Papers).

59. Waldon to Brosseau, October 26, 1925 (box 2, Detroit RTC Papers).

60. Waldon, "Suggested Article for Free Press" (typescript dated November 24, 1923, box 2, Sidney D. Waldon Papers, Detroit Public Library); emphasis mine.

61. Waldon to Common Council, City of Detroit, April 9, 1924 (box 1, Detroit RTC Papers).

62. Waldon to Martin, April 10, 1924 (box 1, Detroit Mayors' Papers, 1924).

63. For a typical report, see Detroit RTC, *Minutes*, January 16, 1928 (box 11, Detroit RTC Papers); see also Waldon to Mayor John C. Lodge, October 25, 1929 (box 1, Detroit RTC Papers); and Detroit Dept. of Public Works, City Planning Commission and RTC, *Report on Proposed 10 Year Program of Street Widening* (Detroit, March 22, 1930).

64. Detroit RTC, *Rapid Transit System for the City of Detroit* (Detroit, August 16, 1926), p. 26.

65. Detroit RTC, *Report of the Rapid Transit Commission to the Mayor's Finance Committee* (Detroit, December 10, 1926), cover letter.

66. Miller-Schorn System to Common Council, City of Detroit, December 14, 1925 (box 2, Detroit RTC Papers).

67. *Detroit News*, January 14, 1926.

68. *Detroit Times*, January 4, 1928.

69. *Ibid.*, January 15, 1928.

70. Detroit RTC, *Report on Miller-Schorn Petition No. 14396, January 25, 1928* (Detroit, 1928); *Detroit Free Press*, July 1, 1928.

71. *Detroit Free Press*, July 1, 1928.

72. In August the council came within one vote of abolishing the commission (*Detroit Times*, August 22, 1928).

73. *Detroit Times*, July 16, 1928.

74. For a thorough analysis of Detroit's subway proposals during the 1920s, see Davis, "The Curious Fate." The bond issue failed by nearly a 3-to-1 margin.

75. *Detroit News*, March 31, 1929.

76. Pope to Richard P. Joy, May 8, 1925 (box 2, Detroit RTC Papers).

77. Detroit RTC *Minutes*, May 6, 1927 (box 16, Detroit RTC Papers). Not all planners resisted piecemeal construction of rapid transit lines. See for example City Plan Commission, St. Louis, *The St. Louis Transit System: Present and Future* (St. Louis, 1920), pp. 16–18.

78. For a summary of the dates of submission and projected costs of proposed rapid transit plans for Detroit, see Detroit RTC, *Minutes*, December 19, 1953 (box 13, Detroit RTC Papers).

79. For a more extended discussion of the failure of public transportation forces to effect rapid transit in Los Angeles, see Thomas, "Mass Transportation for Los Angeles"; see also Mark S. Foster, "The Decentralization of Los Angeles During the 1920s" (Ph.D. diss., University of Southern California, 1971), pp. 111–139; and Foster, "The Model-T, the 'Hard Sell,' and Los Angeles' Urban Growth: The Decentralization of Los Angeles During the 1920s," *Pacific Historical Review* 44, no. 4 (November 1975): 459–484.

80. Los Angeles Board of Public Utilities, *Fourth Annual Report of the Board of Public Utilities, July 1, 1912 to June 30, 1913*, p. 113; James C. Findley, "The Economic Boom of the Twenties in Los Angeles" (Ph.D. diss., Claremont Graduate School, 1958), p. 422; and Robert M. Fogelson, *Fragmented Metropolis: Los Angeles, 1850–1930* (Cambridge, Mass., 1967), p. 185. In 1911 a nationally renowned transportation consultant, Bion J. Arnold, had recommended a subway system, but his ideas gained no serious following; see Arnold, "The Transportation Problem of Los Angeles," *Supplement to the California Outlook* 11, no. 9 (November 4, 1911), pp. 1–8.

81. See Foster, "Decentralization of Los Angeles," pp. 111–119.

82. *Charter of the City of Los Angeles, Adopted by the Electors of the City of Los Angeles May 6, 1924, Effective July 1, 1925*, Art. 1, sec. 3, para. 9, p. 11.

83. Kelker, de Leuw and Co., *Report*, p. 22.

84. *Ibid.*, p. 3.

85. W. H. Pierce to John R. Haynes, October 3, 1925 (box 1, John R.

Haynes Papers, Public Affairs Reading Room, University of California, Los Angeles).

86. *Bulletin of the Municipal League of Los Angeles* 3 (September 25, 1925).

87. S. A. Jubb *et al.* to Board of Directors of the Los Angeles City Club, *Supplement City Club Bulletin: Report on Rapid Transit, January 30, 1926,* pp. 3, 4, 9. Six of seven members of the transportation committee concurred in this negative evaluation. The seventh member, A. F. Southworth, presented a minority report. See *ibid.,* appendix A. See also Foster, "The Western Response," pp. 31–39.

88. Gordon Whitnall, untitled ms. dated September 22, 1925 (Whitnall Scrapbook).

89. Whitnall, untitled ms. dated September 10, 1929 (Whitnall Scrapbook).

90. Los Angeles Board of City Planning Commissioners, *Conference on the Rapid Transit Question, January 21, 1930* (Los Angeles, 1930).

91. Los Angeles Board of City Planning Commissioners, *Annual Report for the Year Ending June 30, 1930* (Los Angeles, 1930), p. 19. In contrast to the enormous fixed costs of building operable transit systems, highway proposals appeared inexpensive. Even more important, many of the actual costs of automobile operation were indirect and veiled.

92. Several transit plans were proposed during the 1930s; none generated a significantly large following. See Thomas, "Mass Transportation for Los Angeles."

93. Foster, "The Model-T," pp. 459–484; see also the chapter on Los Angeles in Sam Bass Warner, Jr., *The Urban Wilderness: A History of the American City* (New York, 1972), pp. 113–149.

Chapter 5

1. Today it appears evident that there was a difference between planners and traffic engineers. According to historian John Hancock, planners considered the impacts of transportation plans upon land-use patterns, the environment, and so forth, while traffic engineers simply drew up street and highway plans when ordered to do so (Hancock to author, October 26, 1979). My own research suggests that distinctions between planners and traffic engineers were extremely fuzzy during the 1920s and 1930s. First, some traffic engineers were just as conscientious as their planner peers in considering the environmental and land-use effects of their highway plans. While a handful of men made their livings as full-time planners with private consulting practices, they did not emphasize their differences from traffic engineers in their personal correspondence or in their proposals. Rather, the two "groups" worked together closely in many

cases. For these reasons, I feel justified in considering traffic engineers to be planners.

2. Blaine A. Brownell, "Urban Planning and the Motor Vehicle in the United States in the Early Twentieth Century" (paper presented at the First International Conference on the History of Urban and Regional Planning, University of London, September, 1977), p. 7.

3. Raymond Unwin, "America Revisited—A City Planner's Impressions," *The American City* 28, no. 4 (April 1923): 334.

4. For details on the range of early conflicts between urban and rural road interests, see Mark H. Rose, *Interstate: Express Highway Politics, 1941–1956* (Lawrence, Kans., 1979), ch. 1; John B. Rae, *The Road and Car in American Life* (Cambridge, Mass., 1971), chs. 3–7; and Philip P. Mason, *The League of American Wheelmen and the Good Roads Movement, 1880–1905* (Ann Arbor, Mich., 1958). Early-twentieth-century professional journals frequently commented on the competition between the two factions; see *Roads and Streets, Municipal Engineering,* and *The American City.*

5. Waldon, "Address before the Society of Automotive Engineers" (mimeographed typescript dated January 9, 1930, box 3, Sidney D. Waldon Papers, Detroit Public Library).

6. Jacob Viner, "Urban Aspects of the Highway Finance Problem," *Roads and Streets* 65, no. 2 (February 3, 1926): 106. It would be virtually impossible to settle the argument over which "side" got the better break. However, the use of road tax revenues was a warm issue in the 1920s that became even warmer in the 1930s. See John C. Burnham, "The Gasoline Tax and the Automobile Revolution," *Mississippi Valley Historical Review* 68, no. 3 (December 1961): 435–459; and Warren J. Belasco, *Americans on the Road: From Autocamp to Motel, 1910–1945* (Cambridge, Mass., 1979).

7. American Automobile Association, *President's Report, Twenty-eighth Meeting,* [June 20–21, 1930], p. 5. See also Rose, *Interstate.*

8. Alvan Macauley, "City Planning and Automobile Traffic Problems" (pamphlet, Detroit, 1925), p. 5.

9. Philip Harrington, *A Comprehensive Superhighway Plan for the Control of Chicago* (Chicago, 1939), p. 16. Chicago transportation historian Paul H. Barrett provided even higher figures. According to Barrett, Chicago spent $450 million on all street improvements between 1913 and 1937 (Barrett, "Mass Transit, the Automobile, and Public Policy in Chicago, 1900–1930" (Ph.D. diss., University of Illinois, Chicago Circle, 1976), p. 469.

10. Harvey W. Corbett, "Different Levels for Foot, Wheel, and Rail," *The American City* 31, no. 1 (July 1924): 2.

11. Arthur S. Tuttle, "Increasing the Capacity of City Streets, with Discus-

sion," *Transactions of the American Society of Civil Engineers, Paper No. 1556* (New York, 1925), pp. 217, 222.

12. *Ibid.*, pp. 238–239. Ironically, however, even Bartholomew occasionally resorted to recommending double-decked streets. He did so the very next year. See Harland Bartholomew, *Some Preliminary Observations on Transit Facilities in the Central Business District with Particular Reference to the Triangle Situation* (Washington, D.C., December 1926), p. 2.

13. Noulan Cauchon, "City Planning and Traffic Congestion," *Roads and Streets* 66, no. 1 (July 1926): 21.

14. Angus S. Hibbard, "The River Area: A Suggested Plan Related to the Chicago Downtown District" (typescript dated March 6, 1923, box 1, William E. Dever Papers, Chicago Historical Society).

15. "And This?" *The American City* 36, no. 6 (June 1926): 803–805.

16. Stephen Child, "Restricted Traffic District Proposed," *The American City* 36, no. 4 (April 1927): 507–510. Some social critics with a keen interest in urban planning were horrified at the emphasis upon mechanical "solutions" to problems of central-district congestion. Lewis Mumford saw such proposals as the product of "lazy imaginations," too narrow to think along larger concepts of creating humane urban environments. See Mumford, "The Next Twenty Years in City Planning," *Planning Problems of Town, City, and Region: Papers and Discussion at the Nineteenth National Conference on City Planning* (Washington, D.C., May 9–11, 1927), p. 56.

17. Burton Marsh, "Traffic Control," *The Annals of the American Academy of Political and Social Science* 113 (September 1927): 90.

18. William P. Eno, *The Science of Traffic Regulation, 1899–1920* (Washington, D.C., 1920), *passim*.

19. Merely thumbing through the traffic-oriented periodicals gives a sense of engineers' absorption with traffic-control experimentation. See, for example, *Municipal Engineering, Roads and Streets, The American City*.

20. Harold M. Lewis, "Metropolitan Traffic Control," *Roads and Streets* 65, no. 5 (May 5, 1926): 277; Lewis, "Routing Through Traffic," *The Annals* 113 (September 1927): 26.

21. Eno, *Traffic Regulation*, p. 3; Automobile Club of Southern California, *A Report on Los Angeles Traffic Problems, with Recommendations for Relief* (Los Angeles, August 1922), p. 25.

22. Auto Club of Southern California, *Report*, p. 25.

23. Miller McClintock, *Street Traffic Control* (New York, 1925), p. 10.

24. John C. Long, "What City Planning Means to the Motorist," *American Motorist* 17, no. 7 (July 1925): 10.

25. John Ihlder, "The Automobile and Community Planning," *The Annals* 116 (November 1924): 199.

26. George A. Damon, "The Influence of the Automobile on Regional Transportation Planning," *American Society of Civil Engineers, Transactions* (New York, 1925), p. 1132.

27. Miller McClintock, "What Does Traffic Congestion Mean to Me?" *Motor News* 18, no. 7 (July 1928): 16.

28. Clarence A. Dykstra, "Congestion Deluxe—Do We Want It?" *National Municipal Review* 15, no. 16 (July 1926): 395.

29. C. J. Galpin, "Better Highways to Relieve City Congestion," *The American City* 28, no. 2 (February 1923): 187.

30. J. C. Nichols, "The Development of Outlying Shopping Centers," *Planning Problems of Town, City, and Region: Proceedings of the Twenty-first National Conference on City Planning* (Buffalo and Niagara Falls, N.Y., May 20–23, 1929), pp. 16–31.

31. *Ibid.*, p. 19.

32. See, for example, John Nolen, "New Towns versus Existing Cities," *City Planning* 2, no. 2 (April 1926): 1–11. By the 1920s, the terms Garden City and New Town were synonymous.

33. Mel Scott, *American City Planning since 1890* (Berkeley, Cal., 1969), pp. 164–165, 234.

34. John Nolen, "Mariemont, Ohio: A New Town Built to Produce Local Happiness, a National Exemplar" (undated typescript, box 4, Justin R. Hartzog Papers, John M. Olin Library, Cornell University); Nolen, "General Plan—Mariemont—a New Town" (pamphlet, Cambridge, Mass., July 1921).

35. Arthur C. Comey and Max Wehrly, *Final Report on a Study of Planned Communities* (Washington, D.C.: National Resources Committee, Research Committee on Urbanism, 1936), p. 454. Ladislas Segoe Papers, Olin Library, Cornell University.

36. See Irving L. Allen, ed., *New Towns and the Suburban Dream: Ideology and Utopia in Planning Development* (Port Washington, N.Y., 1977).

37. Alfred E. Smith, "Building for the Future," *Building Age* 52, no. 1 (January 1930): 37–38; similarly, Nolen claimed Mariemont was a "town built for the motor age" (Nolen, "Mariemont, Ohio").

38. L. Deming Tilton, *A Report upon a Major Thoroughfare System and Traffic Circulation Problems of Washington* (St. Louis, 1927), p. 2. While he clearly endorsed the New Town concept, Tilton did not design any New Town suburbs for Washington.

39. Mark H. Rose astutely observed that downtown interests frequently fi-

nanced major traffic street plans, even regional highway plans, hoping that highway systems leading out from central districts would make their locations more accessible for suburban shoppers and workers (Rose to author, January 4, 1979). But in some cities, even as early as the 1920s, downtown interests were either abandoning their stores for suburban locations or at least opening branch stores. Los Angeles is probably the best example of this phenomenon during the 1920s. See Mark S. Foster, "The Decentralization of Los Angeles during the 1920s" (Ph.D. diss., University of Southern California, 1971), pp. 155–156.

40. *Proceedings of the Sixteenth National Conference of City Planners, April 7–10, 1924, Los Angeles, California* (Baltimore, 1924), p. 10.

41. Daniel Turner, "The Detroit Super Highway Project," *The American City* 32, no. 4 (April 1925): 373.

42. Chicago City Council, Subcommittee on Two-Level Streets, *A Memorandum and Preliminary Report on Elevated Highways* (Chicago, 1928).

43. An excellent example of very modest adjustments to motor vehicles is Ladislas Segoe, *Report and Recommendations of the Louisville Traffic Survey* (Louisville, 1927).

44. "Rapid Transportation for the Great West Side," *Motor News* 19, no. 10 (October 1929): 7.

45. Olmsted Brothers, Bartholomew, and Associates, *Parks, Playgrounds and Beaches for the Los Angeles Region: A Report Submitted to the Citizens Committee on Parks, Playgrounds and Beaches* (Los Angeles, 1930), p. 21; emphasis in original.

46. *Detroit News*, March 14, 1926.

47. John Beeler, "Planning Transportation for the City of the Future," *Electric Railway Journal* 66, no. 13 (September 26, 1925): 528, 530.

48. *New York Times*, December 20, 1928; Gilmore D. Clarke, "Modern Motor Arteries," *The American City* 43 (July 1930): 107.

49. *Root's Motor Digest* 1, no. 8 (February 1912): 10.

50. *Root's Motor Digest* 1 and 2 (1911–1913): *passim*. Letters to the editor frequently complained of just such harassment of "innocent" drivers.

51. Paul G. Hoffman, "Why the Automobile Industry Should Believe in City Planning," *City Planning* 6, no. 2 (April 1930): 96.

52. U.S., Bureau of the Census, *Historical Statistics of the United States, Colonial Times to 1970* (Washington, D.C., 1975), 2: 719.

53. Report of the President, *Proceedings of the 26th Annual Meeting of the American Automobile Association*, June 28–30, 1928, p. 5.

54. "The Automobile Peril Twenty-five Years Ago, and Today," *Public Works* 60, no. 11 (November 1929): 437; see also Morris Knowles, "Rebuilding

Cities for the Motor Age" (paper presented to the Public Safety Section of the National Safety Council, Thirtieth Safety Congress, Louisville, Ky., October 1, 1924).

55. "Safety on Our Highways," *Scientific American* 138, no. 4 (April 1928): 336–337; "When Is the Road to Blame for Accidents—and How?" *Highway Magazine* 19, no. 11 (November 1928): 283–286; S. J. A. Williams, "Safety Considerations in Highway Design," *Journal of the Western Society of Engineers* 31, no. 4 (April 1927): 163–166.

56. Russell V. Black, "The Spectacular in City Building," *The Annals of the American Academy of Political and Social Science* 133 (September 1927): 53.

57. Edward Bennett and Harry T. Frost, *The Axis of Chicago* (Chicago, 1929), p. 17.

58. *Detroit Times,* March 29, 1929.

59. Thomas H. MacDonald, "Parkways for Pleasure and Utility," *The American City* 31, no. 5 (November 1924): 421.

60. Ray L. Cadwallader to Isahel Curtis, May 9, 1930 (box 7, Isahel Curtis Papers, Suzzallo Library, University of Washington).

61. Henry Wright, "The Road to Good Houses," *Survey Graphic* 54, no. 3 (May 1, 1925): 166.

62. Benton MacKaye, "The Townless Highway," *The New Republic* 62, no. 797 (March 12, 1930): 94; see also Nichols, "Outlying Shopping Centers," p. 19.

63. For a challenge to this judgment, see Robert B. Carson, *What Ever Happened to the Trolley?* (Washington, D.C., 1978). In the late 1970s, Carson urged a return to the street railway as a realistic solution to present-day urban transportation problems.

Chapter 6

1. During the 1940s, population-growth figures approached the 1920–1930 averages, at 14.5 percent nationally and 22.0 percent in the cities. Leo F. Schnore, "Metropolitan Growth and Decentralization," in Schnore, *The Urban Scene: Human Ecology and Demography* (New York, 1965), p. 80.

2. U.S., Bureau of the Census, *Sixteenth Census of the United States, 1940: Population* (Washington, D.C., 1943), 1: 32–33, 61–64. Such raw figures do not, of course, reveal important patterns of movement within city boundaries. Urban demographers and sociologists have observed significant patterns of movement from inner-city areas to outlying neighborhoods during the 1930s. The literature on these trends is extensive; a good starting point is Amos H.

Hawley, *The Changing Shape of Metropolitan America: Deconcentration since 1920* (Glencoe, Ill., 1956).

3. A congressional study revealed that the number of federal employees in Washington nearly doubled between 1929 and 1936, increasing from 60,000 to 112,000 (see U.S. House of Representatives, 74th Congress, *Report of the Special Subcommittee of the District of Columbia to Make a Traffic Survey* [Washington, D.C., 1936], p. 533). Historian Lyle W. Dorsett points out that expanding tourism was also an important facet of Denver's healthy growth during the 1930s. See his *Queen City: A History of Denver* (Boulder, Colo., 1977), pp. 217–220.

4. *Sixteenth Census, Population,* 1: 61–64. The similarity of Los Angeles's city and suburban growth figures is partly due to the city's unusual shape. A large part of Los Angeles stretches far out into the San Fernando Valley, some fifteen to twenty miles from downtown. However, several "suburbs" are located within five miles of City Hall.

5. Schnore, "Metropolitan Growth," p. 80. Fringe areas in a few cities experienced large percentage increases during the 1930s. For example, Seattle's suburbs grew at a rate of 53.7 percent, while Washington, D.C.'s, increased 82.4 percent. These gains are largely explained by the fact that both cities began the decade with very small population bases. Seattle's suburbs contained but 55,000 residents in 1930, and they added only 29,000 people during the following decade. In Washington, the 1930 figure was 134,000; suburbs added 110,000 during the 1930s. See *Sixteenth Census, Population,* 1: 61–64.

6. U.S., Bureau of the Census, *Historical Statistics of the United States, Colonial Times to 1970* (Washington, D.C., 1975), 2: 721. Trolley coaches were powered by electricity supplied by overhead wires, but the coaches used rubber tires and were not limited to fixed rails.

7. *Ibid.,* p. 716.

8. Boston Traffic Commission, *Report on Boston Traffic Survey: W.P.A. Projects 15211 and 17024* (Boston, 1939), chart 16. Michigan Highway Department, *Street Traffic, City of Detroit, 1936–1937: W.P.A. Project No. 65-51-2101* (Lansing, Mich., 1937).

9. *Ibid.* But such relatively primitive traffic studies did not produce an accurate picture of Detroit-area traffic. Like most cordon-count studies during the 1930s, this project did not closely examine crosstown traffic, which was undoubtedly growing more rapidly than traffic to and from the central district. While exceptions existed, most studies still focused on the older pattern of traffic flow.

10. Paul Shoup, "Cooperation Is Essential to Meet 1930s Challenge to Transportation," *Electric Railway Journal* 74, no. 8 (July 1930): 431.

11. Quoted in H. V. Wallace, "The Outlook for City Transit," *The American City* 44, no. 2 (February 1931): 138.

12. Hawley S. Simpson, "Mass Transportation," in Harvard University Bureau for Street Traffic Research and Institute of Traffic Engineers, *Program for Traffic Engineering Training School: Outlines and Lectures* (Cambridge, Mass., August 1937), p. 89.

13. "Transit versus the Automobile," *Transit Journal* 84, no. 1 (January 1940), pp. 4–5.

14. In 1900, some thirty million urban dwellers took 4.5 billion trolley rides, an annual "riding habit" of roughly 135 per capita. Forty years later, 74.4 million urbanites took 8.4 billion rides, a "habit" of roughly 113. *Historical Statistics to 1970,* 2: 721; U.S., Census Bureau, *Abstract of the Twelfth Census, 1900,* 3rd ed. (Washington, D.C., 1904), p. 387; *Historical Statistics to 1970,* 1: 8, 11.

15. A. J. Lundberg, "Transit Prospects Brighten," *Transit Journal* 77, no. 11 (October 10, 1933): 375.

16. California Railroad Commission, *Report on the Local Public Transportation Requirements of Los Angeles: Case 4002* (Los Angeles, December 16, 1935), p. 10.

17. An old but first-rate survey of economic thought during the 1930s is Broadus Mitchell, *Depression Decade: From New Era through New Deal, 1929–1941* (New York, 1947).

18. "The Trackless Trolley System," *Seattle Municipal News* 20, no. 30 (June 26, 1930). Seattle purchased its first trackless trolley buses in 1936; see *Seattle Municipal News* 26, no. 32 (August 15, 1936).

19. *Seattle Municipal News* 26, no. 32 (August 15, 1936).

20. Beeler Organization, *Report to the City of Seattle on Its Municipal Street Railway System* (New York, 1935), p. 4. It should be observed that such a recommendation assumed a need to reinforce radial lines of intra-urban travel. The report placed little emphasis upon crosstown traffic needs.

21. Charles Gordon, "Automobiles versus Railways for Urban Transportation," *Electrical Engineering* 50, no. 1 (January 1931): 8.

22. *Denver Planning* 4, no. 3 (November 1931): 5. By mass transportation, it was quite clear that the Denver organization meant electric railways. It should also be pointed out that, while the Denver organization viewed street railways with favor, it never even presented a rapid transit proposal.

23. National Resources Planning Board, Committee on Urbanism, "Report: Transit Facilities and Urban Development," mimeographed, ca. 1937 (box 843, Central Office Files, NRPB Papers, National Archives, Washington, D.C.), p. 18.3.

24. "Recapture of Auto Owner Patronage," *Transit Journal* 75, no. 9 (September 1932): 370.

25. "Automobile versus Street Car," *Electric Traction and Bus Journal* 30, no. 2 (February 1934): 36.

26. American Electric Railway Association, "The Urban Transportation Problem" (pamphlet, ca. 1932), p. 12. The same statement frequently appeared during the 1930s in the pages of the *Electric Traction Journal* and in the Proceedings of the AERA. See also NRPB, "Report: Transit Facilities."

27. Sherwood Andrus to Norman H. Hill, March 2, 1933 (box 2, Detroit Mayors' Papers, 1933, Burton Historical Collection, Detroit Public Library).

28. *Detroit Free Press,* April 9, 1938.

29. Chicago City Council, *A Comprehensive Local Transportation Plan for the City of Chicago, November 22, 1937* (Chicago, 1937), p. 45. One student of Los Angeles transportation concluded in 1939 that streetcars passing through the downtown area on Broadway traveled more slowly than they had during the days of horse-drawn cars in the 1890s! See Evan W. Thomas, "An Analysis of Prospects to Provide Rapid and Adequate Mass Transportation for the Los Angeles Area" (M.A. thesis, University of California, Los Angeles, 1939), pp. 1–2.

30. A. B. Patterson, "The Private Automobile and Its Effect upon Mass Transportation," *Electric Traction and Bus Journal* 29, no. 9 (September 1933): 278.

31. American Transit Association, *Fare Structures in the Transit Industry: A Report of the Committee on Fare Structures* (New York, 1933), p. 165.

32. "Tough Going," *Mass Transportation* 33, no. 8 (August 1937): 227.

33. William Reilly, "Measuring the Market for Mass Transportation," *Transit Journal* 76, no. 2 (February 1932): 64.

34. Burton H. Schoepf, "Are Private Car Owners Taking away Your Traffic?" *Bus Transportation* 11, no. 9 (September 1933): 379.

35. *Bus Transportation* 12, no. 1 (January 1933): 70.

36. "Kidding the Public," *Mass Transportation* 34, no. 3 (March 1938): 67.

37. Boston Elevated Railway Company, *Fifty Years of Unified Transportation in Metropolitan Boston* (Boston, 1938), p. 109; Boston Elevated Railway Company, *Twenty-second Annual Report of the Board of Public Trustees of the*

Boston Elevated Railway Co., Year Ended December 31, 1940 (Boston, 1941), pp. 10–11.

38. "Traffic Congestion: Its Cause and Its Cure," *Mass Transportation* 33, no. 11 (November 1937): 359.

39. "Look Within," *Electric Traction* 27, no. 8 (August 1931): 373.

40. Gordon, "Automobiles versus Railways," p. 6.

41. An influential government study challenges this interpretation. Bradford C. Snell argues that, as early as 1932, General Motors set up the United Cities Motor Transit Company for the avowed purpose of buying streetcar lines and converting them to bus operations. The American Transit Association threatened an antitrust suit, and GM abandoned the attempt. By 1936, however, GM was back in the picture with another holding company, National City Lines. According to Snell, GM's grand design was to motorize trolley lines and profit in the short run by selling buses to the holding company. Bus service was then to be allowed to deteriorate to the point where there would be little public outcry if bus lines were abandoned. See Snell, "American Ground Transport: A Proposal for Restructuring the Automobile, Bus, and Rail Industries, February 1974," in U.S., Congress, Senate, Subcommittee on Antitrust and Monopoly of the Committee of the Judiciary, *Hearing on Bill 1167*, 93rd Cong., 2nd sess., 1974, pt 4, pp. A21–27. Without exonerating GM, I would argue that such charges are largely irrelevant. The point to remember is that street railway patronage was in steady decline for more than a decade before the creation of National City Lines, and that GM's "plot" probably did little to speed up the collapse of trolley systems across America.

42. See Chapter 7.

43. Roosevelt to Thomas P. Henry, October 31, 1938 (box PPF 1641, Roosevelt Papers, FDR Library, Hyde Park, N.Y.). This was, no doubt, just the kind of political rhetoric for which Roosevelt was so famous. Yet this statement, unlike many others, was forcefully supported by New Deal measures on behalf of the automotive–highway lobby (see Chapters 7 and 8).

44. Chicago City Council, Department of Highways, *A Comprehensive Superhighway Plan for the City of Chicago* (Chicago, 1939), p. 21.

45. Couzens to Sidney Waldon, March 19, 1935 (box 5, Detroit Rapid Transit Commission Papers, Burton Historical Collection, Detroit Public Library).

46. "No Need to Worry for 2,000 Years," *Mass Transportation* 35, no. 1 (January 1939): 2.

47. In the late 1930s there was a significant effort by automobile dealer

groups to induce the federal government to buy and scrap old automobiles. See B. B. Ellerbeck to Franklin D. Roosevelt, January 18, 1938 (OF 102-A, Roosevelt Papers). There are many letters promoting this program in OF 102-A.

48. *Facts and Figures of the Automobile Industry, 1931*, pp. 20–21; *Automobile Facts and Figures, 1940*, pp. 14–15; Day Monroe *et al., Family Expenditures for Automobile and Other Transportation: Five Regions* (Washington, D.C., 1941), p. 2.

49. *Facts and Figures, 1931*, pp. 20–21. Los Angeles had the highest per capita registration in 1930, with two cars for every five residents.

50. Hoffman to Roy D. Chapin, April 30, 1934 (box 27, Roy D. Chapin Papers, Bentley Historical Library, University of Michigan); see also Hoffman, "America Goes to Town," *The Saturday Evening Post* 211, no. 44 (April 29, 1939): 32.

51. Sidney D. Waldon, "Address before the Society of Automotive Engineers, January 9, 1930, New York" (typescript, box 3, Sidney D. Waldon Papers, Detroit Public Library).

52. Austin F. Bement to Ernest Hoftyzer, n.d. (box 2, Detroit RTC Papers).

53. *Proceedings of the Annual Meeting of the Councillors of the American Automobile Association, June 16, 1933*, p. 40.

54. Ed Ainsworth, "Out of the Noose" (a series of seven articles, reprinted by the Automobile Club of Southern California, 1938).

55. E. E. East, "Streets: The Circulation System," in George W. Robbins and L. Deming Tilton, eds., *Los Angeles: Preface to a Master Plan* (Los Angeles, 1941), p. 92.

56. Richard Ossenbaugh, "Bicycles Were Once a Traffic Problem," *Rocky Mountain Motorist* 7, no. 5 (May 1936): 4.

57. "Unfit for Modern Motor Traffic," *Fortune* 14 (August 1936): 85.

Chapter 7

1. The few rapid transit proposals submitted to the federal government during the New Deal era were routed directly to Harold L. Ickes of the PWA; if national planners even became aware of them, it was through informal channels. Peter Marcuse argues that the planning profession gave little thought to housing before the 1940s, and he emphasizes the fragmentation within the profession during its early years. See his "Housing in Early City Planning," *Journal of Urban History* 6, no. 2 (February 1980): 153–176.

2. Three scholars have, however, provided a good beginning to that assessment. See Otis L. Graham, Jr., "The Planning Ideal and American Reality: The

1930s," in Stanley Elkins and Eric McKittrick, eds., *The Hofstadter Aegis: A Memorial* (New York, 1974), pp. 257–279; John Hancock, "Planners in the Changing American City, 1900–1940," *Journal of the American Institute of Planners* 33, no. 5 (September 1967): 290–304; and Mark I. Gelfand, *A Nation of Cities: The Federal Government and Urban America, 1933–1965* (New York, 1975), chs. 2–4.

3. Harland Bartholomew, "The Trend of Modern Planning," *American Civic Annual* 4 (Washington, D.C., 1932): 180. While Bartholomew's generalization held true regarding the necessity for planners to recommend *physical* changes, the pressures to recommend humane solutions to urgent social and economic problems were enormous.

4. *Regional Planning Notes,* July 14, 1932 (weekly newsletter of the Los Angeles County Regional Planning Commission, Municipal Reference Library, City Hall, Los Angeles).

5. Robert A. Walker, *The Planning Function of Local Government: A Report to the Local Planning Committee of the National Resources Board* (Washington, D.C.: National Resources Planning Board, July 28, 1939), p. 27. One must be wary of placing too much emphasis on raw numbers. Many cities large enough to need thoroughfare plans did not need any comprehensive public transit plans. Yet it is also true that in many of the 86 cities with transit plans, nothing was ever effected; in most of the other cities, only small portions of the transit schemes were carried out.

6. No doubt many contemporary observers, hopelessly mired in the technical jargon of planning theory, would count this as a blessing, not a liability. Yet in 1937, President Russell V. Black of the American City Planning Institute urged members to unite around "something that is a profession, something with a fairly well defined and peculiar technique." Black to Members of the ACPI, November 11, 1937 (box 28, John Ihlder Papers, Franklin D. Roosevelt Library, Hyde Park, N.Y.).

7. Harvard had offered a Master's Degree in City Planning in 1923; however, it was an option within the Landscape Architecture Master's Degree Program (*Harvard News,* September 3, 1929). Nevertheless, funding for the planning program was extremely uncertain well into the 1930s. In fact, the school of planning nearly terminated operation in 1936 (*Harvard Crimson,* June 3, 1936). The others were Cornell, Columbia, and Massachusetts Institute of Technology. However, a number of other institutions offered courses in planning and quasi-official planning programs. See Norman Johnston, "Harland Bartholomew: His Comprehensive Plans and Science of Planning" (Ph.D. diss., University of Pennsylvania, 1964), p. 245.

8. Henry V. Hubbard *et al.*, *Report of the American City Planning Institute Committee on Professional Education, May 25, 1937*, p. 7.

9. Orton to Frederick Adams, March 14, 1941 (box 2, Justin R. Hartzog Papers, John M. Olin Library, Cornell University).

10. While even planners perceived little need for formalized university training, they did endorse practical training for traffic engineers. In 1939, Maxwell Halsey of Yale University's Erskine Bureau of Traffic Research estimated that, although 500 traffic engineers were working in American cities, there was a demand for 1,000 additional graduates. See Halsey, "Training Traffic Engineers: Origins and Functions of Bureau for Street Traffic Research, Yale University," *Yale Scientific Magazine* 14 (winter 1939): 5.

11. A thorough examination of the varying interpretations of the origins of New Deal thought would require a lengthy bibliographic essay. However, most historians agree on the pragmatic orientation of the New Deal programs. A sampling of these views includes Otis L. Graham, Jr., *An Encore for Reform: The Old Progressives and the New Deal* (New York, 1967), pp. 7–8; William E. Leuchtenburg, *Franklin D. Roosevelt and the New Deal, 1932–1940* (New York, 1963), pp. 337–339; Arthur M. Schlesinger, Jr., *The Age of Roosevelt: The Politics of Upheaval, 1935–1936* (Cambridge, Mass., 1960), pp. 389–391.

12. Walker, *The Planning Function*, p. 65, 67.

13. Brownell, "Urban Planning and the Motor Vehicle in the United States in the Early Twentieth Century" (paper presented at the First International Conference on the History of Urban and Regional Planning, University of London, September 1977), p. 1.

14. Los Angeles County Regional Planning Commission, *A Comprehensive Report on the Regional Plan of Highways, Section 4, Long Beach–Redondo Area* (Los Angeles, 1931), p. 26.

15. Pomeroy quoted in Walker, *The Planning Function*, p. 125.

16. The Roosevelt Library in Hyde Park, N.Y., contains ample evidence of the battles waged between Tugwell and his two critics. See, for example, La Guardia to Tugwell, August 24, 1939 (box 2, Tugwell Papers); and Moses to Tugwell, May 23, 1940 (box 2, Tugwell Papers).

17. Herbert L. Russell, "Practical City Planning Possibilities" (typescript, 1933, box 1, Detroit Mayors' Papers, Burton Historical Collection, Detroit Public Library).

18. Bennett quoted in "Proceedings of the National Conference on City Planning, 1936," in George B. Galloway and Associates, eds., *Planning for America* (New York, 1941), p. 63.

19. L. Deming Tilton, "Preventive Planning," *City Planning* 7, no. 4 (October 1931): 235.

20. Walker, *The Planning Function*, p. 131.

21. *Ibid.*, p. 30.

22. National Resources Committee, "Circular X" (Washington, D.C., May 15, 1937), p. 5, and *passim*.

23. Boston City Planning Commission, *Annual Report, 1940*; Detroit Office of the Controller, *Annual Appropriations, 1930–1940* (Burton Historical Collection, Detroit Public Library), *passim; Annual Appropriations of the City of Chicago for 1932* (Municipal Reference Library, Chicago), pp. 2288, 2664; *ibid., 1934*, p. 1696; and *ibid., 1935*, pp. 3507, 3576.

24. *Proceedings of the Chicago Planning Commission, June 21, 1935* (Municipal Reference Library, Chicago), p. 1569.

25. Detroit City Plan Commission, *Annual Report, 1934* (Detroit, 1935), p. 1.

26. I. S. Shattuck *et al.*, "Highways and Transportation in Relation to Each Other and to Other Planned Development: Preliminary Report of the Highways and Transportation Committee of the American Society of Planning Officials," *Proceedings of the National Conference on Planning Held at San Francisco, California, July 8–11, 1940:* 63.

27. Charles W. Eliot, "The Growing Scope of Planning" (copy of paper delivered at American City Planning Institute, Richmond, Va., May 2, 1936, box 2, Ladislas Segoe Papers, Olin Library, Cornell University).

28. Walker, *The Planning Function*, p. 183. This assessment was confirmed by other sources. The efforts of the Los Angeles planning organizations received both praise and cooperation from interest groups as diverse as the Los Angeles City Club and the Southern California Automobile Association. See, for example, City Club of Los Angeles, *Supplement City Club Bulletin, Report on Rapid Transit, January 30, 1926* (Los Angeles, 1926); *City Club Bulletin,* October 12, 1929; E. E. East, "Streets: The Circulatory System," in George W. Robbins and L. Deming Tilton, eds., *Los Angeles: Preface to a Master Plan* (Los Angeles, 1941), pp. 99–100.

29. For initial probing into this complex topic, see Mel Scott, *American City Planning since 1890* (Berkeley, Cal., 1969); John Hancock, "Planners"; Graham, "The Planning Ideal"; and Paul K. Conkin, *Tomorrow a New World: The New Deal Community Program* (Ithaca, N.Y., 1959).

30. See Ulysses S. Grant III to Sol Bloom, March 14, 1932; Manning to Grant, February 4, 1933; and Grant to Manning, March 16, 1933 (all in box 101, National Capital Park and Planning Commission Papers, National Archives, Washington, D.C.).

31. Graham, "The Planning Ideal," p. 271; and Gelfand, *A Nation of Cities*, p. 97.

32. Mark Gelfand astutely observes that while such rural New Deal programs as the TVA and REA profoundly reshaped the countryside and altered rural living conditions, Roosevelt had little interest in reshaping the city. Hence urban-oriented New Deal programs focused upon urban dwellers, but ignored the cityscape. See Gelfand, *A Nation of Cities,* p. 68.

33. Black to Frederick A. Delano, August 3, 1940 (box 883, National Resources Planning Board Papers, National Archives, Washington, D.C.).

34. NRPB, Committee on Local Planning, *County and Municipal Planning: A Statement of Improved Practices and Procedures* (Washington, D.C., June 21, 1939), p. 65.

35. Galloway and Associates, eds., *Planning for America* (New York, 1941), p. 28.

36. Arthur M. Schlesinger, Jr., *The Age of Roosevelt: The Coming of the New Deal* (Boston, 1958), pp. 27–39; see also Gelfand, *A Nation of Cities,* pp. 68–69.

37. Crane to H. I. Harriman, June 16, 1933 (PPF 2024, Roosevelt Papers, FDR Library, Hyde Park, N.Y.).

38. NRPB, "Interim Report of the Research Committee on Urbanism to the National Resources Committee" (typescript dated July 1, 1936, box 839, NRPB Papers).

39. NRPB, "Disunity of the City" (typescript dated 1937, author unknown, box 842, NRPB Papers).

40. NRPB, *County and Municipal Planning,* p. 1.

41. In recent years, the New Deal's role in the cities has received considerable attention from historians. The literature is massive, but good starting points include Philip Funigiello, *The Challenge of Urban Liberalism: Federal-City Relations during World War II* (Knoxville, Tenn., 1978), ch. 1; Otis L. Graham, Jr., *Toward a Planned Society: From Roosevelt to Nixon* (New York, 1976), pp. 1–68; Lyle W. Dorsett, *Franklin D. Roosevelt and the City Bosses* (Port Washington, N.Y., 1977); and J. Joseph Huthmacher, *Senator Robert F. Wagner and the Rise of Urban Liberalism* (New York, 1968).

42. See, for example, J. Joseph Huthmacher, "Urban Liberalism in the Age of Reform," *Mississippi Valley Historical Review* 50 (September 1962): 231–241; and Richard O. Davies, *Housing Reform during the Truman Administration* (Columbia, Mo., 1966).

43. Roosevelt to Joseph Kennedy, October 30, 1939 (PSF, box 53, Roosevelt Papers).

44. John Nolen, "The City of the Future: Address to the College Club, Boston, Mass., November 20, 1931" (typescript, lecture no. 206, box 14, John Nolen Papers, Olin Library, Cornell University).

45. National Resources Committee, New England Regional Planning Commission, "From the Ground Up" (Boston, 1939), p. 20.

46. NRPB, *County and Municipal Planning*, p. 18.

47. The debate over whether laissez-faire or corporate statism is the more dominant strain in American ideology has developed over decades and has attracted the attention of many historians. Anything more than a listing of the key works would require a lengthy bibliographical essay. The interested reader might begin with Graham, *Toward a Planned Society*, ch. 1; Funigiello, *Challenge of Urban Liberalism*, ch. 1; and Scott, *American City Planning*, pp. 300–311.

48. For example, see National Capital Park and Planning Commission, *Annual Report for the Year Ending June 30, 1932* (Washington, D.C., 1932), p. 6.

49. Carol Aronovici, "Let the Cities Perish," *Survey Graphic* 68, no. 13 (October 1, 1932): 439.

50. I found no direct evidence of such a trend in planning thought. However, the private papers of John Nolen and Justin Hartzog revealed that in the 1920s and 1930s many planners actively promoted planning in the smaller cities and suburbs. See especially box 39, Nolen Papers, and box 4, Hartzog Papers.

51. For a good account of the program's impact, see Joseph L. Arnold, *The New Deal in the Suburbs: A History of the Greenbelt Town Program, 1935–1954* (Columbus, O., 1971).

52. Conkin quoted in Charles N. Glaab and A. Theodore Brown, *A History of Urban America*, 2nd ed. (New York, 1976), p. 277.

53. Norman T. Newton, *Design on the Land: The Development of Landscape Architecture* (Cambridge, Mass., 1971), p. 510.

54. NRC, Research Committee on Urbanism, *Final Report on a Study of Planned Communities* by Arthur C. Comey and Max Wehrly (mimeographed, dated 1936), map 1, ch. 7, Ladislas Segoe Papers, Olin Library, Cornell University. This number is somewhat misleading because it includes such defunct experimental towns as New Harmony, Indiana, and Pullman, Illinois.

55. Urban Land Institute, "Decentralization—What Is It Doing to Our Cities?" (pamphlet, Chicago, 1940), pp. 1, 5.

56. United States Chamber of Commerce, "Balanced Rebuilding of Cities: A Statement Issued by the Construction and Civic Development Committee" (pamphlet, April 1937), p. 9.

57. *Proceedings of the Twelfth National Conference on City Planning* (Cincinnati, April 19–22, 1920), p. 99. For an extended analysis of Bartholomew's intellectual growth, see Johnston, "Harland Bartholomew."

58. Harland Bartholomew, "A Program to Prevent Economic Disintegration

in American Cities," *Planning Problems of Town, City, and Region Presented at the Twenty-fourth National Conference on City Planning* (Pittsburgh, November 14–16, 1932), p. 2.

59. Bartholomew, "The Trend of Modern Planning," p. 180.

60. Harland Bartholomew, "Is City Planning Effectively Controlling City Growth in the United States?" *Bulletin of the National Conference on City Planning* 23 (November 1931), p. 7.

61. Harland Bartholomew, "Problems Raised by Urban Development outside City Limits—How Can City and County Meet Them?" (paper delivered to Second Annual Southern Institute of Local Government, Knoxville, Tenn., October 17–18, 1941), p. 6.

62. In a highly influential book, Jane Jacobs took exception to the view that inner cities were not viable living areas. See *The Death and Life of Great American Cities* (New York, 1958).

63. Bartholomew, "A Program," p. 14.

64. Clarence A. Dykstra, "Congestion Deluxe—Do We Want It?" *National Municipal Review* 15 (July 1926), pp. 394–398.

65. Clarence A. Dykstra, "The Future of American Cities" (address before American Transit Association Convention, Cleveland, September 24, 1934), pp. 2–3. Mark H. Rose and John G. Clark have argued that inexpensive, readily available energy was a key factor permitting decentralization. See their "Light, Heat, and Power: Energy Choices in Kansas City, Wichita, and Denver, 1900–1935," *Journal of Urban History* 5, no. 3 (May 1979): 340–364.

66. Clarence A. Dykstra, "A City Works at Planning," *Bulletin of the National Conference on City Planning* 26 (November 1934): 4.

67. Homer Hoyt, "Urban Decentralization," *The Journal of Land and Public Utility Economics* 15 (August 1940): 273.

68. In some cities this process began well before the crash; Los Angeles's city core was losing businesses to suburban areas by the mid-1920s. See Frank G. Mittelbach, "Dynamic Land-Use Patterns in Los Angeles, the Period 1924–1954" (unpublished paper, Real Estate Research Institute, University of California at Los Angeles, n.d.).

69. Lewis Mumford, "The Plan of New York, I," *New Republic* 71 (June 15, 1932): 121–126; Mumford, "The Plan of New York, II," *New Republic* 71 (June 22, 1932): 146–154.

70. "The Problem of Decentralization and Disintegration in Cities," *The Denver Plan* 7 (Denver, 1941), p. 5.

71. Henry Babcock, "City Growth and Transportation" (speech before the Los Angeles Section of the American Society of Civil Engineers, September 15, 1937), p. 11.

Chapter 8

1. In retrospect, it is evident that proponents of inner-city highways were already winning the battle, as there were large federal expenditures on street repair, road widening, and so forth. However, in the late 1930s relatively few new city highways were being constructed; the same held true for rapid transit systems. The triumph of the superhighway in the inner city would become fully apparent only after World War II.

2. Robert H. Whitten, "The Expressway and the Region," *City Planning* 8, no. 1 (January 1932): 24–26.

3. John Nolen, Jr., "Memorandum on the Traffic, Parking, and Transportation Situation in the District of Columbia" (Washington, D.C., January 30, 1936), p. 4.

4. I. S. Shattuck *et al.*, "Traffic Studies in Relation to City Planning," *Proceedings of the National Conference of Planning, Held at Minneapolis, Minnesota, June 20–22, 1938* (Chicago, 1938), p. 38.

5. American Society of Planning Officials *Newsletter* 6, no. 2 (February 1940): 9.

6. Charles E. de Leuw, *Report on the Proposed Woodward Avenue Subway to the Rapid Transit Commission, City of Detroit* (Detroit, September 27, 1938), p. 30.

7. Los Angeles Transportation Engineering Board, Letter of Transmittal, *A Transit Program for the Los Angeles Metropolitan Area* (Los Angeles, 1939).

8. Geddes quoted in Maxwell Hamilton, "Traffic and Transit in the World of Tomorrow," *Transit Journal* 83, no. 8 (August 1939): 273.

9. Chicago, Detroit, and Los Angeles all developed such plans; these were the only cities included in this study to develop comprehensive transit plans in the 1930s.

10. Charles Gordon, "Transportation as an Element in Urban Rehabilitation," *The American City* 54, no. 6 (June 1939): 88.

11. Waldon to Reading, July 27, 1939 (box 7, Detroit Mayors' Papers, 1939, Burton Historical Collection, Detroit Public Library); emphasis in original.

12. Mayor's Committee on Employment Projects to Frank Murphy, March 17, 1933 (box 7, Detroit Mayors' Papers, 1933).

13. John P. Hallihan, "Things to Be Done in the State of Michigan and Detroit to Enable the Cities to Take Advantage of the Emergency Relief and Construction Act of 1932" (typescript dated September 15, 1932, box 4, Detroit Rapid Transit Commission Papers [hereafter referred to as "Detroit RTC Papers"], Burton Historical Collection, Detroit Public Library).

14. Henry C. Koch, "Finance Transit!" *The American City* 54, no. 3 (March, 1939): 101.

15. Donald M. Baker, "The Transportation Problem in the Los Angeles Area" (speech to the Los Angeles Section of the American Society of Civil Engineers), September 15, 1937.

16. Waldon to Reading, August 18, 1938 (box 3, Detroit RTC Papers).

17. This was one of the chief reasons opponents of rail lines protested all forms of subsidies to rail lines, which symbolized to them an outdated form of transportation technology. These arguments surfaced only occasionally during the Depression, but after World War II, the American Automobile Association became increasingly critical of rail transit. Auto club pamphlets between 1946 and 1960 particularly reflect this view.

18. I. S. Shattuck *et al.*, "Highways and Transportation in Relation to Each Other and to Other Planned Development: Preliminary Report of the Highways and Transportation Committee of the American Society of Planning Officials," *Proceedings of the National Conference on City Planning Held at San Francisco, California, July 8–11, 1940,* p. 48. Mark Gelfand concluded that one of the chief reasons the New Deal had less physical impact on the city than on rural America was that Roosevelt was largely uninterested in the city per se. He catered to numerous interest groups that comprised the urban population, but relief, rather than expensive rehabilitation, was his first responsibility. Gelfand, *A Nation of Cities: The Federal Government and Urban America, 1933–1965* (New York, 1975), pp. 68–69.

19. Nolen quoted in *Regional Planning Notes,* January 14, 1932 (mimeographed newsletter of the Los Angeles County Regional Planning Commission, Municipal Reference Library, City Hall, Los Angeles).

20. Edward M. Bassett, *Autobiography of Edward M. Bassett* (New York, 1939), p. 133.

21. Frederick A. Delano, "Statement before the Zoning Commission, December 4, 1940" (box 12, National Capital Park and Planning Commission Papers, National Archives, Washington, D.C.).

22. John Ihlder, "Population Density and Distribution in Urban Areas" (typescript dated April 25, 1935, box 28, John Ihlder Papers, Franklin D. Roosevelt Library, Hyde Park, N.Y.). Mark Gelfand pointed out that housing experts were actively promoting federal assistance to housing during the 1930s (*A Nation of Cities,* pp. 59–65, 112–136). Hence, they may have been biased against rapid transit proposals, considering them competitors for federal grants.

23. *Washington Post,* April 4, 1937. See also "Mass Transportation Plan for Chicago," *Mass Transportation* 33, no. 12 (December 1937): 395. This argu-

ment opposed implementation of any transportation plan that would permit continued centralization. By implication, however, the automobile provided more flexibility than fixed-rail transit.

24. Boston Municipal Research Bureau, *The Participation of Boston in a Public Works Program under the NIRA* (Boston, August 1933), p. 32.

25. Carroll to Harold L. Ickes, May 14, 1938 (box 146, Harold L. Ickes Papers, Library of Congress).

26. *Washington Post,* October 15, 1941.

27. Los Angeles Engineering Board, *A Transit Program,* p. 14.

28. Detroit Rapid Transit Commission to William M. Bruckner, July 22, 1932 (box 6, Detroit Mayors' Papers, 1936).

29. One excellent example is Donald M. Baker, *A Rapid Transit System for Los Angeles, California: Report to the Central Business District Association of Los Angeles, November 15, 1933* (Los Angeles, 1933).

30. A. M. Proudfoot, "City Retail Structure," *Economic Geography* 23 (1937): 425–428; see also Blaine A. Brownell, "The Automobile and Urban Structure" (paper delivered at American Studies Association meeting, San Antonio, November 5–8, 1975), pp. 9–11, 16.

31. Ihlder, "Population Density," *The Planner's Journal* (supplement) 1 (May-June 1935): 5–6.

32. Charles B. Whitnall, "Land Use Economics," Ninth Annual Session, Institute of Government, University of Southern California, June 14–18, 1937 (typescript, Frances Loeb Library, Harvard University), p. 10. An occasional planner scored the automobile. In 1931, Charles Moore, chairman of Washington's Fine Arts Commission, stated that "everybody seems to worship the automobile with the same awe and fear with which the untutored savage approaches his idol" (Moore to Congressman Roy Britten, March 25, 1931, box 43, Fine Arts Commission Papers, National Archives, Washington, D.C.).

33. National Resources Committee, New England Regional Planning Commission, "From the Ground Up" (pamphlet, Boston, 1939), p. 20.

34. "Greenbelt, Maryland" (ms. ca. 1936, box 1, Edgar R. Herzog Papers, Suzzallo Library, University of Washington).

35. Miller McClintock, "The Traffic Problem in Dollars and Sense," *Proceedings of the Annual Meeting of the Councillors of the American Automobile Association, November 19, 1937,* p. 100.

36. See, for example, "The Traffic Problem," *Life* 5 (July 4, 1938): 51. McClintock, *Street Traffic Control* (New York, 1925), pp. 4–6; McClintock, *Report and Recommendations of the Metropolitan Street Traffic Survey, Prepared under the Street Traffic Committee of the Chicago Association of Com-*

merce (Chicago, 1926), pp. 20–21; McClintock, "Of Things to Come," *New Horizons in Planning: Proceedings of the National Planning Conference Held at Detroit, Michigan, June 1–3, 1937* (Chicago, 1937), pp. 34–38.

37. McClintock's view that autos could be accommodated less expensively certainly was valid in the short run. It would be unfair to blame pre–World-War-II thinkers alone for the extravagant expense of postwar freeway construction, which evolved from the pressures of both selfish interests and sincere public servants.

38. Waldon to Roy D. Chapin, January 28, 1932 (box 19, Detroit RTC Papers). Waldon's ambivalence toward rapid transit and the automobile was due to the fact that he was both an urban planner and a former automobile company executive. He continued his friendships with many of the industry's most powerful people after he left Packard Motor Co. Paul G. Hoffman, president of Studebaker, expressed much the same view in 1934: "Sales resistance to further absorption comes from inability to use automobiles effectively rather than from inability to buy them. Many well-to-do people do not own automobiles, not because they cannot afford to own them, but because, as they will tell you, the ownership lacks advantage. They can use mass transportation more convenient-ly for many of their movements" (*New York Times,* January 7, 1934). For correspondence suggesting Waldon's intimacy with the automobile industry, see especially box 19, Detroit RTC Papers.

39. Chicago City Council, Committee on Traffic and Public Safety, *Limited Ways: A Plan for the Greater Chicago Traffic Area* (Chicago, 1933), 2: 21.

40. Marsh quoted in *Regional Planning Notes,* July 16, 1931 (mimeographed newsletter of the Los Angeles County Regional Planning Commission, Municipal Reference Library, City Hall, Los Angeles).

41. Miller McClintock, quoted in "Unfit for Modern Traffic," *Fortune* 14 (August 1936): 99.

42. U.S., Department of Highways, *Program of Improvements and Operation for the Street and Bridge Divisions* (Washington, D.C., September 8, 1937), p. 2. See also Thomas H. MacDonald, "Roads We Should Have," *Proceedings of the Annual Meeting of the Councillors of the American Automobile Association, November 20, 1936,* p. 66.

43. McClintock, "The Traffic Problem," p. 102.

44. Norman Bel Geddes, *Magic Motorways* (New York, 1940), p. 11.

45. "Traffic," *Life* 4, no. 7 (February 14, 1938): 41.

46. Crandell quoted in "Make L Highways Beautiful," *Motor News* 26, no. 11 (November 1936): 2.

47. Charles M. Noble, "Parkways and Express Highways," in Harvard Uni-

versity, *Program for Traffic Engineering Training School: Outlines and Lectures* (Cambridge, Mass., August 1937), p. 147.

48. Burton W. Marsh, "Express Highways," *Proceedings of the Eighth Annual Institute of Traffic Engineers Held at Kansas City, October 10–12, 1937* (New York, 1937), pp. 61, 67.

49. Justin R. Hartzog, "American Parkway Systems" (typescript dated 1933), box 4, Hartzog Papers, Olin Library, Cornell University).

50. Shurtleff to Hyman A. Enzer, September 11, 1939 (box 1, Frederick A. Delano Papers, Roosevelt Library, Hyde Park, N.Y.). According to landscape architecture historian Norman T. Newton, the initial impetus for beginning the Bronx River Parkway was to clean up a highly polluted and ugly stream. See Newton, *Design on the Land: The Development of Landscape Architecture* (Cambridge, Mass., 1971), pp. 601–607. In fact, a drive along the Westchester system during light traffic periods can be very pleasant even today.

51. Frank W. Clark, speech at dedication of Arroyo-Seco Parkway (typescript dated December 1940, Los Angeles City Planning Commission Library, City Hall, Los Angeles).

52. Chicago City Council, Department of Subways and Traction, *A Comprehensive Plan for the Expansion of the Subway System of the City of Chicago, Including Provision for the Widening of East and West Congress Street* (Chicago, 1939), p. 42.

53. Alden quoted in *Seattle Municipal News* 23, no. 47 (November 18, 1933): 3. This view was shared by L. Deming Tilton, a noted Southern California planner. See Tilton, "Freeways" (mimeographed, n.d., box 2, Regional Plan Association Papers, Olin Library, Cornell University).

54. Newton, *Design on the Land*, pp. 601–607; Waldon to Robert Graham, May 4, 1937 (box 5, Detroit RTC Papers); *Detroit News*, November 15, 1938, August 3, 1939; and John P. Hallihan to Waldon, September 12, 1940 (box 7, Detroit RTC Papers).

55. Paul Barrett, "Mass Transit, the Automobile and Public Policy in Chicago, 1900–1930" (Ph.D. diss., University of Illinois, Chicago Circle, 1976), pp. 636–637.

56. Works Progress Administration, *Report on Progress of the Works Program, June 1939* (Washington, D.C., 1939), p. 168. Of the 2.6 percent of funds spent for non-highway transportation, 2.1 percent was devoted to airport sites. Hence, but 0.5 percent was devoted to all other forms of transportation. The PWA provided $666 million to street and highway projects, and but $123 million for subways and tunnels. In straight grants, the disparity was over ten times as great, $648 million to $48 million! *America Builds: The Record of the*

PWA (Washington, D.C., 1939), p. 281. New Deal historian Lyle W. Dorsett suggested that in aiding road construction New Dealers were probably responding to predominant public preferences rather than the pro-transit arguments of a handful of "elite" planners (Dorsett to author, December 11, 1978).

57. "More Road Building Urged to Stimulate Return to Prosperity," *The American City* 44, no. 1 (January 1931): 94; see also Grover C. Dillman, "Road Building as an Agency of Employment," *ibid.* 47, no. 6 (December 1932): 75–76.

58. Works Progress Administration, *WPA Statistical Bulletin, January 1940* (Washington, D.C., 1940), p. 11. One should avoid overestimating the impact of federal funds on street and highway projects before World War II. As late as 1935 the federal share of all such projects begun since 1925 amounted to just over 10 percent. State, county, and city shares were 31.8, 24.2, and 33.9 percent, respectively. Albert Lepawsky, "Trends in Urban Government" (typescript, box 836, National Resources Planning Board Papers, National Archives, Washington, D.C.), p. 35.

59. Harold L. Ickes, untitled speech presented to the National Conference on City Planning and American Civic Association, October 9, 1933 (mimeographed, box 125, NCPPC Papers, Chairmen's and Directors' Files), p. 7.

60. Any number of studies lead to this conclusion. See in particular Mark Reinsberd, "The Heyday of Highway Benefits," *Interstate Commerce Practitioners' Journal* 30, no. 9 (June 1963): 1153–1168; and Philip P. Mason, *The League of American Wheelmen and the Good Roads Movement, 1880–1905* (Ann Arbor, Mich., 1958).

61. *Proceedings of the Chicago City Planning Commission, June 21, 1935* (Municipal Reference Library, Chicago), p. 1570.

62. Walter H. Blucher, "The Economics of the Parking Lot," *The Planners' Journal* 2, no. 5 (September-October 1936): 115.

63. Thomas H. MacDonald, "The Urban Traffic Problem," *Proceedings of the Annual Meeting of the Councillors of the American Automobile Association, November 16, 1939*, pp. 100–104.

64. WPA, *Report, June 1939*, p. 168.

65. For a sampling of this correspondence, consult OF 129 and OF 139, Roosevelt Papers, Roosevelt Library, Hyde Park, N.Y.

66. Hallihan to Waldon, September 12, 1940 (box 7, Detroit RTC Papers). Hallihan still clung to the idea of center strips for rapid transit on superhighways. For further evidence of the intimacy of Detroit planners with political realities at local, state, and national levels, see Hallihan to Waldon, May 21, 1935; and Robert Rosen to Harold L. Ickes, May 29, 1934 (boxes 4 and 5, respectively, Detroit RTC Papers).

67. NRPB, *American Transportation Policy: Summary Report* (Washington, D.C., October 13, 1941), p. 59.

68. Gelfand explores the intricate maneuverings of housing reformers amidst a melange of competing social welfare interests during the New Deal; see *A Nation of Cities,* pp. 59–65, 112–136.

69. Chicago City Council, Department of Highways, *A Comprehensive Superhighway Plan for the City of Chicago Submitted to Edward J. Kelly and the City Council of Chicago* (Chicago, 1939), p. 29.

70. U.S., Bureau of Public Roads, "Toll Roads and Free Roads," *76th Cong., 1st Session, House Doc. No. 272, April 27, 1939,* pp. 94–95.

71. Harry P. Freeman and George H. Herrold, "Obsolescence in Cities," *The Planners' Journal* 2, no. 2 (March-April 1936): 47.

72. R. M. Devine to C. Earl Morrow, August 17, 1936 (box 2, Regional Plan Association Papers). Devine's assessment of minimum distance for escaping noise was, of course, extremely modest.

73. P. S. Coombs, *Monorail Suspended Airway Lines on the Scale of Efficiency with Los Angeles Transportation Systems* (Los Angeles, ca. 1940), p. 10.

74. Moses to Rexford Tugwell, July 5, 1939 (box 2, Tugwell Papers, Roosevelt Library, Hyde Park, N.Y.). See also Moses to Tugwell, June 15, 1939 (box 3, Tugwell Papers). Yet Moses himself gained fame and notoriety for promoting parkways in the New York City region regardless of human and social cost. A superb (and highly critical) biography is Robert A. Caro, *The Power Broker: Robert Moses and the Fall of New York* (New York, 1974).

75. Scales to C. Earl Morrow, December 30, 1936 (box 2, Regional Plan Association Papers).

76. Washington Cleveland, "Traffic Survey" (typescript dated May 17, 1937, box 23, Ihlder Papers).

77. See, for example, John Keats, *The Insolent Chariots* (Philadelphia, 1958); Kenneth R. Schneider, *Autokind versus Mankind* (New York, 1971); Ronald A. Beul, *Dead End: The Automobile in Mass Transportation* (Englewood Cliffs, N.J., 1972); Lewis Mumford, *The City in History: Its Origins, Its Transformation, and Its Prospects* (New York, 1961), pp. 505–510.

78. Segoe to Samuel H. Eliot, June 27, 1939 (box 14, Segoe Papers, Olin Library, Cornell University).

79. Elizabeth Herlihy, "City Planning in Boston: Address before the Harvard School of City Planning" (typescript dated January 9, 1931, Frances Loeb Library, Harvard University), p. 20. In fact, the Central Artery, constructed after World War II, was essentially the same concept promoted six decades earlier by Mayor John F. ("Honey") Fitzgerald.

Bibliographic Note

Like many of their contemporaries, planners and traffic consultants of the 1900–1940 period often unknowingly frustrated future historians by destroying or losing their professional correspondence. A number of important consulting firms went out of business during the Depression, and their records, too, disappeared. In addition, since most "planners" received few commissions before World War I, and since the "profession" did not make large-scale strides in organization until the 1920s, primary source material on planning thought before World War I is somewhat limited. Fortunately, a number of important transportation studies, City Beautiful plans, and related professional journals allowed me to fill in important gaps. And primary source material covering planning activities after World War I abounds. All things considered, I was heartened to discover a large number and wide variety of primary source materials during my year of research travel.

My two most productive and lengthy visits were to the John M. Olin Library at Cornell University and the National Archives. Cornell boasts a superb planning collection, including the papers of Russell V. Black, Jefferson C. Grinnalds, Justin R. Hartzog, Nelson P. Lewis, John Nolen, and Ladislas Segoe. The Nolen and Lewis papers were the most useful. These six collections reveal a great deal about planning thought throughout the 1920s and 1930s, both in America and abroad. Cornell also holds an enormous collection of the New York Regional Plan Association, which numbers several hundred uncataloged boxes. Due to constraints of time, I only sampled the New York Regional Plan Association collection. At the National Archives, I spent several fruitful weeks examining the well-indexed files of the National Capital Park and Planning Commission, the National Resources Committee, and the National Resources Planning Board, as well as a small collection of Regional Planning Association of America papers. The National Capital Park and Planning Commission files contained important data on planning for the capital from 1924 on, while the other three collections provided excellent evidence of the growing federal involvement in planning at all levels from 1933 to 1940.

A number of other research libraries contain excellent primary source material. The Burton Historical Collection at the Detroit Public Library contained detailed evidence of planning activity in that city during the 1920s and 1930s. The most useful collections included the Detroit Rapid Transit Commission Papers, the Sidney D. Waldon Papers, and the Detroit Mayors' Papers. At the Franklin D. Roosevelt Library, Hyde Park, N.Y., the Frederick A. Delano, John Ihlder, Franklin Roosevelt, and Rexford G. Tugwell Papers contain materials that deepened my understanding of the complex forces guiding federal planning during the New Deal.

Other useful primary sources were scattered. In Chicago, I consulted the William E. Dever Papers and the Chicago Regional Planning Association files at the Chicago Historical Society. The Chicago Art Institute contained useful materials on Daniel H. Burnham's 1909 Plan of Chicago, including originals of the plan itself. The Burnham materials were particularly important, since the plan contained the most ambitious and comprehensive recommendations for any American city in the pre–World-War-I period, and Burnham's views represented the cutting edge of planning thought in this country. In Los Angeles, I uncovered the Los Angeles County Regional Planning Commission Minutes in the Municipal Reference Library in City Hall. In the same library, I accidentally discovered a long-forgotten scrapbook containing many of the unpublished views of Gordon Whitnall, a highly influential local planner who enthusiastically promoted accommodation of the motor vehicle in Los Angeles and across the nation. Also in Los Angeles, the Clarence A. Dykstra Papers at the University of California shed considerable light on the interaction between planners and other reformers during the period from 1913 to 1924.

I found several useful collections in the Suzzallo Library at the University of Washington in Seattle. The Reginald H. Thomson Papers provided useful material on early-twentieth-century responses to rapid transit and the automobile, and also on the politics of planning in Seattle. The Suzzallo Library also yielded the useful collections of Isahel Curtis and Edgar R. Herzog. Although I consulted dozens of additional primary source collections at many other libraries, those cited above yielded my most important evidence.

For purposes of tracing changing planning thought between 1900 and World War I, I relied heavily upon the published planning reports of a few individual planners and a larger number of reports of transportation consulting firms. Fortunately, a number of original City Beautiful plans and the reports of such early-twentieth-century transportation consultants as Bion J. Arnold and Delos Wilcox were available at a few libraries. The Frances Loeb Library at Harvard University's Graduate School of Design contains an outstanding collection of these early reports. The Loeb Library also provided useful information on early efforts to educate a second generation of planners for America's cities. The library at Harland Bartholomew and Associates in St. Louis contains over one hundred city plans developed either by or under the direction of Bartholomew. Perusal of several dozen of Bartholomew's plans enabled me to trace this pioneer planner's rapidly evolving views of urban transportation during the years from 1915 to 1940.

During the preliminary stages of my research, I consulted several dozen professional journals. Among the most useful were *The American City, Bus*

Transportation, City Planning, Electrical Engineering, Electric Traction, Proceedings of the American Society of Civil Engineers, Proceedings of the National Conference of City Planners, Mass Transportation, Municipal Engineering, National Municipal Review, Public Works, and *Roads and Streets.* Several of these journals, particularly the engineering magazines, were critical to my understanding of the slow emergence of planning thought between 1900 and World War I.

Finally, I consulted hundreds of articles and monographs on planning, urban transportation, and related topics. A complete, or even partial, listing would require many additional pages. I have included the most significant secondary sources and have acknowledged my most important intellectual debts in the notes.

Index

Adams, Thomas, 66, 69
Ainsworth, Ed, 130
Alden, Charles H., 165
American Association of State Highway Officials, 96
American Automobile Association, 93, 96, 111–112, 130
American City Planning Institute, 134
American Electric Railway Association, 53, 56, 81, 119, 122, 127
American Petroleum Institute, 174
American Road Builders Association, 81
American Society of Civil Engineers, 63
American Society of Planning Officials, 136, 153
American Transit Association, 120, 124, 148, 154
Annexations, 145
Arnold, Bion J., 37–38, 41
Aronovici, Carol, 144–145
Arroyo-Seco Parkway, 164
Autobahn, 162
Automobiles: and criticism, 3–4, 21, 44, 54, 62–64, 93, 112–114, 125–127, 130–131, 177; and energy sources, 128–129; and federal government, 165–166, 171–173; impact on urbanization, 42, 48–61, 63, 101–106; as new technology, 20–22, 58–60, 110–111, 151, 161; per capita ownership, 59; and planner support, 5, 8, 22, 44, 60–61, 91, 114–115, 158–166, 171; public acceptance, 21, 59, 62, 91, 110–112, 127–129, 158, 160, 161; registrations, 8, 58, 91, 109, 118, 129; in rural America, 21, 62, 113; and safety, 110–112; sales, 58, 59, 62, 118; saturation, 121, 129, 152; and urban congestion, 7, 20, 22–23, 62, 64, 87; and urban mass transit, 21, 22, 44, 60–64, 78, 81–83, 119–120, 126–127, 158–161

Babcock, Henry, 149
Babson, Roger W., 53
Baker, Donald M., 89, 155
Baker, Ray S., 21
Baldwin Hills, Calif., 146
Barclay, Parsons, and Klapp, 38
Barrett, Paul, 165
Bartholomew, Harland, 39, 71, 94, 133, 147–148
Bassett, Edward M., 38, 110, 156
Beeler, John A., 51, 70, 110
Beeler Organization, 122
Bement, Austin F., 129
Bennett, Charles H., 136
Bennett, Edward H., 33, 34, 112
Bettman, Alfred, 28, 37
Black, Russell V., 70, 140
Blucher, Walter H., 171
Bogue, Virgil C., 32, 39. *See also* Seattle, Bogue Plan of 1911
Boston: automobile registrations, 129; planning in, 66, 175; population trends, 46, 116–117; suburbanization, 16; subway plans, 26, 37
Boston City Planning Board, 66
Boston Elevated Railway Co., 74, 126, 156–157
Boston Municipal Research Bureau, 156
Bradway, Judson, 77
Brownell, Blaine A., 68, 91, 135
Bruce-Briggs, B., 4

239